# THE BIRTH OF AMERICAN POLITICAL THOUGHT, 1763–87

# The Birth of
# American Political
# Thought, 1763–87

Dick Howard
*Professor of Philosophy*
*State University of New York at Stony Brook*

Translated by David Ames Curtis

University of Minnesota Press, Minneapolis

Copyright © 1986 by Dick Howard
English translation © The Macmillan Press Ltd. 1989
Introduction to the English edition © Dick Howard 1989
Originally published as *La Naissance de la pensée politique américaine,
1763-1787* by Editions Ramsuy, Paris, 1987.

Published by the University of Minnesota Press
2037 University Avenue Southeast, Minneapolis MN 55414.

Printed in Hong Kong

Library of Congress Cataloging-in-Publication Data
Howard, Dick. 1943–
[Naissance de la pensée politique américaine. English]
The birth of American political thought, 1763–87/ Dick Howard,
translated by David Ames Curtis.
p.    cm.
Translation of: Naissance de la pensée politique américaine.
Includes bibliographical references.
ISBN 0–8166–1832–1.—ISBN 0–8166–1834–8(pbk.)
1. Political science—United States—History—18th century.
2. United States—Politics and government—Revolution. 1775–1783.
3. United States—Constitutional history.    Title.
JA84.U5H6813    1989
320.5'0973'09033—dc20                                              89–20330
                                                                        CIP

The University of Minnesota
is an equal opportunity
educator and employer

For my parents-in-law,
Jean and Hélène Delaquaize

# Contents

# Preface to the French Edition

For an American to write in French a political history of the Revolution that founded his country may be surprising. I should stress that this is a history of a type of political thought that I have discovered only recently. I am by training a philosopher and a Left activist – an activist of that *New Left*, international in scope, that was born in the Movement of the 1960s. The ideology and practice of this Movement were principally determined by democracy. But what it lacked was theory, especially in the United States, where the quest for political democracy seemed odd and where no Marxist tradition existed. A number of us turned to Marxism. Some have since, in frustration, distanced themselves from it; many remained there. Others passed through the various Marxisms to the point of criticizing them from the inside. Having rediscovered our democratic ambitions, we are trying to draw from these a theory that would aid us in understanding their contemporary meaning. Here we cross paths with a certain strand of French thought that itself is also seeking to define modern democracy now that its Marxist illusions have been lost.

The first readings that attracted me to the American Revolution were those known under the name of the 'republican synthesis', as found especially in the writings of Bernard Bailyn and Gordon Wood. What appealed to the leftist in me was that the republican concern for the common good, for a public space and for virtue, differed from the economics-based politics of interests that Marxism had offered. It differed too from the choice of Social Democracy which had stressed the struggle toward social equality and which resulted in neither democratic participation nor a break with the principles of the established order. It contrasted, finally, with that other left-wing option, which always takes the side of the underdog in an unending struggle. Just this choice, now combined with a republican orientation, led me to write this book.

I was also attracted to the American Revolution by Hannah Arendt's book *On Revolution*. Her opposition between the American and French Revolutions intrigued me, in as much as the latter supposedly represented the revolutionary model, even for that New Left to which I belonged. Thinking through the problems posed in practice, I came to different conclusions, and asked myself other questions. Moreover, between the time I began writing this book and the time I finished it, I completed a study on political philosophy, *From Marx to Kant*. The method I have used here has naturally been influenced by that work, although I did my best to let history speak for itself and raise questions on its own.

The reader undoubtedly already has his/her interpretation of the American Revolution – or the War of Independence, as it is often called in France. What I have done is to tell a story while also trying to comprehend it and to let the reader follow its thread and question his or her own preconceived interpretation. I have tried not to weigh down this essay, which is intended as an invitation to reflection, with too many scholarly notes. I cite my sources when I wish to signal what I have borrowed or when it is a matter of an interpretation that might bear further investigation. I have also used the notes to raise questions, to indicate lines of research that go beyond the boundaries of this study or, sometimes, to engage in polemics. There are inevitably some repetitions necessary in a work such as this. I hope to have avoided them as much as possible. I have tried to make this book a reflection on the Revolution and a work of political thought.

The first version of this work was presented at the Ecole des Hautes Etudes en Sciences Sociales in May-June 1985. I should thank François Furet, the school's director, for his kind welcome as well as my audience for their critical attention. I want also to thank Claude Lefort, who encouraged me to continue this project; Lefort's own work, I believe, finds echoes in this text. I also thank Guillaume Malaurie, director of the collection in which this volume appeared, and Sabine Delattre of Editions Ramsay: Both have lent a hand to put into correct French what were too often ideas born of indefinite questions that sometimes were drowning in their own complexity. Pierre-Olivier Montheil has not only translated all the English quotations and done what was necessary to correct the verb tenses, place the adjectives in the right position, and so forth; his questions have often led me to define my thoughts more clearly when his editing had not already done so. A first version of the Introduction appeared in *La Lettre Internationale* in June 1986. [An English translation now exists in the Australian journal, *Thesis 11*.] I thank Paul Noirot for his editorial work on that text which I have developed here in more detail. I have tried to explain the pertinence of this American experience to a French public in an article that appeared in *Intervention* (March 1986) under the title, 'Pourquoi revenir à la Révolution américaine?' This essay was edited by Joël Roman, whom I thank here. [This article, too, is now available to English-speaking readers in *Thesis 11*.]

If I have written this book in French, it is thanks to my wife and to my in-laws, who have aided me in understanding a certain France and another America. And it is to thank my in-laws that I dedicate to them this book.

# Introduction to the English Edition

## REPUBLICANS AND DEMOCRATS

Why did I write about the American Revolution in French? What can the English reader expect from this book? The first question is addressed below in the Introduction to the French edition, which I have retained here, after some hesitation. But more can be said. My original title was 'The Political Theory of the American Revolution'. My French publisher decided that the claim to analyze the 'birth' of a presumably still present entity called 'American Political Thought' would have broader appeal. After all, the French think that 'revolution' is their own; when they refer to them at all, the 'events' in North America are called 'the War of Independence'.[1] Perhaps unintentionally, the French publisher parried potential attacks by a sleight-of-hand which escaped the proof-reader (and the author[2]): the cover to that edition claims to treat the dates '1763–87', while the title page specifies that my concern is defined by the date 'September, 1787'. Only the frontispiece carries the general claim, which is retained as the title here and which defines correctly my intention. In this sense, the French publisher was correct to insist that I am speaking of 'American Political Thought': I do conceptualize a history which is still being lived. These categories are not innocent. To explain them, I need to return to the context in which I wrote this book. In doing so, I will address as well my expectations for the English translation, which depend on assumptions about the nature of contemporary politics.

I was concerned with the political logic, not the causes, of the American Revolution. The usual identification of the concept of revolution with the French Revolution had been put into doubt by historians such as François Furet. The point can be made quite simply. Did that Revolution culminate in 1791 (the Girondin Constitution), in 1793 (the Montagnard Constitution), in 1795 (the Directorial Constitution), in 1799 (the Tribunate), in 1804 (the Empire), or in 1815 (the final defeat)? Did the *social* legacy concealed by these political dates live on, reappearing in 1830, in 1848, in 1871, before its culmination in Russia in 1917? The dates and data can be parsed differently; one can distinguish bourgeois and proletarian revolutions, and add to them the new

20th-century form of national revolutions. The causal account seeks a common denominator, usually economic, with or without a bow to Marxist theories of class struggle. But the unhappy fate of 20th-century colonial (that is, anti-colonial) revolutions, and of the Eastern European 'revolutions' that created a Soviet bloc suggests a different approach. The historian thinking about the past in terms of present-day problems may have recourse to R. R. Palmer's idea of an 'Age of Democratic Revolutions'. The philosopher animated by the same concerns will recall Hannah Arendt's study of the emergence of democratic politics in the American Revolution and its failure in the French Revolution.[3] Both approaches stress the unique logic of *democratic* politics.

If France pretends to be the homeland of revolution, the United States lays claim to democracy with the same legitimacy. That is, history suggests that the concept poses more problems than solutions. When I began this essay, the French left had come to power, jettisoned its revolutionary rhetoric, and was searching for an alternative. Its slogan was 'republicanism', which was intended to capture the heritage of 1789 without its negative consequences. The right-wing opposition replied with 'liberalism'.[4] The words are familiar, but French history gives them a different twist. Nineteenth-century French liberalism, typified by Guizot and the July Monarchy, was the ideology of a bourgeoisie which was opposed to popular democracy. The liberals argued that this would preserve the fruits of 1789 without the repressions of 1793 and Bonapartism. Their radical opponents appealed to the heritage of republicanism, at least until the birth of a proletarian political movement claiming justification in Marxist science. A century later, the left government, which called itself socialist, had rejected this theoretical baggage as well as the myth of revolution. But the rhetoric of republicanism that it tried to introduce was ahistorical; it did not catch the popular imagination. The 'liberal' counter-attack by the right was better armed: it could appeal to triumphant Reaganism's free market ideology. In this context, a return to the origins of American democracy, and its republican institutional form, seemed to be a promising avenue of research. What is republicanism? What is liberalism?

There was an American side as well. I am not a professional historian. When I began my research, I knew no more than the average American about the history of my own country. Perhaps, as a political activist, I knew a little bit more. I knew about Beard and the 'progressive' historians; and I knew that they were replaced by the 'consensus' theory of 'American exceptionalism'. I knew that without reading; I didn't have to read, because the goal of my generation was to create a 'new' history, one written from below, giving voice to the voiceless and restoring conflict to the seamless web of self-congratulation. When I discovered, by accident, in a used book store, the 'republican synthesis' of Bailyn and Wood, my interest was kindled. The French context drew me toward these theorists; but the American side explains why this essay is not simply a reconstruction of that thesis. The New Left, in which I was a participant, had disintegrated. To be sure, repression played a part in it; but the victim was a willing accomplice. The movement decided that it must be truly revolutionary. People grasped at Marxist nostrums, stressing the 'left' identity over the 'new' politics they had sought. The political logic of the 'participatory democracy' of the early Students for a Democratic Society, and the 'civil rights' which shattered the exceptional consensus of the 'American Century', were forgotten. The American left did not understand the political nature of its own democracy.

It is a truism in French politics that the past lives in the present, which seeks to understand itself by relation to it. The assertion is less evident in the United States. In what sense is the revolutionary origin of American democracy present in our politics? In telling the story of the American Revolution to a French public unfamiliar with its twists, turns and even its consequences, I proposed an answer. I constructed a narrative that conformed to their expectations: problems posed at one moment suggested solutions which, in turn, posed new forms of these same problems. The narrative turned around three problems: sovereignty, its representation, and the republican democracy, which appeared to be an almost Hegelian synthesis.[5] Within each of these divisions, a similar movement appeared. The moments of this triadic development presented history as 'lived', as 'conceived' and as 'reflected upon'. I added a fourth chapter–'History Rethought'–to underline the fact that the 'synthesis' is not a final unification. For the same reason, I have included here an Appendix, which is the text of a lecture given in Paris at the time of the publication of the book, to stress that the revolution did not end with the ratification of the Constitution. That 'reflection' suggests that the French truism is valid for the United States as well.

The claim that a unique form of republican democracy emerges from the American Revolution needs qualification. The assertion could mean simply that the political experience of the revolution created that republican democracy. But a stronger formulation is suggested by my narrative, which implies that this republican democracy *is* the revolution itself. This broader interpretation clarifies the presence of the American revolutionary past today. Contemporary political debate turns around the distinction between liberal rights protected by 'a government of laws' and a communitarian ethos which seeks to restore a kind of 'civil religion'. But the debate is not without ambiguity. The appeal to rights insists on republican constitutional guarantees; the call for community insists on the democratic foundation of such rights. But republicanism appeals also to a civic conscience, while democracy can come to demand the protection of individual rights (or 'entitlements'). Republicanism criticizes rights that cloak private interest, but its use of the state to enforce the abstract universality of law violates democratic representation. Democracy appeals to community, but neglects those excluded from its miniature sovereignty. The debate goes on; the Revolution is not a 'synthesis' solving all problems of politics. The revolution continues. The republican or the democratic aspect may come to the fore at one or another moment; but its counterpart is never completely suppressed, nor should it be.

The political presence of the Revolution points to a methodological difficulty in my narrative. What explains the move from the 'reflected' solution to a new form of 'lived' history? Why does one or the other aspect of the revolutionary experience re-emerge? Is the continuity imposed by the theorist who reconstructs the past in terms of a present? If that were the case, the possibility of other historical choices would be eliminated; history would be a force for conservatism, preaching the kind of philosophical resignation typified by Hegel's evocation in the *Philosophy of Right* of the 'owl of Minerva' which takes flight only after the fact, 'at twilight'. This kind of teleology can be avoided by a method which preserves the openness of the historical moment in which political choice can occur. History as 'lived' does not eliminate the conflicts out of which it emerges. This is the sense in which the Revolution is still present. Were I to change the title my French publisher bestowed on this book, I would speak of the *origin* of American political thought. This category has a specific philosophical weight, whose explanation will help the reader to understand the theoretical underpinnings of my argument. This methodological clarification will explain in turn the interplay of theory and politics, then and now, as it emerges in this book.


QUESTIONS OF METHOD

What *is* a revolution? Neither its preconditions nor its results explain the advent of an experience which is at once a rupture with the past and the foundation of a future whose horizon remains open. Preconditions

xvi        *Introduction to the English Edition*

imply evolution; results point back to a cause. Revolution must be conceived as *originary*; it is not a result of the past, nor does it determine causally a future. Of course, a revolution does not take place outside of history; and of course, it must be studied with the historian's tools. But the philosopher cannot help but wonder: what *is* this newness? Although the historian seeks to determine its uniqueness, the very quest for determinations denies the creativity of revolution. Material determination explains by explaining *away* its novelty. Nor can recourse be taken to the consciousness of the actors, as individuals or as a putative collective subject. They find themselves in a situation, try to adjust their actions to (or against) it, understand themselves within its frame. But revolution is not some 'thing' which can be intended by an actor; revolution forces actors to pose the question of meaning at the same time that it gives to their actions a meaning that they may not have intended. In both of these senses, meaning is not something objective which could in principle be calculated by a rational actor or comprehended by historical reconstruction. If that were its criterion, no revolution would take place; revolutionaries would be utopians, romantics, or fools. But revolutions occur; we can understand them. How?

Human action can be described either in terms of the conditions of its genesis or in terms of the normative meaning which gives it intersubjective validity. In normal conditions, either of these moments suffices to explain action. Behaviour is considered rational according to its context or in terms of the meaning which the actor attaches to this context. There are, however, moments when the two explanations appear to conflict. The determination of meaning is no longer self-evident; the context for action is not clear. It may be that behaviour has materially altered the context, which no longer fits the previously valid framework of meaning. The materialist would suggest that rational actors will modify their criteria of validity to make sense of the new context. This is easier said than done. It may just as well be the case that changes in the framework of meaning engendered a new interpretation of a context which has remained substantially unchanged. The idealist would suggest that rational actors will modify their behaviour in accord with this shift. But this no more explains revolutionary action than did the materialist. Both positions could just as well explain the absence as the presence of revolution. The phenomenon appears irrational, accidental, a failed adaptation rather than the origin of the new.

These are not abstract possibilities; the materialist and the idealist are encountered within the study of revolution. Their failure to explain it suggests a provisional definition of revolution as the *unity* of genesis and validity. The materialist and the idealist separate genesis from validity, explaining the one as determined by the other. The only difference between the two methods is the relative weight they assign to each pole. As opposed to such reductionist methods, explanation of revolution as originary entails a new *relation* of genesis and validity. A brief illustration will be helpful here. I assign a major role to the Declaration of Independence, at the same time that I point to the material necessities which led to its promulgation. This does not imply that the Declaration played a causal role. I also stress the difference between the general principles it announces at the outset, and the concrete historical arguments it adduces for the necessity of a rupture. This does not imply that the ideas of the Declaration determined future development. Neither the history of colonial quarrels with England, nor the normative ideals of the colonists explains the revolutionary rupture, any more than either of them determines the shape of the next phase of the Revolution. The Declaration is *symbolic*; it institutes a new frame of meaning within which the now sovereign United States must both act and understand its own action. As the unity of these two aspects the Declaration is *originary*. It crystallizes a new sense of the past *and* poses new questions for the future.

This interpretation of revolution as originary suggests a distinction between politics and what I call 'the political'. Simply put, the political is that which gives sense to any given political practice; it is the symbolic matrix which is both its condition of possibility (that is, its genesis) and the framework establishing its legitimacy (that is, its intersubjective validity). This implies that although the pre-revolutionary colonists practiced a politics which some would call democratic, that judgement is based on a presupposition about the nature of democracy. Politics makes sense only within the framework of the political. Colonial politics was not a sort of acorn from which the oak of American democracy evolved. But one must be careful. A critique of such evolutionary materialism that views the politics of principle practiced during the quarrel with England as the ideological grain from which the new democracy sprouted is equally unsatisfactory. The same problem appears when critics of such idealism seek the germ of democratic politics in the struggle between the colonists and their British (and domestic) opponents. It reappears if the critic stresses instead the unintended consequences of the politics of self-interested resistance by a colonial élite. All of these accounts are bound to the frame of traditional politics; they fail to capture the *revolutionary* nature of American democracy because they do not pose the question of the political.

The political is a *modern* phenomenon[6] which emerges with modern revolutions. The destruction of the old order calls for a new one; but it does not provide its norms or define its path. The old order was a material context *and* a framework of meaning. Now everyday experience becomes problematic; the question of its sense is posed. Of course, the old norms and practices do not simply disappear; but the horizon against which they appear is no longer sharply defined. This situation parallels the one within which the philosophical programme known as *hermeneutics* emerged. As the Enlightenment penetrated society, it put into question the sense of the tradition; a technique for its reappropriation had to be developed. Hermeneutics is a method which was developed first for written texts but then broadened to deal with contexts of meaning including those of human behaviour.[7] The practice of interpretation within the problematic of Revolution takes the form which I describe by the categorial distinctions between history as lived, conceived, reflected and rethought. Revolutionary history as lived presents the originary structure; it is conceived with regard to its validity claims, and reflected in terms of its genetic conditions. The moment of reflection is *not* an Hegelian synthesis. The originary structure from which the process began – the problem of the political – remains present in the conceived and reflected moments; that is why the process moves on. This presence of the originary moment explains also why the rethinking of history is part of the revolution.[8]

I do not thematize this hermeneutic in this book; it is used in an intuitive manner, to guide the reader through an historical narrative whose implications are theoretical, and ultimately political. The three sections into which the work is divided elucidate practical problems lived, conceptualized and reflected upon by the Americans, and rethought by their heirs. It becomes clear that the question of sovereignty entailed the problem of representation; both of them point to the still-present dilemma of republican politics in a liberal and democratic society. The same hermeneutic method which articulates the three principle sections reappears within each section, whose culmination in new practical problems suggests that the rethinking is not simply theoretical. If this were the place for self-criticism, I would propose some modifications in the presentation. In particular, the third section could have treated the Philadelphia Convention as lived history, the *Federalist* as its conceived form, and the institutional arrangements that emerged in the first years of the republic as its reflected moment. I did not follow that procedure because I wanted to make clear that the reflected moment is *not* a synthesis. The symbolic nature of sovereignty in the *Federalist* develops my interpretation of the Declaration of Independence. It explains the sense in which American republican institutions are democratic, and how American liberalism differs from its European forms.[9]

The objection to an hermeneutic approach is that it cannot explain the 'cause' that generates the revolutionary process and/or provides it with the norms that it seeks to incarnate. The materialist and idealist interpretations make revolution either one-sidedly necessary or an irrational leap. From what position, or on what basis, does the narrator reconstruct the story? The hermeneutic method asserts that the presence of the revolution as the horizon within which the narration occurs justifies its account. But interpreting revolutions is not the same as elucidating literary texts. For example, at the conclusion of the Seven Years' War, the French Foreign Minister predicted that the victorious English colonies would eventually demand independence; but he did not expect this to take the form of a revolution. A more explicitly hermeneutic model presented by a historian of the 'imperial school', Andrew C. McLaughlin, encounters the same problem. He interprets the dialogue of the deaf which led the Americans to problematize the political as the result of an inability to understand the new 'federal' relations between the colony and the mother-country. British economic practice was based on mercantilism; its political theory was founded on its domestic constitutional principles. The colonies sought in vain to synthesize this opposition during the years that led to the rupture, but the weight of tradition was too strong. Neither side could conceive or reflect upon their federal relation – until its form emerged finally in the Constitution of 1787.[10] This makes revolution simply the explicit realization of implicit relations; it neglects the revolutionary discovery of the political question that founds democratic politics.

The hermeneutic approach cannot provide a causal account of revolution. It can only elucidate a process of practical questioning in which the sense of experience is torn from its traditional bounds. There is a virtue in this apparent vice; the hermeneutic reconstruction does not propose a final synthesis. The originary tension that was present at the outset remains, in different forms, at the conclusion of the story. American history did not end in 1787; the legacy of the Revolution permits a reading of that history, and permits the present to continue its writing. The hermeneutic method does not imply the 'end of ideology' that dominated liberal historiography in the 1950s. That approach argued that the destroyed tradition which made necessary the emergence of the modern question of the political in the form of revolutionary demands has been recreated in the form of a democratic 'civil religion'. But that assertion has to be interpreted in the context of the history of the Revolution. If democracy has become a tradition, it takes the form of the institutionalized process of questioning that *is* the Revolution. But this civil religion is *symbolic*; its existence confirms the attempt to interpret revolution in terms of the political. Democratic politics is the action of society upon itself which is made possible by the mediation of the political. This is why democratic politics does *not* exclude the social demands which the liberal synthesis degrades to the status of 'ideology'.

## THEORY AND POLITICS

This history of the American Revolution is also an attempt to formulate a more general political theory. The central category, the political, appears first as the problem of sovereignty, whose achievement with independence must then be realized through representative forms which are in turn defined by republican institutions whose practical basis must be democratic in order to conserve the sovereignty which was only declared in 1776. The development of this general theory is traced in the Americans' debates and in their institutional experience. The republican solution appears as the unity of the political theory of the old Whigs–for whom history is the struggle of Liberty against Power–and the Whigs–for whom politics presents the movement of a well-organized society. But the democratic complement to the republican political forms has to unite two forms of action whose nature and foundation appear contradictory: the political praxis of virtuous republicans oriented toward the public good, and the social practice of democratic individuals motivated by private interest. The democratic republic has to mediate and preserve both public and private liberty. This challenge was new; it had no precedents in classical political theory. The Americans' solution is not contradictory; its structure is *originary*. It was imposed not only by the Revolution; it defines also the conditions of modern politics.

The relation of a modern theory of the political to concrete political practice has to be specified. I skirted that problem in the book by developing the theory by means of an historical reconstruction.[11] But if the argument that emerged from the historical account is more than just descriptive, it must show that the hermeneutic reading permits also the political practice that one might call 'writing'.[12] This is why I have included here an Afterword, which suggests that the birth of political parties and the development of constitutional jurisprudence fulfill this function. Neither of these institutions was caused by the revolutionary experience; both were *new* political forms that cannot be reduced to developments of the traditional matrix. My analysis specifies the practical implications of the hermeneutic method. Both institutions provide means for dealing with the implications of the apparently contradictory originary structure. To the moment of genesis corresponds the problem of particularity: what are the specific problems, interests, institutions with which politics must concern itself? After all, not everything is, or ought to be, grist for the political mill; private freedom has to be preserved if the democratic individual is to be other than a member of mass society. On the other hand, to the moment of intersubjective norms corresponds the question of universality: how do the particular problems which enter the political agenda acquire legitimacy in a society of democratic individuals? After all, the individual is more than simply a self-seeking monad; the citizen of the republic cannot accept the privatized deformation of the *res publica*.

The problem cannot be solved simply by institutional means. Political parties and constitutional jurisprudence are not the only form in which the originary structure of the political can be concretized. These institutions can be distorted, one can come to dominate the other. Other institutional forms can exist, and have existed, in the American and other democratic republics. What history has produced is not the only thing that could have been created, or that will be invented by society as it works on itself. Because of its originary structure, the political can never be institutionalized once and for all; there is no single or simple practice or institution which is adequate to it. The symbolic can never be fully and completely translated into reality. This is what the critique of totalitarianism had taught (some of the) French left by the 1980s, and what (some) French historians have learned about their own Revolution.[13] A revolution which attempts to incarnate in reality the Good Society is condemned to failure, or to worse. But the American case suggests that the irreducibility of the political does not imply the impossibility of a just politics. The abandonment of the French model of a revolution which imposes change on society does not entail acceptance of the *status quo*. A just politics, in Cornelius Castoriadis' phrase, is one in which the question of justice can and must constantly be posed anew. As such, it recalls the democratic republican politics that is supposed to be the American civil religion.

My argument seems to have returned to the point of departure (if not the origin) of my preoccupation with American history and contemporary politics. Have I formulated my own variant of Louis Hartz's 'liberal tradition'? Conflict is integrated within a harmonious developmental pattern whose shape is determined at the outset. There is no place for fundamental opposition, let alone for a revolution which would not only overthrow the particular interests hiding behind the formal frame of republican government but would transform the structures which permit those interests to remain in power (and to use their power to exploit other peoples as well). At best, my interpretation seems to allow for liberal meliorism and individual moral stands. Collective democratic action is institutionalized in party machines which claim to be representative; political participation in the decisions that affect daily life is handed over to a sacralized Constitution. The litany could go on . . . and instead of writing a new chapter in American politics, I would have 'erased' all of the other options to which American history was open as well as the injustices – of which slavery is the most glaring, and whose legacy is still present – whose real existence my symbolic synthesis neglects.[14]

Such a criticism would miss the point. A 'democratic republic' is not simply a democratic society nor is it the formal institutions that define its political superstructure. The usual understanding of a democratic society takes the form of interest group pluralism in which political institutions preserve the freedom of each group to form and to agitate for its own private concerns. The model is often taken to be Madison's argument in the Tenth *Federalist.* But that implies that the republican institutional frame offered later in *The Federalist* is either superfluous or a further (superstructural) guarantee of liberal-pluralist private social interest. There is no need to rehearse the details of the interpretation of *The Federalist* that I have offered in the text. I try to show how the particular form of representation of the sovereign people created by the American republic makes necessary its democratic political practice. The republic is not built simply (or scientifically) on the division of powers which check and balance one another. More important is the facts that none of the powers, nor even their united action, can claim to incarnate the popular will. In Claude Lefort's phrase, the place of power is empty; power is everywhere and nowhere. Because the political is symbolic, the democratic republic can never be fixed in a given institutional or social structure. Democracy is necessary because society must constantly question the pretension of any institution *really* to incarnate the *res publica*, the republic.

With *this* argument, I have indeed returned to the origin of my questions: the civil rights movement and the movement for participatory democracy. Rights and participation are the most general formulations of the moments of normativity and genesis whose unity was defined as originary. Neither suffices by itself; when the civil rights movement turned increasingly to the courts for constitutional remedies, it died as a political movement for a democratic society; when the New Left stressed participation at the cost of institutional change, it imploded into the personal or exploded into 'revolutionary' gesture. The dilemma reproduces the conflict between the liberal and the communitarian, the republican and the democratic legacies of the American Revolution. The same theoretical problems are present in everyday practice. A recent essay by Karl E. Klare provides an illustration. The adversary model of labour relations insists on the individual rights of the worker; the co-operation model stresses the economic benefits to be gained in a workplace free from antagonism. Klare demonstrates that both positions are justified. He proposes a perspective that he calls 'workplace democracy' as a means to avoid the one-sided technical solutions. Not only is he right to refuse the dichotomy; he also is aware that 'workplace democracy' is not a once-and-for-all solution. His essay concludes with questions, rather than a formula for its achievement. The questions point to the need for a *politics*; the correctness of both techniques suggests that such a politics will be based on both rights and participation.[15]

I have not solved the problems that led me to write this book. It is enough here to have given theoretical form and historical grounding to these political questions. Neither theory nor history can deliver more. They can elucidate, but never explain exhaustively the dilemmas of politics in a democratic republic. They can point to the irreducibility of the political, and can criticize the necessary failure of any attempt to incarnate the Good Society. This does not imply satisfaction with the *status quo*, or the impossibility of social and political change. Understood correctly, the originary or symbolic nature of the political makes *necessary* precisely that struggle for change which is at once the foundation and essential nature of a democracy. Democracies, like revolutions, can be deformed. They can reify the political, or they can lose sight of it. There is much in contemporary America that outrages, scandalizes, and saddens the democratic republican. Moral indignation is no more useful than moral imprecation. The task is to understand the origins of the political and to change – not it, but a society which refuses to practice democratic politics.

## APOLOGY TO THE HISTORIAN

The reader will see that I owe an enormous debt to the historians; but the historian may find that I have not paid in full. Offering this essay now to an Anglo-Saxon public, I have to ask myself what changes would have been made had it originally been written in English? In all honesty, I am not certain that I would have dared to do so; after all, I too live in the academy, and my research has profited from its division of labour and imposed standards. (That hesitation may explain, too, why I did not undertake the translation myself.) The professional historian will, I hope, criticize more my exclusions than my arguments and reconstructions. It is tempting to take advantage of this Introduction to justify myself, just as I found myself wanting to rewrite parts of the book as I reviewed the manuscript of the translation. But what's done is done, and this Introduction should serve only to clarify what I intended to do.[16]

As history, the major weakness of this book is its neglect of the material conditions in which American politics developed. The presentation of the pre-revolutionary situation is no doubt too general; differences among the colonies are not developed in detail. Similarly, the experience of the war years could have been analyzed in greater breadth and depth. The Americans had expected a brief war, from which England would shrink when it realized the cost; while the English came to count on a war of attrition to dampen colonial ardour. The Americans did suffer, more than I indicate. Richard Buel, Jr. aptly titles his study of the Connecticut experience *Dear Liberty*; he wants to understand how the republican ardour of 1776 became the conservative politics that made Connecticut a bastion of Federalism into the 19th century. My presentation of the experience of the Confederation once the war ended is also open to criticism. To supplement my sketch with a discussion of Madison's essay on 'The Vices of the Confederation' was perhaps only a resort to expedience. The 'bankruptcy' of the Confederation was, after all, *real*. It was due to the costs of the war, but it was the result of a basic economic imbalance (to which the loyalist Samuel Seabury had pointed in his polemic with Hamilton shortly before independence): America was a colonial economy. This fact had material, and psychological, consequences which political theory could not ignore.

I can justify these historiographical weaknesses by the theoretical nature of my project. Others are more troublesome. I discuss the various popular political institutions that developed during the debate with England, but I do not follow out their role during and after the

Revolution. For example, the non-importation programme that worked well at the earlier time gave rise to divisions when it was tried during the war. The same difficulty confronted popular attempts at price regulation in the face of inflation. There was recourse to Committees of Public Safety during the war since, despite the principle of legislative domination, some sort of executive agency was needed. Relations between the national army and the local, supposedly volunteer, militias are not developed in my narrative. Nor do I evoke the development of forms of guerrilla warfare, the taking of hostages, or the attempt by what was no doubt a majority somehow to find a place between loyalism and revolution. As a result, my discussion of the debates concerning the ratification of the Constitution could be criticized.

Despite these limits, I have tried to flesh out my political story sufficiently to avoid the reproach of distortion while at the same time presenting a theoretical interpretation which is, so far as I can tell, and despite my debts to others, new. This brings me to two final criticisms, made by Richard Buel, Jr., which permit me to underline once again the aims of this book. Did I overstress the role of James Otis, while giving short shrift to the more important theoretical arguments of Daniel Dulaney and John Dickinson? Did I give too great weight to the Declaration of Independence, which was in effect only the crowning of a *fait accompli*, imposed ultimately on Congress by the presence of Howe's fleet in New York? I stressed Otis' arguments because I wanted to make clear the sense in which the American Revolution gave birth to a specifically *modern* politics. That is why Otis returns as a point of comparison later in the narrative, whereas the arguments of the others cannot serve that function. The same reasons explain my interpretation of the Declaration of Independence, which serves to make concrete the theoretical argument about the *symbolic* nature of the political. The stress on the Declaration is justified also by the role that it has played in the arguments of later American radicals, who want to find in it the material basis for a radical theory of democracy. As my arguments suggest, I do not believe it can play that role.

I have enjoyed writing this book, and admit too that I even enjoyed rereading it! I tried to find a style which, like the events I was narrating, preserved the open, experimental nature of the revolutionary process. And I confess as well that writing the book was far more a learning experience than was researching it: whatever I had learned from the historians had to be put back into the context of an ongoing political debate, in which choices were weighed, consequences evaluated, positions justified. In this sense, the book stands also as a practical lesson in political *thinking* as well as a theoretical argument about what has been thought.

It remains to thank those without whose help this book would not have come to fruition. A first version was presented at the Ecole des Hautes Etudes en Sciences Sociales in May-June 1985. François Furet, director of the school, as well as my receptive audience, provided encouragement to continue. Claude Lefort, whose ideas find echoes in this text, was particularly helpful. Guillaume Malaurie and Sabine Delattre of Editions Ramsay, as well as Pierre-Olivier Montheil, helped rework the text of the French edition. Further encouragement was provided by Antonin Liehm, editor of *La Lettre internationale*, in which a first version of the Introduction appeared, and by Joël Roman of the journal *Intervention*, in which an earlier essay, 'Why Return to the American Revolution?' was published. Joël Roman also provided critical help with the Afterword to this English edition, which was first published in *La revue Française de science politique* (and whose English translation now appears in my *Defining the Political*).

Preparation of this English translation was greatly aided by David Curtis, who provided far more than simply a rendition of my previous text. His queries forced me to tighten the arguments in this version; his rigor drove me to specify my assertions and to document my notes.* I had hoped that it would be possible to include here a more substantive Translator's Introduction, in which David Curtis would develop many of the arguments that he presented to me over the course of our collaboration. As that was not possible, I have tried to take into account some of his suggestions in the present Introduction. I am aware that I have not been able to do full justice to his positions, and can only hope that he will publish his arguments in due course.

Finally, if I wrote this book in French, it was due to my wife and to my parents-in-law, who have helped me to appreciate a certain France and another America. This book is dedicated to my in-laws as a small gesture of thanks.

Dick Howard
22 September 1988

---

* As indicated in the Preface to the French edition, I proposed here an essay, not a scholarly text. Consequently, the footnote apparatus has been reduced to a minimum. I hope that the professional historian will not take umbrage–even though my rigorous translator would have liked me to supply the missing links in more cases than I have.

# Introduction

A REVOLUTION?

It is a commonplace that the United States is a country without history, that it has no memory, that it scorns tradition, and that it is always seeking out the new. The energy, the optimism and the pragmatic spirit of the American people have their source in a faith that precedes experience; the destiny of America is felt as something natural, nay even predestined. But this robust attitude should not conceal anxieties and doubts equally rooted in the American character. A great 19th-century historian once said that the more the Frenchman, the German or the Englishman knows his culture and his history, the more he is French, German or English. But what about the American? How can s/he know him/herself? Is s/he the product of his/her Revolution? Before answering these questions we must pose another one: was there a revolution? In what way does the experience which unfolded over a period of 24 years between 1763 and 1787 alter the received view of the American, of his/her society, of his/her politics? Does its nature make us rethink our political ideas, our idea of the political?

The American Revolution passed through three phases, which developed around three problems: first of all, that of sovereignty; then, once independence was declared, that of the institutional forms through which this sovereignty could be represented; and finally that of the incompatibility between the political principles elaborated at the outset and the new institutional life established in the country. These three phases correspond successively to the immediately *lived*; to the *conceived*, which gives form to this first experience; and to the *reflected*, which integrates the first two.

Was there truly a revolution? Or is there, on the contrary, only a simple continuous process which begins with resistance against the Constitution of the freest country in the world, England; which then passed through the constitutional experiences of a country at war, only to be transformed in and through the new conditions of peacetime; and which culminated, finally, in a Constitution that remains in force two hundred years later? Are there no backward steps or leaps forward during these phases? Should one analyze each phase on its own before totalizing them under the concept of revolution? By what right does one try to merge under this one term such a diversity of actions, some of which were based on economic interest, others on the defence of traditional liberties within a liberal empire on its way to modernization and others still whose motivation was religious, even idealist in inspiration? One could provide a Marxist-like explanation, or one could appeal to Locke, to Montesquieu, or even to the theories of natural law. Some people will see a continuity in motivations, others will discover a learning process with anticipations of the new as well as backward steps. Some will separate the 'good' revolution from what followed and will talk of that work as being confiscated, while others will boast that they have opened a new era whose horizon extends to infinity.

Since 1789, the radical political transformation that a society operates upon itself has taken the name 'revolution'. Sometimes the French Revolution is opposed to the North American one, which is said to have been fought to gain independence but without transforming its institutions (except for eliminating the reference to the King) or its socio-economic relations. This American model (which some tried in the 1950s to sell to the now independent former colonies) is said to be based upon the demand for political liberty whereas the French Revolution is supposed to have tried to create, nay to impose, social equality. This difference in turn would explain why the American Revolution became decentralized whereas the French remained Jacobin even after the Jacobins had been eliminated. In a word, the American Revolution is said to have limited itself to political transformations, giving free rein to private initiative (or egoism), whereas the French sought a thoroughgoing transformation of society. The concept of *revolution* would then signify a total transformation of society and of the individuals that compose it. Politics would be the means; society, the end.

The thesis of two revolutions was formulated explicitly by Burke's translator – and later Metternich's secretary at the Congress of Vienna – Friedrich Gentz. His *The French and American Revolutions Compared* was immediately translated into English in 1800 by John Quincy Adams, the son of President John Adams, and employed during the electoral campaign that year, in which his father was opposed by Thomas Jefferson. The political form of Gentz's thesis served the forces of reaction in Europe; in the United States its function went beyond this partisan end while also fulfilling it. As early as the Declaration of Independence, contemporaries on both sides of the Atlantic did not hesitate to affirm that a revolution had occurred in America. Claude Fohlen notes that in France at the time the expression 'American Revolution' was more frequently used than the term 'War of Independence'. In America, this initial certainty was replaced by doubt as history put past victories into question. For some, the revolutionary break had been sealed by the Declaration of Independence; for them, the revolutionary process is reduced to the struggle against English tyranny between 1763 and 1776. For others, the important thing was the actual conquest of independence, crowned in 1783 by the Treaty of Versailles; for them, the Revolution was realized in the armed struggle through which the unity of the 13 independent colonies was forged. Finally, during the debates over the ratification of the new Constitution of 1787, neither its advocates nor its opponents hesitated to appeal to the 'principles of the Revolution' in order to support their own arguments and to launch an attack on those of their adversaries. But the questions the Americans were posing to themselves were not only partisan in character; questions of principle, of political philosophy, were at stake.

The principles to which all groups appealed were generalities, not only inherited from English colonial experience but also gleaned from the political history of humanity, of which the Americans showed their fondness throughout this period. Divergent and even contradictory meanings could be hidden under words like 'republic' or 'liberty' – not to speak of negative or pejorative concepts such as 'tyranny' or 'corruption', labels that were frequently abused. In an impressive flowering of political analyses were mixed together concepts developed with a thoroughly Newtonian boldness and pride. These concepts appealed to a transhistorical experience, drawn from the Greeks and Romans (and, of course, from the Bible) and brought up to date by reference to recent events in English history. The Americans developed arguments that were at once pragmatic and quite logical; one could use the lessons of history as one wished, the important thing was to prove one's point.

Theoretical, logical and pragmatic, the Americans were also an active, religious, adventurous people. They inhabited 13 colonies of differing cultures and institutions, sizes and economies, pasts and futures. They never had experienced political unity, and the unification produced by the Declaration of Independence was above all defensive. So far as it had a positive form, it centred on political theory, and existed as an intellectual opposition to the measures being undertaken by the new British Empire. But the heteroclite nature of the ideas underlying this unity became apparent when it came to applying this theory to the task of establishing independent political institutions. Locke's contractualism or the theory of natural law facilitated criticism but neither view had any idea of how to go about setting up positive institutions – for a people cannot enter into a contract with itself. The objective of establishing a virtuous republic activated popular participation, but it was a truism of classical political theory that a participatory democracy threatened to degenerate into tyranny if an adequate modern form could not be found. The republican idea, accepted by all, was not necessarily democratic in character; it was conceived of as the triumph of the common good over private individual interest, following the Spartan model, or else as the replacement of a corrupt, politically-dependent aristocracy by a meritocracy which could be considered as a natural aristocracy. But the creation of an aristocracy, whatever its foundation, was out of the question in a country that had just freed itself from old Europe.

Whatever the internal theoretical difficulties, the Americans were independent, and they believed they were republicans. But they also knew from political history that a republic is condemned to a continuous flight forward. They knew that republican virtue is always menaced. The Protestant tradition they had inherited served only to heighten their doubts and fears. The source for the regeneration of the virtuous republic was supposed to be found in the community and in the religious life and traditions of this sparsely urbanized country which lacked large industries but which nevertheless was active and energetic. This oft-repeated idea served as a retort to Montesquieu's thesis that a republic can survive only in a small territory. The revolution, in short, was the achievement of a state of independence that would guarantee local autonomy. But if a community becomes closed upon itself, it may engender narrow-minded, petty forms of behaviour incapable of forestalling an internal collapse and thus disproving the idea that independence had created a great, unified country with an open frontier. There thus arose another option, which replaces virtue with institutions capable of maintaining it. The Americans were prepared for this, thanks to the intense political life to which the independence of the 13 colonies and the Articles of Confederation had given birth. The new system, established upon an extended territory, was instituted through the Constitution of 1787. Was this the crowning of the Revolution . . . or its confiscation? A republic in which interest replaces virtue: was this not to reproduce just what they had reproached in the English mercantile empire when it seemed to threaten their liberties?

## THE REVOLUTION CONTINUES

The adoption of the new federalist Constitution of 1787 put an end neither to the Americans' doubts nor to the Revolution itself. Its advocates were accused of being counter-revolutionaries and budding tyrants who wanted to overturn the noble principles established by the Declaration of Independence. The national system that replaced the decentralized Confederation was perceived as a confiscation of the rights not only of the States but also of their communities and of the citizens whose voices would be drowned in a vast, but well shored up, ocean. Unity was achieved in part because everyone knew that George Washington, the 'Cincinnatus' who had led their armies to victory before retiring to his farm, would be the first President. But the preparation of the first elections without Washington revealed the existence of political parties – something the Constitution had not foreseen. The designation of John Adams of Massachusetts as president, with the Virginian Thomas Jefferson as vice-president, was the occasion for a dispute which the development of the French Revolution, supported in general by the Jeffersonians and criticized for its excesses by the friends of Adams, made into a question of principle.[1] Congress's adoption of the Alien and Sedition Acts gave Adams' government the power to censor the press and muzzle public opinion. In response, Virginia and Kentucky, under Jefferson's leadership, voted resolutions authorizing these States to annul federal laws with which they disagreed. Claiming the right to nullification based upon States' rights,[2] these resolutions became heavier with consequences when the Civil War approached, as the frontier moved west and the slavery question became acute. Before this test had to be faced, however, the Americans scored a first in political history: Jefferson won the 1800 elections, and a peaceful transfer of power was achieved. The implication was that society knew that it was divided and yet remained united. But this meant that the Republic could no longer be defined by the existence of a common good shared by all.

The political system ratified in 1800 by this transfer of power was, nevertheless, challenged constantly during the next 60 years of expansion leading up to the ultimate test of the Civil War. Despite Washington's admonitions in his *Farewell Address*, where, in the name of a nationalist isolationism, he warned his fellow citizens against intervening in European affairs, the War of 1812 saw England once again fighting against its former colonies. This war was far from unanimously popular, even after the taking of the Capitol – which was now located in Washington – and the burning of the White House. A Convention of New England States meeting in Hartford threatened to secede in 1815. In 1824, following the three great Virginians – Jefferson, Madison and Monroe – a son of these same New Englanders was returned to the White House. But John Quincy Adams remained there only four years; he was beaten by the new spirit (and the new economy) of the West as embodied by Andrew Jackson, the hero of the Battle of New Orleans. Jackson ran as a son of the people, and his inauguration to the presidency was a popular festival which symbolized the people's return to power. The Revolution was again the order of the day. This time, however, it took socio-economic forms, for example in Jackson's epic struggle against the National Bank. But the most serious peril lay at a deeper level: would the new States created by westward expansion be free or slave? So long as the South and the West were tied by reciprocal economic relations, the problem did not become explosive. But the railroad and the new worldwide commercial position of the industrial North compromised this alliance.

The bloody Civil War which freed the slaves and preserved the national Union can be interpreted in terms of the grid furnished by the experience of the Revolution. The priority given to national unity over States' rights seemed to echo the arguments of the federalists, who wanted to replace the loose Confederation with a national State. But President Lincoln's Gettysburg Address, which every American school-child learns by heart, begins with the strophe: 'Four score and seven years ago, our forefathers founded . . .' In other words, Lincoln dates the founding of the Republic from 1776, the year of the Declaration of Independence. Undoubtedly he was thinking of the preamble of this Declaration: 'We hold these truths to be self-evident, that all men are created equal, that they are endowed by their Creator with certain unalienable rights . . .' But Lincoln was not the only one to refer to the experience of the Revolution. The Southerners could invoke the Virginia and Kentucky Resolutions, which were inspired by Jefferson. They could also point out that, after all, the colonies had rebelled against English oppression and that the Declaration had affirmed the right to revolution as one of the fundamental rights of man. Moreover, as the iconoclastic Marxist historian, Eugene Genovese, has shown, these Southern cavaliers could claim to be the heirs of republican values for which the excessive, egoistic and exploitative capitalism ruling in the North had shown its contempt.

After the war southern Reconstruction gave way to westward expansion. The question of the Revolution was posed once again in 1893. Frederick Jackson Turner's *The Frontier in American History*, takes as its point of departure the fact that the conquest of the continent has been accomplished. But going beyond the frontier had been a trait constitutive of the American character. The existence of an always open space meant that the young republic would not repeat the classic cycle of political theory through which a young and courageous nation conquers an empire only to have its new wealth set it on the path toward corruption. America had saved itself from this temporal death by a continuous spatial movement. For some, expansion had to be pursued further by opening up new frontiers. This policy, symbolized by Theodore Roosevelt, culminated in the conquest of the Philippines and Cuba and opened the doors of China. This was the beginning of an American imperialism that claimed to be civilizing in character but whose psychological motive is to be found in the republican thought that guided the Revolution.

Against Roosevelt's conquering republic, militant populism dreamed of returning to an America founded on the individualistic and communitarian principles of the Declaration of Independence. The populists were isolationists in foreign affairs but were violently opposed to the new economic giants symbolized by the trusts and their entrepreneurial chieftains, the 'Robber Barons'. Even though the populists were defeated, their cause has remained present in the American mind. It is found again in Woodrow Wilson's 1916 re-election campaign, mixed with a current of state reform that recalls the spirit of 1787, and then once again, in an identical manner, in the New Deal of Franklin Roosevelt. And then, when the Welfare State found that it had feet of clay, the populist spirit reawakened, this time in the form of a *conservative* politics which does not neglect the opportunity to appeal to the origins of the republic. The vitality of this originary spirit, coming from the depths of the myth of a constantly to be recreated frontier, explains why the question of the American Revolution remains topical today, even though it may seem buried in history books. The encounter of the problematic of the historian with a recurring demand from society gives to the work of the researcher a philosophic dimension, that of an open history, of the self-interrogation of American society.


THE REVOLUTION AS HISTORICAL OBJECT

As we follow the Revolution through the three stages of its development we will also analyze how historians have thought through this history. Their manner of apprehending the events, the outlook they have chosen for interpreting them, and their own implication within contemporary history all go to show that history, *nolens volens*, is a philosophical and open discipline. The first school of historians to rethink the closing of the frontier and the singularity of the American experience looked at the Revolution in terms of its relation to European history. Around the same time and in the wake of the populist movement, a 'progressive' school emphasized popular participation in the Revolution as well as its democratic character. This school projects its criticism of the trusts onto the events that led to the Constitution of 1787, which they interpret as a *coup d'état* engineered by certain interest groups against the people. After 1945 came a critique of these progressives, along with a new positive interpretation, known as the school of American 'exceptionalism' or 'consensus'. This school reactivated Tocqueville's thesis that the United States had the luck to be born liberal. According to this view, the institutions of 1787 were modelled on the national character; every participatory reform, every attempt to renew the country's alleged virtue, could only be illusory in this middle-class democracy. But this continuity thesis poses anew the question of the Revolution.[3]

The historians' questioning of the Revolution is therefore above all philosophical. This, indeed, is the way the Revolution itself had been lived during an era when, as Douglass Adair has remarked, history was essentially the search for the universals that shape the way people lived in society. The political principles upon which Americans leaned were drawn from history, but their legitimacy was philosophical. As such, the debate among historians cannot come to an end: the Revolution cannot be reduced to an event, its meaning does not exhaust itself in any institution, its outcome is not limited to the social sphere. The Revolution is *political*; it institutes new political relationships, going beyond both the material interests that grow within and beneath these new relationships and the inherited schemata through which people try to understand their life as a collectivity. The question of the Revolution is *philosophical*; it challenges the institution of a new world in which the concepts of power, of law, and of the individual that lives them are transformed. More precisely, it is not the question that is philosophical but rather the Revolution that questions us, due to the fact that in our own way we still are participants in it.

Recent historiography of the American Revolution seems to have taken account of this philosophical dimension almost without knowing it. The pioneering work of Bernard Bailyn and Gordon Wood aroused enthusiasm, for a while, for what has been called the 'republican synthesis'. But this work has not been followed up.[4] Bailyn attempted to trace the political logic articulated in the pamphlets published during the long conflict with England prior to independence. He developed a (sociological!) theory of his own historiography in an article published several years after his key work, *The Ideological Origins of the American Revolution* (1967). Using the ethnographic method of Clifford Geertz, Bailyn argued that the political logic he had uncovered became an ideological framework that served to twist the meaning of each action by the English into that of an aggression, so that reconciliation became impossible and the crisis was aggravated. Ideology functioned as a sort of grammar permitting the colonists to interpret a world that was becoming alien to them. It encouraged Americans to defend themselves and to free themselves from a corrupt and menacing England. But this ideology provided no suggestions as to what should be put in its place. This is why Bailyn's study stops with independence, which he describes in socio-psychological terms.

Gordon Wood's work, *The Creation of the American Republic, 1776–87* (1969), completes Bailyn's analysis. Wood studies the ups and downs of the ideology Bailyn discovered from the point where this ideology begins to take on institutional forms. What was valid for interpreting the power of others is no longer applicable in a country where popular sovereignty is the foundation for its institutions such that it needs only to be protected against itself. Since the role of ideology is to throw a veil over experience, time is needed for it to decline in influence. Here Wood's method differs from the approach taken by Bailyn. Wood shows how the new meaning of the revolutionary experience is formed. The ideology analyzed by Bailyn partakes of this experience without exhausting it. Other theories coexist with that of the 'republican synthesis'; all of them correspond to the interests involved and permit an understanding of them. Wood follows this complex experience and its contradictions as they emerge in the drafting of constitutions for the 13 newly independent States; he shows, further, how people rebelled against the new institutions in which popular liberty was supposed to be anchored; and he traces the slow birth of a new form of political thought which blossomed finally in the Constitution of 1787. The result, according to Wood, is a new type of political thought that goes beyond classical politics to found politics in society itself. Politics becomes sociology.[5]

The sociologizing of the political to which Wood's analysis leads is not unanimously accepted. One can grant, with Bailyn, that the ideology of the Americans preceded and determined the actions they undertook. Political thought would therefore relate anew to, and transform, the social relationships in which it is rooted. Thus Pauline Maier describes, in *From Resistance to Revolution* (1972), how the people, manipulated by economic interest groups at the beginning of the conflict with

England, became aware of their power and of their political capacities. The class of artisans and workers then becomes the force that defends the Revolution when economic interest groups are tempted to compromise with Parliament. These new citizens adopt as political concepts ideas that the economic interest groups were using merely as rhetorical slogans. They transform them into reality and turn them into a political power.

But Maier does not broach the question of what institutions would be able to embody this new reality and would be able to preserve, and even reinforce, this new strength. Hers is a sort of plebeian version of the thesis of J. G. A. Pocock, whose *The Machiavellian Moment* (1975) traces the ups and downs of the republican idea (and ideal) from Florence to Venice, rediscovering it in the English Revolution, and then in the rebellious colonies. The crucial point in this vast panorama is the dialectic that Pocock elucidates between the republican *virtù* of Florence and the institutionally guaranteed serenity of the Venetian republic that endures beyond the accidents of its history. Pocock proposes a new answer to the question whether the principles of 1776 are opposed to those of 1787. For him, the inspiration of republicanism did not die in 1787; politics has not been replaced by sociology, commerce has not replaced virtue as the foundation of the republic. Republican thought will arise again in the course of the history of this reputedly liberal, if not downright capitalist, country. The argument is attractive for a country that has never known a serious socialist movement or a true conservative movement.[6] But the challenge set by Gordon Wood – how to institutionalize the whole revolutionary experience – has still to be met.

## THE REVOLUTION AS PHILOSOPHICAL SUBJECT

During the years when the American political system was becoming established there was no genuine opposition to the Revolution. Not that all Americans were united around a project for the future or that their society was homogeneous in a way that prevented conflicts of interest from forming within the overall revolutionary movement. Quite the contrary. The Revolution was violent, and it did not hesitate to curb its real or imagined enemies. It seemed to go too far for some, to stop too soon for others. The leaders of one phase lost their influence and their position as the energies freed up thanks to the break with old habits overflowed the boundaries within which these leaders hoped to contain them. The historian of the Revolution rediscovers in each town, region or State all the forms of personal, economic, social and political conflict found everywhere else: vanguard parties, a polemical press, coalitions that do not distinguish between personal interest and that of the common cause, personal conflicts masked by political verbiage, military men seeking to gain civilian power, financial and land speculation. And the historian discovers too that the Revolution did not benefit everyone, and that those who felt cheated were not about to let things go by without a fight. Nonetheless, there was no genuine opposition.

The fact is that the Americans all shared the same ideology – Whig thought[7] – but differed on how best to realize it. English in origin, Whiggism in its general form was broad enough to contain ideas drawn from Antiquity as well as from the Bible, from the French Enlightenment as well as from the scientific revolution. As a philosophy of history, it describes an evolutionary process characterized by the slow and progressive triumph of Liberty over a Power that always seeks to extend its domain. At the outset, it is supposed, the Norman Conquest destroyed the ancient liberties of the Saxon people. Progress began when the Magna Carta was wrested from King John in 1215. The Lords, and then the Commons, little by little, take back their old liberties at the expense of a monarchy whose power is based on the control of executive functions centralized in the Court. England's true Whig liberty will be assured finally when the three social estates are integrated into and balanced within Parliament; English sovereignty will then be founded upon the 'King in Parliament'. The political theory of Whig thought thus opposes Liberty, as embodied in the assembly, to Power, as represented by the executive.

In this context, there was no genuine opposition in America because resistance was based upon the right to self-government confronted with invasive English power. The English were represented in the colonies by governors, named by London, who controlled the upper chamber. The lower, or popular, chamber had little by little extracted the right to control its own financial affairs. The members of this popular chamber considered themselves a meritorious élite, in sharp contrast to an aristocracy dependent upon British political favours. This indigenous élite appealed to Whig thought in order to justify its slogan, 'No Taxation Without Representation'. The result was a broad alliance against English policy, at least during the first phase of the revolt. But things were not so simple, as Maier shows, in as much as Whig ideology evolved as the conflict developed. What is more, had not English history been marked by two revolutions in the 17th century, one of which had cost the life of a king and established a republic whose excesses, in turn, had brought about a new tyranny?

The first English revolution, begun in 1640, seemed to confirm the dangers inherent in the Whig conception of how liberty is achieved. The republic had been undermined by more radical currents; democracy had been instituted only briefly, and tyranny had followed, precisely as classical political theory since Aristotle and Polybius had foreseen it. Whig thought had to alter its vision; the simple dichotomy between power and liberty had to find a balance that would allow for the establishment of a stable as well as a just government. The so-called 'Glorious' Revolution created the conditions for this altered goal, and the Walpole government achieved the desired stability soon thereafter. As for justice, the success was less striking. Certain Whigs, who expressed their opinions in the celebrated newspapers of Addison and Steele, *The Tatler* and *The Spectator*, criticized the Court and the aristocrats in the name of what we would identify today as the rising bourgeoisie. They were referred to, without the slightest appearance of irony, as the 'polite Whigs'. And they were not the sole opposition.[8]

The English opposition in the 18th century was grouped under the label 'Country', to distinguish them from the Court. The Country was united only in its criticism of a system whose motor was, to use their language, 'corruption'. This corruption, however, could cut two ways; it could characterize the behaviour of the Court but also that of the people. The corrupt Court sought to extend its power; it found in the people willing, indeed equally corrupt, accomplices, ready to sell themselves in order to obtain favours from the Court. Opposition factions were split in their analysis of the fundamental cause of this corruption as well as on the manner in which it should be remedied. One of the factions, which corresponded to the interests of the landed aristocracy, blamed the Court. The other, which corresponded to the interests of an urban and commercial stratum, found the root of the evil in the people. The slogan of 'the republic' was the only cement holding together their efforts to achieve an eventual common programme. But this shared concept concealed divisions. Among the aristocracy, Bolingbroke's supporters adhered to a programme that could be summarized by the title of his essay, *A Patriot King*; the other faction, the Old Whigs, which included a strong Puritan component, insisted upon the virtue that a citizen in a republic was supposed to exhibit. It was this last trend that left its mark in America, that Protestant, Puritan country of pilgrims which had no king.

It is admittedly somewhat anachronistic to designate the system desired by the opposition by the concept of the republic. This was not the term of choice in the speech of the era, but confusions and inconsistencies within the opposition authorize this conceptualization of its goals. Americans did not talk about the goal of a republic before 1776; but thereafter it became a household word which we must analyze in order to understand the terms of the debates and the respective political choices that were made. The intuition of a Tom Paine, according to whom a republic was simply a government without monarchy which aims at realizing the common good, did not help much when it came to framing constitutions and designing free institutions. A country that was strongly influenced by a sober Calvinistic religiosity could not – as Paine had done – gamble everything on the basis of an optimism which assumes that people are already virtuous and that they become corrupt only under the effect of bad institutions. The American conception of a republic had to include not only guarantees of liberty but also stimulants for virtue. The republic had to be able to protect itself from its own negative inclinations.[9] Thus, the winning of autonomy from the English was not in itself a full realization of the revolution.

The Americans' republican model was first of all based on the English system which the Americans knew quite well both in theory and in practice. But for this very reason, their analyses were confused. They mixed together principles drawn from sources as different as Montesquieu and Locke, Harrington and Hume, natural law and common law as codified by Blackstone. Although this thought did not play an important role, one can follow the Americans' logic by starting with Rousseau's statement that 'all legitimate government is republican'. But one must then draw the consequences of his definition of a republic: 'any State ruled by laws, under whatever form of administration this might be: For only then does the public interest govern, and public affairs mean something'. The American conception of popular sovereignty that emerged from the first stage of the Revolution corresponded to Rousseau's idea of the general will, so that 'in order to be legitimate, the Government must not be confused with the sovereign, but be its minister: Then Monarchy itself can be a Republic'. But the difficulties begin when Rousseau rejects the idea that the general will can be represented. The English roots of the American experience led it down another path. The distinction between the sovereign and the government was worked out only at the end of the journey.

The concept of a republic as the American Whigs understood it included three different aspects whose political implications gradually became apparent during the course of the Revolution. This experience was necessary for Whig thought to be capable of criticizing itself and adapting itself to the new conditions of a new world. This continuous self-criticism, in deeds as well as in theory, distinguishes the American revolutionary experience from that of the French, who were confronted by a real opposition seeking to restore the old order. Thus, a disappointed partisan of the Revolution, Noah Webster, wrote in 1787: 'The jealousy of the people in this country has no proper object against which it can rationally arm them – it is therefore directed *against themselves*, or against an invasion which they *imagine* may happen in future ages'.[10] The root of this jealousy is, of course, Whig ideology. The Americans could free themselves from it only when they became aware that it is imaginary. At the end of that process, the general will or the *res publica* would be replaced by justice as the goal and legitimation of the republic. From it was then born a form of political thought freed from the old imported categories that grew out of an experience of servitude. But we have not yet come to that point. Indeed, we may still, today, need to reflect on our foundational experience in order to realize it.

The classical republic had at first been the *res publica*, the common and public 'thing', as opposed to private affairs where private interest dominated. The republic was the sphere of the political where liberty dictated its own law. This was the sense in which John Adams defined it in his important pamphlet of 1776, *Thoughts on Government*, as a government of laws and not of men. But Adams did not specify the institutional means whereby these laws could be drawn up. He left aside the question of virtue, which cannot be presupposed but which is necessary if public liberty is not to be replaced by private interest. Such a republican government could be monarchical or aristocratic, but Adams was opposed to the English government because of the corruption that in practice distanced it from the model. A government of laws could be opposed also to participatory and democratic self-government to the extent that in the latter case the people would be both judge and interested parties in public affairs at the same time. But Adams could not have recourse to the usual alternative, namely, the one granting representation to a sort of aristocracy which claimed to obey the requirements of republican behaviour and to contribute to the discovery of the common good. That model was too abstract.

Another definition of the republic furnished the first elements of a response. It is well-known that England did not (and still does not) have a written Constitution. Its social structure is called its Constitution, which combines and organically unifies the three constituent parts of society (the estates) in the political functions of the monarchy, the Lords and the Commons. All three, and therefore their specific virtues, are represented in Parliament, the incarnation of sovereignty and therefore of the common good for all. This means that the structure of the republic depends in the last instance upon the structure of the society it is supposed to govern. When the Americans' jealous and unending practice of self-criticism proved to them that their new world had brought forth new and democratic social structures, they had to revise this image of the republic. The theory of mixed government, founded upon an organicist and corporatist image of society, had to be replaced with another one, capable of taking into account the egoistic, self-interested, non-virtuous character of individuals. It was necessary to transform the nature of law and to revise one's conception of justice.

A third formulation of the concept of the republic begins, then, with the recognition of the social changes that had put the organic connection between the social and the political into question. Basing itself on the simple definition of the republic as a government of laws and defining the common good simply as liberty, this theory returns to the original Whig vision. It defines the republic as the institutional form capable of preventing Power from overflowing into the sphere of Liberty. In America, a twofold slippage occurred. On the one hand, liberty of religious conscience became the model for virtue; but this freedom is private, and the virtue that it delineates may follow the same path. On the other hand, this tendency toward privatization went hand in hand with the process of social democratization that came with the separation from the monarchy and its artificial political divisions. The republic would then be the political form that guarantees private freedom, including therein the freedom of socio-economic interests. Privatized in this way, virtue would no longer have a place in the political sphere – or if it is not excluded, the sphere of the political is itself absorbed by private interest.

Like us, the contemporaries of the Revolution asked themselves whether a republican politics based on public virtue could be made compatible with a commercial society based upon the private interest of the abstract and isolated individual. We rejoin here the challenge posed by the progressive historians: is the foundation of an independent capitalist economy the necessary conclusion of the American revolution? And if the capitalist economy, with all its defects, is the product of a political revolution, can it be remedied by politics? But what kind of politics? Or should one develop instead a social revolution as the only kind that can avoid the dangers of a politics based on private interests?

But can the Revolution be reduced simply to its effects? Should we not rather seek to define what this new politics, made possible by the Revolution, is opening toward?

## THE REVOLUTION AND POLITICAL MODERNITY

This analysis of the Americans' experiences of republicanism seems to weaken the thesis that contrasts the American and French Revolutions in terms of political versus social changes. In a depoliticized America, society is distinct from its political representation. Private interest is legitimated by political institutions that are incapable of imposing limits on it. The attempt by republican politics to transcend social interests is replaced by a politics that combines these interests and adds them together; as such, it can take on a liberal or neo-conservative hue. According to the latter orientation, the separation between society and the political depoliticizes social conflicts. The search for justice is relegated to the private sphere, and the end of ideologies is thus justified. Moreover, democratic participation is replaced by a technocratic politics that cannot speak its name, for it believes that it is based on the eternal laws of the market which it wishes to liberate from the political distortions imposed by the Welfare State. On the other hand, the politics of liberalism, which is based upon the same separation of the political and the social and upon the same economic market, makes a virtue of necessity: political life in the United States appears to it as the perpetual self-transformation of economic society, a sort of permanent revolution preserved by constitutional mechanisms which guarantee that no branch of government can claim to embody and thus impose its measures in the name of the popular will.

The distinction between the social and the political therefore seems to be the foundation of modern politics. But things prove to be more complex in light of the American Revolution. Jürgen Habermas, for example, proposes a thesis that can be designated as that of the two revolutions turned upside down.[11] According to him, what is at stake are two interpretations of the philosophy of natural law. For the French, natural law was an ideal to be realized, by force if necessary, whereas for the Americans it was a real state of affairs which could only be distorted by political intervention. Thus, for example, Burke, who attacked the rationalist pretensions of the French Revolution, took on the defence of the American colonists in their debate with England. On this interpretation, the American Revolution would be a conservative restoration whose ethics were thoroughly anti-modern and anti-political in character. The French Revolution would then be the only truly modern one, for it sought to impose a single, united will upon a disparate society. American liberty, often opposed to French equality, would be an archaic form which has no place in a modern society. Had not Hegel said that the State does not exist in the United States? And are not the Americans right to use the term 'administration' to designate the government in Washington?

The Whig ideology which the Americans used in their interpretation of English politics postulated the existence of a Power distinct from social freedom. According to the classical model, this power was considered necessary to the existence and cohesion of society. But this model is pre-modern, as were many of the Americans' arguments against the English. The Americans were using a corporatist tradition, with its ideal of natural equity, and its idea of a moral economy; they were opposing morality to the political autonomy into which they wanted to fit their society. Their attitude was that of fearful provincials confronted by the modernization of an empire. John Dickinson, the 'Farmer from Pennsylvania', expressed the attitude of these provincials quite well when he said, 'A free people therefore can never be too quick in observing, nor too firm in opposing the beginnings of *alteration* either in *form* or *reality*, respecting institutions formed for their security. The first kind of alteration leads to the last'.[12] And this same Dickinson concluded one of his refutations of pre-1776 English policy in a satisfied tone with the simple statement: 'This I call an innovation; and a most dangerous innovation'.[13]

The American Revolution thus appears as the result of a thoroughly conservative attitude. But American institutions seem to rule out a conservative attitude. Noah Webster had explained the difficulty: American politics was based on an imaginary representation characterized by jealousy and a levelling spirit. Once free, however, America was confronted with an unprecedented situation to which neither classical theory nor its Whig variant applied. Power and Liberty were henceforth one; liberty had to become self-sustaining. This new structure could easily be misunderstood, for it appears that each institutional representation of liberty is merely a new manifestation or incarnation of the old tyranny. But this is to condemn modern politics in the name of a pre-modern theory. A modern structure, whether it be political, aesthetic, scientific or religious, is characterized by autonomy, its immanence. The Whig image of the world was pre-modern; functioning in a free America, it could only condemn the very liberty that it believed to be its foundation and its goal.

The American Revolution began with Whig theory and culminated in its radical reversal. Instead of protecting Liberty against Power, the sovereign and independent nation saw itself obliged to invent institutions, forms of power, that would guarantee liberty. An immediate form of representation claiming to be the incarnation of liberty, such as the English Commons, was excluded since liberty was itself now in power. Yet America's plural society, with its multiple interests, could not be embodied directly in political institutions. The people in their plurality–the preamble of the Constitution of 1787 speaks in the name of 'We the people'–are the foundation and the limit for political acts. The situation recalls Rousseau's intuition concerning limited government, but limited in this instance by a changing plurality in which interests combine with each other in a variety of ways. The plural people reserves and preserves its political judgement. It does not claim to speak in the name of any principle or to dictate eternal truths; and it cannot claim to be truly unified in one class, institution or single interest. The ultimate political authority, the Constitution, is considered a norm: it is neither a reality nor an actor on the social scene.[14] Society changes itself by reference to that Constitution which serves as a symbolic mediation permitting it to define its specificity and to understand the goals which it pursues. This non-real, symbolic status of the political ensures that the Revolution has no end, in both senses of the term.

If this revolutionary structure fulfills the requirements of modernity, why does its contemporary form leave something to be desired? Beyond the criticisms that one can address to American society, the important thing to point out is that nothing prevents that society from changing through an appeal to politics–but not to the model of politics furnished by the French Revolution. It is not a matter of government intervention, but of action undertaken by society upon itself through the symbolic mediation of the political. Change is readied when two demands are met: that of universality, proximately embodied by law and in the last instance by the Constitution; and that of a particularity that permits the social expression of this universality. This particularity must at the same time be able to make a claim to universality. This is what we lived, for example, during the Civil Rights Movement, when social actions (for example, sit-ins) made manifest a contradiction between the positive laws of the country and its Constitution. But this movement suffered a double setback, when social action neglected this universality and became simply another competing interest group; and when those who appealed only to constitutional law thereby separated themselves from their active social supporters. Change in American society cannot come from above, but neither can it deny the political. The history of two hundred years of institutional life in the United States could be presented in terms of this simple affirmation.

The American Revolution is modern because it results from, and it invites, society's action upon itself. Pre-modern politics, subjected to the image of an organic society, saw stability as its priority. It could not help but be conservative in actual fact. The politics inaugurated by the American Revolution is founded upon an open and changing society motivated by interests; it can only be dynamic, active and pragmatic.[15] Modern politics is inaugurated by a political *revolution*. This origin raises problems on both the theoretical and the practical levels. Must the economy dominate society, as it tends to do in capitalist societies? Economic interest is not necessarily justified under all circumstances. How can political authority allow society to give itself another yardstick for its actions, other norms? It seems clear that political institutions create the space and the relationships within which capitalist relations are embodied. But if these institutions have a meaning that is above all symbolic, how can one define and undertake social change? The answers to these questions will not be found in this study, but one will come to understand the basis for asking them and the necessity for posing them. It is not a matter of determining whether the Revolution was good or bad, whether it went too far or not far enough, whether it was more authentic than the one in France; it is a matter of apprehending it as an originary revolution which is our legacy.

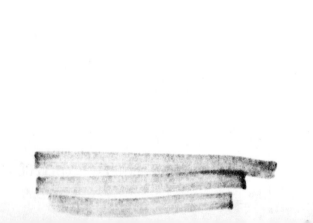

# Part I
# Toward Independence: Sovereignty and the Rights of Man

# 1 History Lived: The Birth and the End of the First British Empire

## COLONIAL PREMISES

The English colonization of North America began slowly and without a precise political goal. Some emigrated in order to practice their religion freely, others did so for reasons of simple self-interest. Nor were there only English colonists in this New World. Competition between European powers extended to this far-off shore. New York was taken from the Dutch in the 17th century, leaving the field open for the Anglo-French rivalry to which the Seven Years' War put an end in 1763. Part of the continent's southern regions and the area along the great Mississippi River – which became French Louisiana, but which Napoleon sold in 1803 to the newly-independent country – were then controlled by Spain. Nor should we forget the existence of an indigenous population, which was sometimes reduced to the role of pawn in the struggles between the various colonizers, but which also sought to defend itself before it was finally pushed back and brought to the point of near annihilation.[1]

The 13 English colonies had few political ties with each other beyond their common dependence upon the Crown. For this negative unity to constitute an independent political reality, a shared symbolic space born of the question of sovereignty and therefore of liberty had to be created. But until then, and for more than a century, the colonists, separated from their country of origin by an ocean, worried first and foremost about their own survival. Politics concerned only a tiny minority, and the great debates about identity and liberty concerned only the Churches (which thus produced a religious conscience capable of taking a political form). As in the case of the formation of an independent political reality, this point of departure, wherein politics played no explicit role, would have a symbolic effect later, when the Church contributed to the spirit of independence. But for the moment, each colony lived more or less on its own, relating to the others only through the intermediary of the British. For these reasons, loyalties were concentrated on the local and regional

23

levels; and relations with England were lived in a more immediate way than were relations with neighbouring colonies.

The first colonization efforts (in Virginia beginning in 1609, in Massachusetts starting in 1620) were interrupted by the English Revolution of 1640–41, which led to the execution of Charles I and aroused in many of those who were inclined to emigrate a hope for a profound transformation of English society. When these hopes were dashed and as this transformation appeared limited to changes in political personnel[2] after the end of Cromwell's dictatorship–which, moreover, justified the classical fear that democracies degenerate–colonization resumed at an even faster pace than before. The population, which in 1650 was only around 50 000 inhabitants scattered along the Atlantic coast–this being less than the number of colonists in the Caribbean Islands, whose sugar production was more lucrative and whose parliamentary lobby was more powerful–then increased very rapidly: to 250 000 in 1700, 1 170 000 in 1750, 1 593 600 in 1760, and finally 5 000 000 in 1800. This growth could not help but influence the way in which the colonists viewed their place and their role in the Empire, and in history. It also testifies to the material transformations in their lives and in their towns.

Demographic growth in the colonies of North America was an expression of a profound change in the economies of the European nations, although it was still barely perceived by economists and even less by politicians. The centre of the Western world was shifting irresistibly from the Mediterranean toward the Atlantic. And while the idea of a continental empire remained alive in the political imagination, the transatlantic interests of the European nations were rendering anachronistic the hopes nourished by the royal houses since the failure of Henry IV's plans, which continued to nourish the imagination of philosophers in the age when Rousseau and Kant still dreamed of 'Perpetual Peace'. The age-old competition between the Hapsburgs and the Bourbons no longer made much sense. Then began a second 'Hundred Years' War', which would end only with what Robert R. Palmer and Jacques Godechot name the Atlantic democratic revolutions, of which those of North America and France are only the best known.[3] This shift in the axis of international political relations was to have an effect upon social relations within each nation, beginning with the economy but not limited to that aspect of social life.

Mercantilist thought sought to take into account the new ties being established by the phenomenon of continuously expanding world trade. This theory included two components, one economic and the other political, whose contradictions were not often perceived at the time. The central idea was that a country's foreign trade should bring in a surplus in liquid assets. The goal of earning such a surplus was justified on the political plane by the fact that this surplus could be cashed in on the level of inter-State relations. But on the economic plane, this politically valuable surplus was obtained through the export of real exchange values produced within the country. Putting a mercantilist policy into work on the plane of foreign relations therefore had domestic political repercussions. Such repercussions could be dampened somewhat by a policy of colonization. But the building of an economic empire depended, in its turn, upon the success of mercantilist policy. This gordian knot was cut by the Glorious Revolution which, from this point of view, ended only in 1694 with the foundation of the Bank of England and the stabilization of the national debt, which consecrated the socio-political domination of the commercially-oriented Whig gentry. Empire building could finally begin.

Whig power, at its apogee under Walpole, resolved the contradiction between mercantilist economics and politics only at the practical level. It is often thought that Locke's theory had been formulated in order to justify the Revolution of 1688 and that this theory provided the Glorious Revolution with its theoretical legitimation.[4] But, the terms of the debate at the time do not support that view. There was indeed an opposition which criticized the new commercial society (and the military policies accompanying it); but it arose later, around 1730. This opposition united the divergent interests of artisans, manufacturers and urban professionals with those of an aristocracy reacting against the devaluation of its landed wealth that resulted from the appearance of new financial forms of wealth. The opposition's unity was expressed in the theory that contrasted, in classical terms, the virtuous political republic to an egotistical commercial society. This unified opposition, the 'Country' party, was the rival of the 'Court' faction. Before looking at their counterparts in America, we should stress the paradox entailed in this situation. The Court party, whose programme was radical and innovative in economic matters, was socially conservative; the Country party, on the other hand, was conservative on economic questions but radical when it came to social matters. Neither group succeeded in harmonizing their political conceptions with economic theory. Both claimed to be the heirs of the Whig Revolution, which they interpreted in different ways, even though they both proceeded from shared premises.

The 1688 Revolution which overthrew James II was justified by the classical republican tradition, which recognized a right to resist tyranny.

In its classification, this did not contradict but complemented the Whig premises. Whig theory, in its broadest sense, imagines a society organized and directed by a power to which liberty must always serve as a counterbalance. The Whig monarchy brought into being by the Glorious Revolution was supposed to incarnate the three components of society – monarchic, aristocratic and democratic – and their respective virtues – energy, honour, good sense – and to integrate them into a political nation wherein social harmony and political institutions converged toward a single goal: the *res publica*, this common good that founds the 'Commonwealth'. However, this classical ambition was contradicted by mercantilist reality. Commerce, growth and individual interest had no place in the classical view. The classical republic was not intended to deal with the tasks faced by a commercial power. The republican ethic could not coexist for long with the new dynamics of the economy. The generality of the republican conception allowed diverse interests to join together temporarily under its banner. This unity was broken in North America rather than in the mother-country, with consequences that challenged the foundations of the classical theory of politics.

The American colonies participated only from afar in British political institutions, but they profited directly from Britain's economic life. Americans felt themselves to be profoundly English, sometimes more English than the English. It was as if their distance from the homeland created in them the need for an identity which had to be expressed not in economic but in political terms. If one adds to this the enduring influence of the Protestant religion, one understands why each political initiative on the part of the colonists necessarily had to be accompanied by a theoretical legitimation addressed *urbi et orbi*. The Americans become Whigs by conviction, ferocious republicans jealous of their English liberties; they take seriously the ideological battles of the English, amplified by distance and simplified by isolation. And yet they are, at the same time, good, commercially-oriented Whigs, differing in this respect from the colonists of the rich Caribbean Islands as well as from the British conquerors of India (definitively won by the English near the end of the Seven Years' War, which had also confirmed English supremacy over North America). Such as it was, then, American unity before the onset of the movement for independence was built only upon adherence to a contradictory combination of mercantilism and republican Whiggism.

In fact, differences between the colonies were more evident than what united them. The imperative of rapid growth was not achieved everywhere at the same pace. The policy of encouraging immigration was sometimes paradoxical. With an abundance of cheap land, wage labour was relatively scarce and it cost dearly. The indigenous populations resisted the colonists' plans; they were hunted down so as to take their land. The trip to the New World was a difficult one which could tempt only the needy or the adventurous to leave Europe; and when they arrived, they had to be retained. Colonists were offered land against payments that were monetary, in kind, or simply symbolic. In some instances lands were granted by the King to noble landowners, following the feudal model; this was the case, for example, in Pennsylvania and in Maryland. These attempts to copy the feudal model onto a virgin world did not easily pass the test.[5] A variation on the system of apprenticeship–indentured servants–experienced a greater success. Poor emigrants were shipped over at the expense of some already established colonist or of ship captains hoping to profit from the resale of the indentured servant's contract upon arrival in the colonies. Myth has it that many were able to become established at the end of the period of indenture. But the reality seems to be less happy, as testified by the high mortality rate during the voyage over, and by the obligation of these indentured servants to carry a sort of internal passport as soon as they arrived. This harsh situation is also testified by the fact that many of these indentured servants preferred to join the army rather than remain with their masters–a liberty the English Parliament had enshrined in law despite the contrary provisions of colonial legislatures.

If the Northern workforce tended to be supplied by indentured servants, the South was characterized by the practice of slavery. Granted, the triangular trade with the Antilles and Africa was for the profit of English merchants; American participation was mostly limited to transfers between the colonies. Slavery did not really begin to amount to much until the middle of the 18th century. At that time slaves constituted 22 per cent of the colonial population, around 459 000 souls. They were basically concentrated in the South because of their supposed ability to withstand the heat. Thus one finds in South Carolina a population that was 60 per cent black, in Virginia 41 per cent, and nearly a third in Georgia and in Maryland. In the North, the State of New York was in the lead with 13.7 per cent, followed by Rhode Island with 7.6 per cent, New Jersey with 7 per cent and Delaware with 5.2 per cent. I will not enter into the debate concerning the respective social conditions of slaves from North America, those from the islands, and those from South America; nor will I study the complex psychology of a slave society which claims at the same time to be republican and Whig. The slavery question did arise from time to time among the Americans, but it took a civil war for slavery to be abolished by law . . . and longer still for the change to enter into American mores.

The slave South claimed to be the inheritor of the feudal ethic and of the 'cavalier' spirit that was opposed to the unmannered and egotistical ways of their Yankee neighbours to the North. The real situation, however, generally offered less of a contrast. Distinctions of rank were not hereditary, depending instead upon favours conferred by the government. Nor were there great disparities between rural poverty, urban destitution and a well-off class headed by a new stratum of entrepreneurs. In fact, one finds instead a rather egalitarian rural society. Cities like Philadephia and Charleston grew principally because they were open to the backcountry, whereas the large city of Boston tended to stagnate because its rural areas were already overpopulated. Socio-economic distinctions remained flexible, for the dearness of labour permitted manual labourers to leave at any moment and go cultivate land of their own. The rich therefore had to work to maintain their station. Pragmatic comforts rather than luxury and ostentation were favoured. Claims to distinction by birth did not generally exist in this land ruled by the spirit of enterprise and autonomy. Since such distinctions, of course, existed anyway, they were justified by the idea of a natural aristocracy based on talent and merit. The latter psychological factor has continued to play an increasing role in the history of the country.

This generally egalitarian structure was neither universal nor was it fated to be eternal. The Northern colonies felt crowded by continued population growth. They lacked the lands required to install a new generation. In the South, the lands along the fertile river banks became increasingly scarce; a few large landowners monopolized these areas to the detriment of newcomers and even of middle-sized plantation owners. In both regions, speculation in frontier lands inevitably ensued. This could only lead to political problems that would upset the state of social equilibrium seemingly established around 1750. It also engendered conflicts between and among the colonies whose boundaries were often ill defined. The colonists appealed to the home country or its designated governors to mediate these disputes. At this point economic and political interests became linked with the social question, which depended in the last instance on the good will of the English governors since they named the councillors, judges and other magistrates. The overlapping of different levels thus complicated the problems, whereas from afar these problems appeared to be simple administrative matters.

The stability of the colonial structure was doubly disturbed by political considerations. On the one hand, the colonists who had moved on to cultivate new lands found themselves far removed from the centres of decision-making power. The colonial legislatures took advantage of English indifference and of the distance that prevented England from getting too involved in local affairs to deal with most internal matters themselves. Their position of strength derived above all from the fact that governors' pay and the cost of their civil list had to be voted on by the locally elected legislative body. The frontierspeople, who were often of non-English origin or of a different religious faith than the Easterners, felt they were victims of political discrimination whose consequences they bitterly resented. This led to various movements of discontent. Some, such as the Paxton Boys in Pennsylvania in the 1760s or the Regulators in North Carolina in the early 1770s, took up arms. Later on others supported the English during the Revolution, seeing it as merely an armed coup undertaken by their neighbours to the East who wanted to preserve the historic privileges that were slipping through their fingers as colonization extended toward the West. This acrimony between the frontier West and the prosperous East marks the entire political history of the United States.

The other political question engendered by westward expansion was intercolonial in nature. The various Charters establishing the colonies were often vague, even contradictory, notably on the issue of their western boundaries. Thus, groups of speculators acquired at low cost or by means of bribes vast lands straddling colonial boundaries. Nor was it rare to find several companies of speculators claiming ownership of the same tract of land in the regions that were to become Kentucky and Ohio. Men such as the old Benjamin Franklin of Pennsylvania or the young Virginian soldier, George Washington, found themselves involved in such disputes. Mediation by England was required as the framework within which these conflicts could be settled. The problem was all the more thorny, however, because these lands were also claimed by the French and the Spanish. A definitive solution presupposed colonial independence, for the status of each colony emanated from a charter granted by the King along the lines of those possessed by medieval corporations. These lands were subject to England, whereas claims to rights and ownership implied the existence of a sovereign power capable of disposing of them. A non-arbitrary disposition of frontier tracts of land could come only with independence . . . and then only with difficulty, as will be seen.

Before turning to the political debate among the colonists, we must first consider briefly the psychological premises behind their arguments. These premises were above all religious. There were only two legally established Churches – the Quakers in Pennsylvania and the Congregationalists in New England – and their positions of strength had already been breached by the rapid growth of small sects. As early as 1636, Roger Williams left Massachusetts and founded the colony of Rhode Island in order to live according to his religious convictions. His pamphlet, *The Bloody Tenent*, vigorously defends freedom of religion.[6] Williams was not the sole dissenter, and the religious persecution that was rife at that time is well known today in the examples of the famous Salem Witch Trials. Belief in religious tolerance, which would finally triumph, was not the fruit of a rational and premeditated plan but was rather a result imposed by circumstances. The fact that America was an immense territory offering the potential of asylum would play an important political role only later on, when the authors of the Constitution of 1787 had to confront the classical idea that a republic is suitable only for territories of a small size. For now, to the benefits of the New World were added the heritage of the English political tradition, the Toleration Act of 1689,[7] as well as the effects the philosophers expected from '*le doux commerce*' on people's morals. Instead of establishing religious liberty under the militant slogan of '*écrasez l'infâme*', it was thanks to the activity of the various religious sects that religion itself came to be opposed to all domination over the conscience of the believer. The churches could therefore be on the side of independence, just as economic interest groups would be.

The fact that no single church was legally established demonstrates again the post-feudal situation of the colonies in which every established hierarchy was illegitimate. As a result, the faithful were led to take charge of community affairs. Further, the role of religious ministers, like that of all outward authority, was limited. The Church tended to govern itself. Ministers were engaged by contracts whose term lasted only one year and which were renewed according to the will of the flock. The Puritan Congregationalists, for example, thus evolved from a pure, harsh and hierarchized religion toward an open social institution ready to enter into theological and practical compromises. The visible church tended to replace the mystical body of the invisible church: religion became a social fact. Strict New England began to resemble the other colonies while these other colonies, through a similar movement, saw the birth of institutionalized religions which were little by little erected by their socio-economic position of authority into a new 'Establishment', secreted in this case by society itself, rather than named by political authority.

This social institutionalization of religion provoked tensions in a society where, for lack of an autonomous political class, religion tended to fill the void. The colonists grasped their identity only from the standpoint of their place in a sort of historical theology of redemption—of which there were two versions, one secular, the other religious. In this way one can speak, for example, of both Puritan and Pilgrim fathers. But the two versions also contradicted each other, creating a tension from which American politics suffers to this day. The secular history corresponded to the inception of a new 'Establishment' in which the presbyterial institution came to enjoy a social position that authorised it to exercise semi-political functions of control and leadership. The more spiritual or mystical history could totally bypass institutional politics, but its appeal to resignation and virtue could also find echoes in the classical and republican political tradition which favoured the practice of virtues that the Americans had borrowed from their English cousins.[8]

These two histories were bound to merge and then diverge during the 'Great Awakening' of the 1730s and '40s, which, on a different scale, is comparable to the birth of English Methodism or of Pietism on the Continent. (Americans seem to repeat this kind of religious awakening at regular intervals up until the present time.) The intellectual life of the colonies had assimilated the rational and scientific empiricism of the Enlightenment to a type of religious thought that had eliminated all 'enthusiasm'. The austere Puritanical conscience was systematized, the outward forms of salvation analyzed and codified. Theological training left nothing to be desired when compared, *mutatis mutandis*, with a strict Jesuit upbrining. But this Protestant training did not prepare the minister to deal with the psychological effects of the new commercial and demographic expansion with which he was confronted in the rapidly changing colonial society. The Awakening was prompted by rational theology itself. It challenged the doctrine and especially the institutional structure of the Church, but replaced them with nothing save the subjective faith of the believer. The new Establishment was shaken; individualism triumphed, rebellion itself was legitimated. Then, in reaction to the extreme consequences of the anarchic individualism of this religious conscience, and notably to the intolerance of a subjective faith incapable of recognizing the rights of others, the value of tolerance was again recognized. The Awakening had seen its day and departed, at least for a while. It changed terrain and soon became political.

Although in 1750 theological reflection had gained a stranglehold over all creative forces, a new movement was developing. With economic growth came the birth of new professions. Some Americans left to study in England and Scotland[9]; others attended the new American universities founded at this time. Moreover, the colonists also participated in the movement of the Enlightenment, and in the politico-economic rivalries that triggered the Seven Years' War, called the 'French and Indian War' in the colonies. From all this emerged a new way of thinking and of thinking about oneself, which culminated provisionally in the idea of independence, advocated by some, accepted by others, and rejected by many. The attitude of each group toward this idea depended, in the last analysis, on the way in which it lived the new socio-economic conditions that had been created.

## LIVING THE PRESENT

One might have thought that the conflicts among land speculators would have been resolved through recourse to English arbitration. But such mediation was impossible because of the self-governing structures that had been established in the colonies while the mother-country was not paying attention. Save in proprietary colonies like Pennsylvania (where the Penn family designated its officers), England named a governor who directed matters on the local level through the intermediary of an upper house nominated by him and a lower house chosen by the inhabitants in more or less democratic fashion. This structure was overseen by the Board of Trade and Plantations in London, whose director, however, did not have the rank of minister. Parliament worried about North America only sporadically. The supervisory control exercised by London was therefore episodic, distant and inconsistent in character. Little by little the lower, popular houses took their fate into their own hands. This was not, however, an affirmation of popular independence; the legislatures were controlled by a colonial élite, concentrated in the East of each colony and preoccupied above all with commerce. Those who made up these popular chambers of the colonial legislatures did not differ greatly from those who sat in the upper chamber, except that their positions depended upon the popular will. Yet this difference mattered a great deal; it permitted the legislators to believe themselves to be a natural aristocracy based on merit, as opposed to the upper house, which tended to be an aristocracy in the traditional, European sense of the term. The implication of this difference was that the upper house was dependent on political favours, its social position was not justified; indeed, its dependence could even awaken suspicions of 'corruption'.[10] The lower house sought to assert itself by using its power over the budget, and it succeeded in so far as the salary of the governor–and the appropriations for his civil list–depended upon its decisions.

Meanwhile, England was interested principally in its commercial relations with the colonies. The colonies could govern themselves as they saw fit so long as they did not challenge the trading practices through which the home country made its profit. As a result, during a period of over one hundred years the Board of Trade and Plantations vetoed only 469 of the 8563 laws voted by the colonial legislatures. On the other hand, in the economic field England imposed two series of measures, known collectively as the *Navigation Acts*. The first enumerated the goods the colonists were forbidden to manufacture (iron products, hats, certain woolens, and so forth) in order to prevent them from competing with the mother-country. As an offsetting factor, the second series of measures granted subsidies to encourage the production of commodities necessary to England's prosperity and to the maintenance and protection of its fleet (such as timber in the North to build masts, or indigo from South Carolina). Furthermore, the enumerated products could only be transported by English ships and to English ports. This kind of regulation of domestic production does not seem to have provoked much protest; indeed, it is difficult to determine whether England or the colonies profited more from these arrangements. In general, however, British policy was conceived as a way of orienting the flow of trade in the direction suggested by the logic of mercantilism. Thus, the *Molasses Act* of 1733 taxed the sugar from the Caribbean Islands that New England colonists distilled into rum. Later on, according to the same logic, England forbade the colonies to issue their own money. This was especially disturbing to the South, whose perpetually indebted planters benefitted from the accentuation of inflation that came with each new issuance. (This prohibition also troubled the poor farmers in the West who lacked the cash needed to pay their taxes and settle their debts; but the West did not carry much political weight in the colonial system.) This question of monetary emission arose frequently during the growing conflict with England, and even after independence (when the West would play a greater role). Beyond its economic effects, this problem had political implications. Its resolution could not take place within the logic of mercantilism, for it depended upon settling the question of sovereignty.

Although contested in one respect or another, these mercantile regulations did not at first stir any protests based upon principle. Each colony had its agent in London, where he represented its interest by mobilizing, if need be, the support of English merchants whose prosperity depended upon commerce with his colony. This task was relatively simple since, for example, in 1772, 36 per cent of English exports and 37 per cent of English imports involved the North American colonies. One gets the sense of the role of the agents from the fact that among them were people like Franklin and Lee on the American side and Burke on the English side. When their mediation proved ineffective, other, more direct means could be employed back in America: principally smuggling, made easier by the vast distance from England and the sheer immensity of the colonial territory. And if an English patrol came upon a crew of smugglers, English law guaranteed a trial by a jury of one's peers, which, among Americans, invariably threw out the case. Until the 1760s both the formal and the informal system worked quite well; the colonies were growing, Whig politics was gaining strength, English commerce was prospering. But this harmony was not to last; the interests of the two parties within what was beginning to be called (especially in the colonies)[11] an Empire were entering into conflict. The colonists came to feel that England was suddenly beginning to conspire against them, or rather against what they took – once again, in terms of their general political theory – to constitute the principles of the Empire.

The outbreak of the Seven Years' War not only marked the beginning of the end of the Continental European Empires; its outcome finally made clear to England the nature of its empire, at the same time that it revealed to the colonists their own status as a colonized people. Once the French were defeated, the American colonists became disinterested in the war. They continued their smuggling operations in the French Caribbean (a practice they had never really given up, even during the hostilities). Once the French were chased off the continent, nothing stood in the way of westward expansion; colonization beyond the Appalachians could be resumed. But, England did not see things the same way. The war had cost it dearly; expanded protection of the colonies could cost still more. England therefore decided to limit colonization west of the Appalachians, disappointing colonial speculators. The later *Quebec Act* of 1774, which ratified this policy did not only disappoint speculators; the government had the clever idea of conciliating the French remaining in '*la Belle Province*' by offering them religious liberty. This added spiritual insult to the injury of material loss, for the colonists – as good heirs to the Glorious Revolution – held tightly to the banner of anti-popery and feared above all else the establishment of an official religion. That the new king, George III, was counselled by Bute, a

Scot reputedly sympathetic to the Stuarts, did not bode well for future good relations between the colonies and the young Hanoverian monarch, even though he was the first of his line to be born in England.[12]

The experience of war showed that the Americans and the English hardly knew each other before their alliance against the French and the Indians. They shared a culture and language, but they practised them on different shores. The Americans believed they were English and ardently insisted upon their English liberties. But when Americans and English found themselves side by side in battle they were shocked – the former by the aristocratic pretensions exhibited by the officers (but also by the soldiers), the latter by the coarseness and egalitarian good-naturedness prevailing among the soldiers (but also among the officers). This disappointment was well expressed by the young George Washington, who returned from military service both enlightened and disillusioned. The colonists and the British had become aware of their different statuses. This psychological disillusionment was only the beginning of the misunderstanding that would come between them.[13]

The victory of 1763 was far from definitive; England knew that measures would have to be taken to reduce its debt and to enable it to resist the next attack.[14] But, English landed property was already highly taxed; the Whig representatives, who dominated the Commons, had to find other fiscal resources. Since the colonies owed their new freedom to the English victory and since, moreover, they still required English protection along the frontier, Parliament decided that they would have to contribute to the common cause through the payment of additional taxes. The kind of taxes to be paid and the method by which these taxes were imposed marks a new stage in the evolution of the British Empire. These measures constituted, so to speak, an institutional reflection on one hundred and fifty years of unreflective colonial policy. They are often presented as if they were aimed at substituting a new form of slavery for the liberty formerly granted to the colonists. To imagine the English so stupidly provocative would be to let oneself be deluded by colonial rhetoric. The end of the war brought with it an economic depression in the colonies which served to aggravate the events that followed, but this was not their cause. The real situation is more interesting because, like the people who made it, it is capable of reflecting upon itself at certain privileged moments.

# 2 History Conceived: The Birth and Ends of American Independence

## TOWARD UNITY

The colonies were 13 in number and proud of their respective sovereignties. They had their schools, their universities, their élites; they differed from each other by their respective climates and soils, industries and commerce, pasts and religions; they shared only their status as colonies, of which they refused to take cognizance. When a colonist, even after the separation from England, spoke of 'my country', he was referring to Massachusetts, Virginia, Rhode Island or Maryland. The sole effort at union undertaken by the colonies dates from 1754 when, reacting to the French threat, delegates met in Albany, New York, to propose a plan for a unified defence that would in no way reduce the autonomy of each colony. This 'Albany Plan' (of which Franklin was one of the principal authors) had no sequel.[1] Later, in 1775, when the Continental Congress was on the verge of declaring independence, Joseph Galloway tried to use the failure of the Albany Plan to justify the need for reconciliation and to prove the impossibility of achieving sufficient colonial unity to combat the power of England. But a certain revolution in people's minds and in their institutions had occurred between 1754 and 1775. The 13 colonies had been forced by events to conceive their unity.

In his autobiography, John Adams situates the beginning of the Revolution in 1761 during a trial brought against a merchant accused of smuggling. The lawyer for the defence, James Otis, challenged the legality of the English measures authorizing customs seizures upon which the charge was based. These measures, the Writs of Assistance, conferred upon customs officials the right to call upon the military for aid. Although this did not alter the content of English customs policy, this change in the method of its application, which suddenly allowed stricter enforcement of the regulations against smuggling, shocked long-held colonial sentiments.[2] In his argument for the defence, Otis tried to turn the case into a question of political principle. He saw in it a violation of a natural equity which pre-exists and is superior to positive parliamentary law. At the same time, he called upon Parliament, that much admired instrument of English liberty, to put an end to this error. He thus transformed a judicial case into a political affair and at the same time suggested that a just policy was inspired by principles higher than positive law. According to Otis, the power of Parliament was absolute but not arbitrary. But the lawyer drew the justification of this theoretical assertion from a still pre-modern theory of national sovereignty, one that is more reminiscent of Bodin than of Hobbes, of Coke rather than Blackstone.[3] This contradiction would become unravelled in the course of time, but only slowly.

Another pre-modern legal argument had already been in the political news the same year in Virginia. The salary of religious ministers in this colony had always been set by the colonial legislature and paid in kind in the form of barrels of tobacco. But, with the price of tobacco rising, the legislature decreed in 1759 that the ministers would be paid in cash that year. The ministers appealed successfully to London to have this measure annulled. In a lawsuit filed by one of the injured ministers, a young lawyer, Patrick Henry, denounced the principle of intervention by London in the domestic affairs of the colony, attacking the King himself, whom he accused of having become a tyrant and of thus having annulled the right to obedience owed to him by his subjects. Aided by a predictably understanding Virginian jury, the plaintiff obtained a ruling that granted only a symbolic payment of damages of one penny. Patrick Henry was to become one of the fieriest advocates of independence, then governor of Virginia, and finally one of the opponents of the new Constitution of 1787. According to him, that Constitution struck a blow against the sovereign rights of the States which he was already defending in 1761. The structure of his legal argument at both moments bears witness to his pre-modern corporatist spirit, but also to its radical implications when consistently applied. Such pre-modern arguments had to be transformed by the logic of the events that came to found a modern American society.

The treaty of Paris, which ended the war in 1763, was not unanimously accepted by the English political class. George III, who became monarch in 1760 just as Wolfe was obtaining his victory in Canada and Clive was gaining his in India, saw himself obliged to name a new ministry led by Grenville. Among other things, Grenville undertook to put colonial affairs in order. When an Indian revolt (Pontiac's Rebellion) broke out in 1763, English troops were sent to suppress it. Grenville then passed a series of measures concerning both the organization of the Empire and the settlement of England's fiscal difficulties. Westward expansion in America was limited, and English troops would henceforth be stationed there. The colonies were prohibited from issuing money. An attempt was made to re-establish a hold over the customs serivce. Particularly important was a decree that transferred the jurisdiction of customs cases to military admiralty courts whose seat was located in Halifax, Nova Scotia. On top of this, a bill known as the Sugar Act or Revenue Act of April 1764, set new tariffs which had to be paid in sterling since the Currency Act had eliminated local money. Regulatory measures were voted to enforce these acts. They overturned accepted legal procedures by protecting informers and shielding customs agents from all accusations of false arrest. Finally, there were rumours of a possibility of a new tax whose objective would be purely and simply budgetary.[4]

The colonists' response came quickly. At first it took the form of pamphlets and articles in numerous colonial journals. James Otis developed the argument from his 1761 defence plea and published it under the title of *The Rights of the British Colonies Asserted and Proved.* Otis went immediately to the theoretical heart of the question. What is the foundation of political authority, he asked? It is neither property nore divine grace, not force nor even a contract. If there is a foundation, it can only reside in the immutable will of God whose laws, visible in nature, do not change. A government therefore cannot be arbitrary or depend upon the contingent will of man. Thus, even though the will of Parliament commands our obedience, it is itself limited by a higher truth, a natural equity. Since English institutions were arranged in such a way that the power of Parliament included also a judicial power (the Executive Court) Parliament could and therefore should, according to Otis, invalidate unjust laws. Otis' pamphlet thus remained within the framework of English law, at least according to Otis' understanding of it. Although his views were not shared by many, and were pre-modern in character, his argument would be taken up later in a modified form when the colonies tried to establish a basis for their own judicial institutions. What Otis called a natural or higher law came to take the modern form of a Constitution, founded upon the will of the people and separate from the acts of this or that government whose power it both creates and limits. But such a theoretical development took time and experience.

The reactions of the colonial merchants were more practical. That of Rhode Island Governor Stephen Hopkins may serve as an example. His *Essay on the Trade of the Northern Colonies,* which was written and published at the request of the legislature of his colony, attempted to prove that England was acting against its own economic interest. Furthermore, although he was defending the North's point of view, Hopkins also sought to show that this outlook coincided with Southern interests. Beyond the economic demonstration, Hopkins also drew upon political theory. He sought to show that the English legislation violated the rights granted to the colonies in their constitutional charters. Although this argument appealed once again to pre-modern principles, in so far as it granted sovereignty to corporative bodies constituted by the State, Hopkins' reference to history also drew on a distinction between legislation dealing with trade matters and that relating to internal or domestic taxes. This is a modern distinction between, on the one hand, a fiscal policy aimed at managing the Empire from the point of view of the colonies' interests as well as of those of England and, on the other hand, taxes aimed at producing revenue for the home country not only at the expense of the financial interests of the colonists but also and especially at the expense of their political autonomy. This distinction was to play a large role in this first phase of the conflict. It suggests in practical terms the difference between the concrete situation of the colonies and that of the mother country. But this affirmation could not yet be clearly formulated as constituting a fundamental difference. In retrospect, all that can be seen is a first attempt at a solution to another imperial conflict – the one that gave birth to the concept of the Commonwealth in the 19th century. At this point in the story, however, no one was thinking in those terms.

The opinions of the merchants were no more united than was political opinion.[5] Another political faction in Rhode Island answered Hopkins through the pen of Martin Howard. His *Letter from a Gentleman at Halifax* was based on doctrine inherited from the Glorious Revolution. The foundation of the modern State comes from the fact that it incarnates a single, unified will. In England, this will is that of Parliament.[6] For Martin Howard, the obedience due to the will of Parliament makes the protests of the colonists ridiculous. The twin affirmation of their domestic sovereignty and of the fact that they belong to the Empire is a contradiction in terms, the affirmation of an *imperium in imperio*. Howard was right; the political and legal science of his time massively supported his judgement. But this science was in contradiction to real interests. Many of the colonists were opposed to the English measures for pragmatic reasons or on grounds of personal interest. The pragmatic opponents, of whom the future Massachusetts governor, Thomas Hutchinson, furnishes a telling example, were privately opposed to these measures while at the same time being unwilling publicly to challenge the ultimate authority of Parliament. They could work behind the scenes, but they would later face other difficult choices, for English policy brought the debate continually back into the public eye.

Prime Minister Grenville had already alluded to the idea of a new tax requiring a stamp duty on newspapers, legal papers, certain commercial transactions, and even on the sale of spirits. This tax already existed in England, where it functioned well. It was politically astute, for the only alternative was to increase land taxes – which were already at the point of saturation – or else to re-evaluate land values which had been set in 1692 and privileged certain landowners who, of course, had managed to get themselves elected to Parliament. Moreover, this stamp duty was easy to collect since every unstamped document was *ipso facto* illegal. The attitude of Benjamin Franklin, at the time one of the colonial agents in London, toward the Stamp Act bears witness to the elegance of this fiscal solution. Rather than protest against this measure, Franklin undertook to obtain for his friends posts as stamp vendors! He came quickly to regret this act of generosity. Fortunately for Franklin, he soon had the opportunity to win back a favourable opinion from the colonists by his testimony at a parliamentary inquiry on colonial resistance to this same tax.

Parliament decreed that the Stamp Act would take effect on 1 November 1765. Colonial reaction was immediate. New actors entered the stage: lawyers and journalists whose interests were affected, as well as tavern owners, similarly affected. In Virginia, Patrick Henry seized on the occasion at the end of the legislative session, when most of the members had already gone home. He declared that Tarquin and Julius Caesar had had their Brutuses, Charles his Cromwell, and that the Americans would not let things go by without a fight. He proposed seven resolutions aimed at affirming the principle of *No Taxation Without Representation*. The formula was well chosen. Although three of his seven resolutions were rejected by the legislature, all seven were published in the press, including the press of other colonies. Thus the uniform and general fiscal policy constructed so artfully by Grenville gave rise to effects that he had not expected. A unified colonial movement began to form. Even those who would become loyalists could accept Henry's principle, for this was clearly an *internal* tax designed not simply for regulating commerce within the Empire. The Empire's jurisdiction over trade was the sole power the colonists were willing to recognize as being in the jurisdiction of Parliament, which could only act for the common good of all.[7]

More important than pamphlets and petitions to Parliament was the appearance of spontaneous movements of protest against the Stamp Act. In all the colonies people organized as tempers rose. In general, the élite of merchants and liberal professionals took the initiative and led the actions of a crowd ready to act. They were vigorously supported by the ministers, whose sermons adroitly mixed the religious with the secular. The right to resistance was championed so strongly that it may be said to have become a duty. Those who were charged with the responsibility of selling the stamps were taken to task, their houses were broken into and their persons were threatened. The crowd forced them to renounce their royal commissions under penalty of being run out of town or subjected to the colonists' favourite form of punishment: tarring and feathering. The success of the operation was all the more striking in that physical violence was the exception rather than the rule. The colonists began to learn how to participate directly in public affairs; the protests went beyond the élite circle which until then had tended to dominate colonial politics. They were real mobs, but since they did not encounter any resistance, they did not have to act violently. Thus, they could act in a controlled manner. The experience of this measured participation by the crowd influenced the attitude the élite adopted later on when democratic demands were raised.[8]

The protests against the Stamp Act also affected intercolonial relations. James Otis introduced a resolution in the Massachusetts Assembly proposing that a circular letter be sent to the other colonies, inviting them to a general congress (named the Stamp Act Congress), which was to be held in October in New York. Nine colonies sent representatives; three others tried to send delegates but did not succeed in overcoming the veto exercised by their governors (whose authority they still respected). The resolution agreed upon in New York affirmed, for instance: 'III. That it is inseparably essential to the freedom of a people, and the undoubted right of Englishmen, that no taxes be imposed on them, but with their own consent, given personally, or by their representatives'. This recalls Patrick Henry's formula, but another resolution went further still: 'IV. That the people of these colonies are not, and from their local circumstances cannot be, represented in the House of Commons in Great Britain'. The representatives from the colonies admitted that they had previously paid such taxes, but considered them as a 'gift freely consented to by the people'. All this, of course, was presented under the form of a humble petition addressed to His Majesty and to Parliament. On the level of political theory, there was nothing accidental or fortuitous about this loyalty. Indeed, the concept of a 'gift freely consented to' corresponds to the political realities of the pre-modern world in which the colonies were only corporations whose existence depended upon the will of the king.

The justification of the English measures appealed to political theories accepted by all at the time. Grenville's secretary, Thomas Whately, provided this explanation in a pamphlet entitled, *The Regulations Lately Made Concerning the Colonies and the Taxes Imposed upon Them, Considered*. Whately developed especially the theory of virtual representation. Since the single, unified will of the nation is incarnated by Parliament, which aims at the common good, each member of the Empire is therefore represented in the decisions taken by this authority.[9] After all, large metropolitan areas, such as Sheffield and Manchester, had no representatives in Parliament. To say that everyone must be directly represented in person amounted to a denial of the principle of representation as it was then conceived by political theory. More important, virtual representation was also justified in as much as the representatives themselves were subject to the laws they enact. But this obviously was not the case for taxes affecting the colonies alone, as the fourth resolution of the Stamp Act Congress, cited above, affirmed in its own language. But to reject the idea of virtual representation meant that one did not belong to the nation, that one had other, particular, interests opposed to the common good of the Empire. This was a step that no one yet wanted to risk taking. It therefore was necessary to find other arguments before challenging this postulate, which reflected the common sense of the time.

The two kinds of responses the colonists gave to the assertion of virtual representation and to the Stamp Act were based on this concept. The first is found in the theory proposed by Daniel Dulany in his *Considerations on the Propriety of Imposing Taxes in the British Colonies, For the Purpose of Raising a Revenue, by Act of Parliament*. Dulany noted that in principle Americans could not be represented in Parliament, which implied, according to common law, that they were exempt from parliamentary taxes. More important still was the fact that this form of taxation violated the colonial charters, which granted internal autonomy; Dulany proposed to exercise this internal autonomy actively and thus to justify the creation of industries in the colonies. This last theoretical argument, although founded on the pre-modern concept of corporatism, was quite tempting to the colonists, who were frustrated by

English mercantilism. The consequences of making positive use of colonial autonomy, however, could not yet be made explicit. More important was the fear that acceptance of one tax would lead to the imposition of still others, given the weight of the English debt.

A pamphlet, by John Dickinson, offered an argument similar to Dulany's, but without its positive implications. He noted simply that Portugal benefitted from the protections of the English mercantile system without this giving the English the right to impose taxes on its citizens. In the same vein, Richard Bland, in *An Inquiry into the Rights of the British Colonies*, appealed both to the law of nature and to the colonial charters. The result of this contrast showed that the doctrine of virtual representation was completely unsuitable to the colonial experience. According to Bland, the colonies are subject only to the will of the Crown; they are independent states, tied to the Crown but possessing their own independent representative institutions. Parliament can pretend to apply its laws to the colonies, and it can even impose these laws by force; but this does not mean that it has the right to do so. The colonists are therefore not virtually represented like the non-voters of Sheffield or Manchester. Bland's assertion that the colonies depend only on the Crown is both an expression of corporatist theory and a step toward the recognition of their sovereign autonomy, because, according to Whig doctrine, Parliament represents the national will while the Sovereign King adds only a, so to speak, symbolic legitimation to its decisions. But it would take almost another decade before the consequences of Bland's argument would be recognized by Thomas Jefferson in his pamphlet, *A Summary View of the Rights of British America*, whose publication in August 1774 made famous its author and led him to be chosen to draft the Declaration of Independence.

The theoretical conclusion of these refutations of the doctrine of virtual representation could be deduced only after the colonists gave a practical and pragmatic form to their protests. They knew quite well that the interests of English merchants conformed to theirs. They had used this fact already in their agitation against the Sugar Act to show that England had no justification for imposing taxes on them since these taxes did not contribute to the maintenance of the Empire. On the contrary, according to the mercantile system's own logic, English prosperity depended upon them. Thus, confronted now with the Stamp Act, some thought of the tactic of the boycott as a way to win the support of those affected in England. But how could they assure the co-ordination and unanimity necessary to the success of this inter-colonial project, unprecedented except for the failed Albany Plan a decade earlier? Toward the end of 1765, after the mass actions against the stamp agents, the colonists created Committees of Correspondence which took the collective name of 'the Sons of Liberty'. Once again mixing across social lines, these Committees had leading members of society for their officers, their troops being made up of artisans or small merchants. Once again, their actions were strictly defined in advance so as to avoid all chance of degenerating into uncontrolled violence. And once again they justified their actions by appealing to constitutional principles. This kind of organization carried the seeds of a new form of struggle. It was important – not so much for its capacity to mobilize in order to block certain actions but, rather, for its ability to convince people to continue business as usual, without the use of the obligatory stamps whose distribution was halted. Their success meant that America had the experience of a society functioning with neither a legal government nor legal forms; it prepared the ground for a new theory of the relationship between the social and the political.[10] But here, too, it took time and experience before this conclusion was drawn. The radical opposition did not seek innovations in political theory; it had to act quickly because it was aware that the continued disruption of the import trade, which was increasingly disturbing commerce and the jobs that depended upon it, would sooner or later destroy the unity of their movement. Indeed, this is what the royal Governor of New York and other opponents were counting on. Theory would come later.

The colonial reaction against the Stamp Act was successful. After the fall of the Grenville ministry, Rockingham's, which was more open to the influence of manufacturing and trade interests, abolished the Stamp Act. But this abolition had its price. The same day, Parliament voted the Declaratory Act of March 1766, which stated that Parliament had 'full power and authority to make laws and statutes of sufficient force and validity to bind the colonies and people of America . . . in all cases whatsoever'. This last phrase was, of course, the Trojan Horse by means of which the ministry still hoped to win acceptance for the taxes needed by England. The colonies had to react. An English radical, David Hartley, advanced the idea that English sovereignty was that of the Crown and not the Parliament; but he had no more success than had Richard Bland, whose argument was developed along the same lines. But the affirmation of parliamentary sovereignty in the Declaratory Act changed the attitude of the colonists toward the Empire, of which they had taken pride and had felt themselves members with full rights. Indeed, the 'rights of an Englishman' had a very concrete meaning, especially for the merchant class. But its signification was changed when another use was made of it by Parliament. The movement toward revolution began with a demand for rights which could be called 'conservative'. Its argument was based on principles that were pre-modern. It began now to take on a more radical meaning as it demanded more abstract and general rights. Crucial to this development was the fact that the protest movement continued even though the colonists had won their case, as far as their material interests were concerned. The Declaratory Act, more than any concrete English policy, drove the colonists forward, from political practice to a new theory of that practice, and finally to a new and modern political practice.

## THE CONFLICT THEMATIZED

The dispute was resolved only on the surface; petty issues came to take on an unusual importance, as if the two parties had decided to play on each other's nerves. As Burke put it in a declaration which nonetheless supported the Americans' cause, 'they snuff the approach of tyranny in every tainted breeze.'[11] The fact that militant action had won over Parliament ought not to be underestimated when one tries to grasp the meaning of the issues underlying this contentiousness. The colonists refused to compensate the victims of the violent crowds led by the Sons of Liberty. The colony of New York refused to grant aid to the troops stationed there, despite a law voted by Parliament in 1765. The Rockingham government was soon replaced by the friends of Pitt (who had become Lord Chatham). But the pressure on Parliament to lower English taxes forced the hand of the minister of finances, Townshend, who proposed a new fiscal bill in June 1767, accompanied by a new tightening of the customs service, whose administrative headquarters was transferred to Boston, the most troubled of the colonial cities. But it was another, graver measure that forced Americans to rethink their own theoretical self-understanding. It was proposed that the receipts from these new taxes be used to pay the salaries of the Crown's agents in the colonies. As a result customs officials surely would become more aggressive and arbitrary. But, most important, the colonies had acquired quasi-independence, and their assemblies enjoyed a rather broad freedom of action, in large part due to their control over the salaries of their governors, judges and other English representatives. They therefore had practical reasons for acting; and this reaction had to be justified by an adequate theory.

A first interpretation of the new situation was provided by John

Dickinson in his *Letters from a Farmer in Pennsylvania to the Inhabitants of the British Colonies.*[12] The Townshend Acts imposed customs duties on certain goods (lead, glass, paper) that the colonies did not produce. As if he sought to provoke the colonists, Townshend insisted that these were *external* taxes aimed at regulating commerce, and not internal taxes on the incomes of the colonists. The tactic forced Dickinson to redefine the concept of a tax from a new standpoint. His fourth Letter defined it as any measure, whatever the pretext, aimed at putting receipts from the colonies into the pocket of the home country. From this standpoint, the Townshend Acts were as unjust as the Stamp Act. Dickinson proposed as a rule of analysis for any taxes that might be introduced the 'intention' of the legislator. Even granting the possibility that one could know the true intention of Parliament, this negative solution remained unsatisfactory, for Dickinson affirmed at the same time that the colonies belonged to the Empire. 'We are but parts of a whole; and therefore there must exist a power somewhere to preside, and preserve the connection in due order. This power is lodged in Parliament . . .' How was this statement of parliamentary power to be reconciled with the refusal of its right to impose certain taxes on the colonies? Dickinson had only a vague response: the colonies were 'as much dependent on Great Britain as one free people could be on another'. But in what sense were the colonies free? Dickinson provides no explanation. Dulany had previously raised the question whether or not powers granted by an inferior institution constituted a limit on those of a higher one. An answer was required. Federalism would be the solution, but that would come only in 1787.

The theoretical principles of the unity of the Empire seemed to retain their hold over people's minds, but practice made the situation more unstable. The resolution of non-importation, which was the colonists' response to the Townshend Acts, had the same popular success as the resistance to the Stamp Act. This new form of resistance was again supported by the efforts of the Sons of Liberty, whose discipline and autonomy of action brought about a *de facto* situation of dual power. Distinguishing between violence, which they rejected, and coercion – or the 'formation' of public opinion, as they called it – they helped to create a real spirit of unity among the different colonies. Meanwhile, the English contributed to the mood of unrest by their ill-considered means of carrying out the Townshend Acts. The battle against smugglers was turned into a form of harassment whose immediate effect was to rally to the colonial cause rich merchants like Henry Laurens in the South and John Hancock in the North. Ambitious and petty customs officials helped to alienate American affections. The *Liberty* and *Gaspée* affairs, named after two detained ships, were the most celebrated. A pamphlet by Laurens described his difficulties in great detail. Parliament responded to the colonial agitation by dissolving the New York Assembly and demanding that the Massachusetts legislature apologize for having had the temerity to send a circular letter describing its grievances to the other colonies. The colonists were forced to ask themselves what good it was to have one's own legislature if it was treated this way? Furthermore, the presence of troops – which the colonists refused to house, notwithstanding the Quartering Act of 1765 – was a useless provocation since the troops were not numerous enough to intimidate the colonists, and had in any case been prohibited in advance from any serious engagements.

The tension that had been building finally exploded in radical Boston when, on 5 March 1770, the taunts and threats of the crowd provoked the British troops into reaction. Their intervention ended in what was called the 'Boston Massacre'. The story of the massacre tends toward the anecdotal (the victims were few in number and order was quickly re-established), but it sheds light on the state of mind of the colonies when it is compared – as the colonists did – to the unfolding of the Wilkes affair in England. Wilkes was a radical who had been elected to Parliament, which, however, refused to certify his election. A new election returned him to office, but Parliament still refused to accept him; the same sequence occurred yet another time before Parliament finally decided to grant the election of . . . his opponent! A case brought against Wilkes' newspaper, *The North Briton*, for publishing false and defamatory information was already a *cause célèbre*. Then a demonstration in support of Wilkes was broken up by provocateurs; shots were fired and a child was killed. The colonists could clearly see parallels with their own situation – the more so when, in New York, Alexander MacDougal, the author of an appeal for support of the non-importation movement against the Townshend Acts, was arrested for the excesses of his remarks. Already pressed to develop a theory that would define their place in the Empire, and driven to justify their claims on grounds that were not simply economic, the colonists tried to relate anecdotes and instances of harassment to their political theory. This return to theory was all the more necessary since, on the home front, things were not going well. The non-importation movement did not mobilize all social strata to the same extent. The artisans, newcomers on the political scene, were generally enthusiastic. But the merchants were divided between their opposition and a desire not to suffer economically as a result of the virtuous self-denial that was implied by the tactic of non-importation. To understand the thinking of the colonists the fact that their grievances were not so enormous, that they had already made Parliament back down several times, and that many of the conflicts arose from their own provocations or their insubordination should be stressed. Although they opposed English policy under the pretext of defending historical or constitutional rights, the colonists were challenging the functioning of an empire from which they nevertheless profited, even to the point of smuggling contraband products to the enemy during wartime. A typical example comes from Georgia, which was demanding help from English troops against the Indians on its border at the same that it was declaring its opposition to the taxes meant to cover the costs of this operation. How could they justify themselves? Certainly not by appealing to Whig political theory, considered by everyone as the *ne plus ultra* of progress, liberty and justice, and whose symbol was the Glorious Revolution. That theory presupposed not only the sovereignty of Parliament but also the existence of a common *res publica*, shared by the colonies and the home country. But, Dickinson had already popularized the idea that the relations between the colonies and England were those of two *free* peoples. The next move was to draw the consequences of this statement without recourse to 'the rights of an Englishman' or any other pre-modern concepts.

To understand the action of the colonies, we need to turn to political theories employed during the first English revolution, and which had led an underground life since then. These theories, which are called 'Commonwealth' or 'republican humanism' or 'civic virtue', were inspired by a long tradition that remained latent in the thought of the commercial Whigs in power. The term 'Old Whig', which is frequently used to describe them, implies that this theoretical current conveyed a critical orientation. The basis of that critique was an image of society as a bipolar structure in which Power and the people were opposed to one another asymmetrically. Power is accepted as a necessity in light of the finite and sinful nature of man. But this power is opposed to liberty, at whose expense it always seeks to grow. Liberty must therefore always remain vigilant against the threat of a plot aimed at subjugating it. The critical aspect of Old Whig thinking sees this conspiracy against liberty as a permanent danger because man's sinful nature renders him susceptible to corruption. Liberty is lost when it lets itself be led down the path to corruption. Such corruption occurs when Power hands out posts, honours or material advantages to men whose finite nature explains why they are ready to sacrifice their liberty for such material things. At this point, Power becomes potentially tyrannical; Liberty must redouble its vigilance and the era of suspicion begins. This theory of suspicion is confirmed in turn by that other science on which the colonists placed great weight: the political experience of the ages. The cycle of political corruption had been described already by Polybius; Roman experience demonstrated how real it is.[13] It was logical to think that the British Empire was on the Roman path toward decline; that would explain the way it dealt with issues like the Wilkes affair and, more generally, its colonial policy. Such was the attitude the colonists, worried about the future but at the same time proud of not yet having undergone the moral decline evident in the unjust and tyrannical actions of their English cousins. The sociological conflict thus became political because it was seen as the stage of the historical struggle between Good and Evil. This moral dimension sheds light on the dynamic behind the first phase of the conflict, as well as on the support provided by a large proportion of clergy. The latter could see in English policy a punishment for the sins of the American people, who had become too rich and who had abandoned their old moral ways; and the resistance against the English could appear to it as a collective act of purification restoring the virtue which had momentarily succumbed to the temptations of English corruption.

This Old Whig analysis helps explain the surprising unanimity of the reaction in the 13 previously divided colonies, as well as their sensitivity to apparently mild English measures. But this does not explain how Americans passed from a negative unity against these English measures to a state of independence capable of creating new institutions no longer dependent upon the English model (which, it should be stressed again, represented in everyone's eyes the most perfect form of free government). It was also necessary to go beyond a pre-modern politics founded either on morality or corporatist legal theory. Old Whig thought carried with it a critical understanding of politics. That understanding rendered two services to Americans embarked upon a quarrel which did not seem to leave room for an ideal solution. It permitted them to understand why, from the English side, the material interests that had until then dictated the conduct of the Empire no longer carried the same weight. Having become an Empire, free England was seen to be on the path toward decline. On the American side, the Old Whig analysis masked material interests behind appeals to virtue and to the common good of the Empire. With the help of their theological views, Americans could feel that they were a chosen people whose salvation coincided with the preservation of liberty. Old Whig thought thus allowed for an explanation of the English actions and for a justification of those of the Americans.

## TOWARD ACTION

The American protests and the economic effects of the non-importation movement once again won over the English Parliament. The Townshend Acts were repealed in the spring of 1770 . . . except for a tax on tea. Despite the efforts of some uncompromising militants, non-importation collapsed quickly. This doubly discouraged the leaders of the movement. On the one hand, the rapid collapse of non-importation clearly resulted from jealousy and egotism; everyone rushed to participate in the coming resumption of trade. The diehards were found especially among artisans, for while the merchants suffered from the boycott the artisans stood to profit from it and might even be able to develop their own businesses as a result. The same individualist attitude appeared at the intercolonial level, where each colony sought to pull out quickly to avoid any losses.[14] Had their previous collective action been guided by republican virtue or had they co-operated only under internal or external pressure? Meanwhile, the new actors on the scene, who had sprung up nearly everywhere, were being replaced by the better known leaders of the old élite.

The ebbing and the end of the movement were a sign that the Americans were no longer men of principle ready to sacrifice all, as they had been five years before when the withdrawal of the Stamp Act had been accompanied by the theoretical defiance of the Declaratory Act. The leaders recognized that work must be resumed at the grass-roots level. The years 1770–73 were generally calm. In Massachusetts, the quarrel between the legislature and the governor, Thomas Hutchinson, continued, but without exciting popular passion. Elsewhere the return of prosperity calmed people's spirits. Only the Committees of Correspondence were active. In Massachusetts, where the legislature was stalemated by the machinations of Hutchinson, who proclaimed loud and clear the Whig theory of Parliamentary sovereignty, it was the Boston Town Meeting that set the public tone, for example, with the pamphlet entitled *The State of the Rights of the Colonists*. This pamphlet asserted that, on the basis of a natural law, people entered into society freely and that they also had the right to leave it freely whenever they were oppressed. The pamphlet then detailed the grievances of the colonies and invited other towns to discuss them, either adopting the proposal as is or adding new grievances of their own. More than a hundred towns responded. Some historians see here already sketched out the form taken a few years later by the Declaration of Independence. But the affirmation of the existence of a natural law does not suffice to justify a revolutionary break.

It was the English who forced the pace of events in 1773, for reasons completely alien to their quarrel with the colonies. The giant and politically powerful East India Company had come into financial difficulties. To help it unload its accumulated stocks, the government authorized the company to sell its tea directly instead of through American agents. This policy allowed the company to sell its tea more cheaply than the cheap contraband Dutch tea which the Americans were in the habit of drinking. How should one understand the import of this new English measure, which had aroused opposition even within Parliament? The Old Whig moralists once again found themselves allied with the colonial merchants. Here was tyranny! Here was corruption! And here was England showing that it was ready to annihilate not only formal freedoms but also the quite material ones of American commerce. It was necessary to reply, this time through action.

The colonial reaction was unanimous: prevent the tea from being sold! The non-importation reflex, co-ordinated by the Sons of Liberty, worked well. In Philadelphia, plans to unload the tea cargo were opposed by a determined crowd who forced the English captain to give up his efforts. In New York, the unloaded tea was stored in a municipal building and placed under the guard of the Sons of Liberty before an angered crowd threw the tea into the harbour. In contrast to the other governors, Hutchinson, who claimed to be personally opposed to this English measure, but was angered by the publication of his private papers, refused to concede on principle. His obstinate refusal opened the way for the famous 'Boston Tea Party', during which about a hundred men, dressed as Indians and acting under the leadership of some solid citizens, boarded the British ships, carefully opened only those casks that were filled with tea, and then emptied their contents overboard. The action took place efficiently and peacefully, without any intervention of troops, before a crowd gathered nearby to witness the proceedings.[15] The English reaction was far more violent.

When it learned the news of the Tea Party, Parliament voted a series of laws known in the colonies as the 'Intolerable Acts'. Some were purely economic in character; the port of Boston was closed, the Quartering Act was reimposed. The political measures were of greater importance; the Massachusetts charter was revoked, the power of the governor was increased, and the administrative Council was henceforth to be named in London instead of locally. Legal matters dealing with British personnel in the colonies were transferred to English courts. These political measures confirmed suspicions awakened by ten years of harassment and skirmishes. Here was tyranny finally showing its true face and its underlying intentions! Here was the choice between liberty and slavery! The Intolerable Acts were the point of no return. The colonies could no longer appeal to their commercial allies in England, for these merchants, twice burned by colonial boycotts, had now found other outlets. In any case, the King did not want to back down. He insisted that the withdrawal of the Stamp Act had only increased colonial pretensions. As Commander-in-Chief in the colonies, General Gage suggested that he should suspend the coercive acts, to which George III responded simply: 'Either we master them or else we will have to set them free and treat them as foreigners'.

The time for pamphlet writing had passed; unity now had to manifest itself in action. But action also depended upon unity. One can say in retrospect that it already existed in the experience of the last few years, but it could not be taken for granted, especially after the defections that followed the collapse of the non-importation movement in 1770. Radical fervour therefore had to be tempered in order to assure the spirit of unity without which the resistance movement would remain divided, ineffective and bound to fail. This corresponded perfectly to the plan of the old, more or less loyalist – or simply disoriented – élites who were trying to regain control over the movement or to divert it from a path that seemed to lead it too far. The call for a Continental Congress therefore pleased everyone. The first Continental Congress met in September 1774 in Philadelphia. Although everyone was in agreement on the gravity of the situation, the advocates of independence did not have a majority, for those who still wished for reconciliation had made an effort to get themselves elected to the Congress in the hope of being able to forestall any radical and irrevocable decision.

Both sides jockeyed for position. The Declaration of Rights about which they debated was itself an expression of their indecision. The radicals wished to base their arguments on natural law whereas the moderates, who were hoping for reconciliation, appealed to the charters of the colonies and to the English Constitution itself. These two orientations correspond to the distinction between pre-modern thought and an attempt to analyze the modern State. The practical consequences of this theoretical distinction were now becoming manifest. The Declaration adopted both points of view, despite the strong impression left by the pamphlet of the young Thomas Jefferson, *A Summary of the Rights of British America*. According to him, the unity of the Empire passed through the Crown and not through the Parliament, thus justifying the legislative independence of the colonies. This thesis was familiar; it had already been advanced by Franklin, and then by Bland, but Jefferson's argument no longer was based on pre-modern premises. According to him the first colonists were free people who had not lost their liberty by leaving England. On the contrary, they had the natural right to build a new and free society in America; and if they had freely accepted English law, they could also freely rid themselves of it. Their allegiance to England was therefore only symbolic; it no longer was a question of the kind of participation in the Empire accepted by Dickinson and Dulany when they spoke of external regulations and internal taxes. One still hears an echo there of contractualist thought founded on the theory of natural law. That type of thought could justify independence once it was acquired – as it had allowed Locke to justify the Glorious Revolution – but it was not useful at this stage, since the conflict was still unfolding within the English Empire. Jefferson's approach came to have practical importance once the time for conciliation had passed.

The First Continental Congress concentrated principally on concrete measures. It was decided to issue an order of non-importation beginning 1 December 1774, and if that did not yield results, to impose a non-exportation campaign beginning 10 September 1775 (a date agreed upon so that the Southern producers could sell their harvests – this being a first indication of a division in colonial interests). The 'Association' – a theoretically interesting choice of words – created in order to set the non-importation campaign in motion (and to replace the Sons of Liberty, which did not have a legal status), became the basis for a new legality as the conflict developed. The crowd, spurred on by vague ideas of a 'moral economy', had transformed itself into a political actor. The Association came to constitute, in Pennsylvania for example, the basis for the government of the colony when independence was declared.[16] Meanwhile, non-importation was a success. English imports to the colonies fell 97 per cent from the previous year's levels. The colonists hoped for the support of English radicals, allied with the British merchants whose intervention had already been felt in the struggles against the Stamp Act and the Townshend Acts. But the King was determined to react forcefully. He condemned a 'traitorous corres-pondence, counsels and comfort of divers wicked and desperate persons within this realm' and demanded his subjects 'to use their utmost endeavours to withstand and suppress . . . rebellion, and to disclose . . . all treasons and traitorous conspiracies which they shall know to be against us, our crown and dignity'. The lines of battle were thus drawn. The conciliationists of the Chatham group – who wanted to apply to this case the subtle distinction used in 1745, *viz.*, that there was a rebellion in Scotland and not that Scotland was in rebellion – arrived too late.

In the colonies, the question of independence was finally posed in clear terms by Thomas Paine's famous, pamphlet, *Common Sense*, in January 1776. Paine demolished the final tie linking America with the Empire, its feeling of affection for the Crown. The King and his ministers were one and the same enemy; it is against the monarchy and for the republic that one must stand. Paine did not bother himself with Old Whig or republican jargon about a mixed or balanced constitution, or about the inevitable corruption of which Polybius was the philosopher and Roman history the example. His argument was of an extreme simplicity in comparison with the verbal juggling acts of the previous years, which sought to remain both in the Empire and nevertheless free. The only authority to which Paine appealed was common sense; his only quotations were extracts from the Bible. Starting from a state of nature in which everyone lived freely, Paine compares a social state, in which a thousand ties knit together relations of mutual aid, to a government that is established because these free men are not angels. But Paine does not go on to defend a mixed constitution. Government is created only to guard against human depravity; thus it has no positive function, its role should remain minimal. This limited government must be simple, non-bureaucratic, cheap. Society is capable of self-management so long as no one intervenes. Commerce functions in Paine's harmonious world as gravity does in the world of Newtonian science. On the basis of this image of a natural social state, Paine returns to the concrete situation of the colonies by demonstrating that they have no need of England in order to assure either their prosperity or their future. Then, resuming his rhetoric and recalling the story of Samuel in the Old Testament book of *Kings*, he ends his pamphlet with a vigorous attack on monarchy and on all aristocratic distinctions that block the emergence of talent and merit. Finally, Paine recalls once again the fate of the Hebrew people, this time in a positive way; America is vested with a historic mission, its cause is that of all humanity. The democrat Paine concludes here on a republican theme: 'for the time *hath found us*', he proclaims; *we* must assert *ourselves* before being dragged down by corruption and decadence.

Tom Paine's pamphlet is remarkable for many reasons. His argument is quite abstract when compared to the debate over empire that unfolded during the previous decade and a half; but at the same time this argument, with its Lockian and republican resonances, is also modelled on colonial realities. Paine had lived in America for only 14 months when he published his pamphlet; he did not know the theoretical details of the debates that had allowed the colonists to raise the question of their independence, and he did not bother to inform himself about them. Instead, he participated actively in the radical politics of the artisans of Philadelphia. His pamphlet is thus quite distinct from the development of the revolutionary mentality as well as from its crystallization six months later in the Declaration of Independence. His pamphlet found an echo especially among common people, the artisans and small farmers of the West. Although they applauded its practical effects, advocates of independence of the stamp of John Adams opposed the simplistic or utopian message of his pious and naïvely optimistic thoughts about natural law. And indeed, once independence was declared, Paine did not play a leading role in the institutional politics of the new republic (although he remained active, at the local level and through his writings). On the other hand, his depiction of a state of nature in which everyone lives freely, and of a society capable of self-management, did find its place, if not in American reality, at least in the symbolic imagination on which this reality is nourished. Some came to see in it the birth of an economic liberalism whose praises were sung by America in the 19th century. For them, Paine became the ideologue of a new middle class of artisans seeking to assert themselves by what they do and not by what they are. It is true that he is one of the few pamphleteers to invoke free trade as a replacement for Newtonian gravitational forces in a new science of politics.[17] But the appeal to Scripture and the call to the destiny of the New World was of greater importance. Should an island govern a continent, Paine asked? The other biblical reference, the attack on hereditary nobility and parasitic government, was also an invitation to domestic reform after being liberated from the English yoke. But Paine did not distinguish such social reform from the independence-oriented politics inspired by *Common Sense*.

Tom Paine envisaged a radical democracy. He knew that he would be accused of preaching anarchy, and his pamphlet offered not only an economic analysis but also a political project. This constitutional programme is, to be sure, rather confused, as several contemporary critics, who did not publish their criticisms at the time, emphasized.[18] Reading these criticisms now, one sees the outlines of a distinction between democracy, which Paine praised, and the republican institutions that the new United States would later adopt. But we are not yet at that point. Although the war had begun with the battles of Lexington and Concord in April 1775 and although the Second Continental Congress had decided to raise an army, the *Declaration of Causes and of the Necessity of Taking Arms* which Congress voted on 6 July 1775 ended, nevertheless, with an affirmation of the desire to remain in the Empire. One would still have to wait another year and hear many more debates, of which the most important were between Massachusetts (David Leonard) and Novanglus (John Adams), the Westchester Farmer (Samuel Seabury) and The Farmer Refuted (Alexander Hamilton). The pessimists feared economic chaos, war, division among the colonies and civil war in each. Whoever won, a disaster seemed to them inevitable. Other responses insisted on the fact that people like Samuel Seabury were not pro-British but rather lacked sufficient confidence in their fellow citizens. As Seabury himself said: 'If I must be enslaved let it be by a king at least, and not by a parcel of upstart, lawless committeemen'. But the experience of the last 15 years of struggles and debates proved precisely the contrary: the colonies were capable of self-government.[19] Nevertheless, even the radical John Adams continued to affirm in his *Novanglus* his faithfulness to 'King George III, whom God preserve'.

# 3 History Reflected: The Declaration of Independence and the Question of Sovereignty

## BEYOND REBELLION

The break was slow in coming. Experience had ripened, but the reflection which would reveal its meaning did not yet crystallize. Both camps in Congress hesitated. The conciliator from the old Pennsylvania establishment, Joseph Galloway, proposed that a written Constitution, settling relations with the Empire, be drafted. He envisaged a Parliament elected by the colonial legislatures and presided over by an officer named by the King. On every issue concerning both England and the colonies, either this body or the Parliament in London could propose a bill, but it would not become law unless approved by both. But the Galloway proposal was not made public; Congress met behind closed doors, votes were counted by colony, and Galloway was supported by only five votes against six in opposition. But the die was not yet cast. Galloway abandoned the élitist approach that had characterized colonial politics; he appealed directly to the public in *A Candid Examination of the Mutual Claims of Great Britain and the Colonies: with a Plan of Accommodation on Constitutional Principles*. This pamphlet justified his constitutional project on the basis of the same commonplaces of parliamentary sovereignty drawn from Whig sources to which his opponents appealed.[1] The reflection that would bring a break therefore had to be founded on a philosophical basis capable of creating a different political system than that of the English. To break with that system, the freest and most admired in the world, was not easy. But the fact that Galloway had decided to engage in a public debate suggests the distance travelled in ten years. Henceforth, political questions were not only public matters but matters for the public.

On the theoretical plane, Galloway was right. What was needed was a new theory that could prove its ability to convince nascent public opinion. The foundation for this theory had already been worked out in a pamphlet by James Wilson, written in 1770 but published only in 1774, when the temporary calm that had accompanied the collapse of the non-importation movement was again broken. Wilson's *Considerations on the Nature and Extent of the Legislative Authority of the British Parliament* granted the theoretical impossibility of two sovereignties coexisting in a single empire. Nevertheless, he stated, two representative legislative bodies existed and functioned *de facto* within this Empire. How could the rights of each be specified? The idea of internal legislation versus external commercial legislation had already been invoked, but Townshend had in turn relied precisely upon this distinction. Dickinson's *Farmer* had therefore contested the foundation of this argument, but without being able to advance any further positive claims. Wilson saw that he had to shift ground radically. He posed the question of the general goals of any government. Speaking in the language of natural law, Wilson affirmed that the obligation of government is to assure and to increase the happiness of its citizens. This led to the practical question of whether this happiness was better guaranteed by the English Parliament or by the colonial legislatures. Wilson had no doubts about the answer. Although a certain 'Salus Populi' objected to Wilson by distinguishing between the happiness one actually enjoyed in the Empire and that which the Empire could in principle contribute, the new question itself, rather than any possible responses, was to influence future developments.

The break with England had to be accompanied by the creation of a new political authority in the colonies. The Continental Congress had not been convened in order to accomplish this task. Its role was defensive in character: the organization of passive resistance and the formulation of petitions to the King and to Parliament. The presence in the Congress of a large number of advocates of reconciliation is explained in part by the fact that its members were chosen by the colonies and thus obviously represented the establishment. On the other hand, radical Massachusetts and the Cavaliers of Virginia made common cause to turn Congressional decisions in their direction. What was called the 'Lee-Adams Junto'[2] did manipulate certain decisions, such as the one to move the meetings from the official State House of Pennsylvania to the more modest Carpenters' Hall, or the election of Charles Thomson as permanent secretary of the Congress. On substantive matters, however, another logic held sway for the moment. After the colonies' violent and near unanimous reaction to the Tea Act, conservatives thought it was better to participate in a Congress, where matters could still be debated, rather than to leave things to the passion or the violence of popular opinion. That is why the advocates of reconciliation returned to the Second Congress, despite the failure of the Galloway plan during the first.[3] But this prudent tactic assured that this *national* Congress would assume a role that previous attempts at unifying the 13 colonies had not been able to acquire. Although each colony jealously maintained its authority, it now coexisted with a new national authority forming around Congress.

The First Congress had met for only six weeks and its most important decision was easily taken. Following the success of the campaigns against the Stamp Act and the Townshend Acts, the Congress called for a non-importation campaign and, if that action had no effect, a non-exportation campaign starting the following year. Having voted for the creation of the Association that put non-importation into effect, the members of the Congress chose to return home and take care of local problems. The country as a whole was in a *de facto* state of war but local interests predominated in these delegates' minds. This attitude was typical of colonial behaviour. It is neither as paradoxical nor as naïve as it might appear at first sight. On the one hand, the roles of the Congress and of the central authority were to be only temporary and above all symbolic. This authority was to replace another one against which people had risen because it was interfering in local matters, whereas in fact self-government had existed since the beginning of colonization. The new central authority was necessary only as a guarantee for the *legitimacy* of decisions already taken at the everyday level by those directly affected. That legitimation had been assured previously by Whig political theory and the institutions that it founded. Now Congress was assuming this function, although the theory that would serve to explain and justify its role would be worked out only later, in the form of the new republican federalism of the Constitution of 1787. For the moment, in the press of action, the *symbolic* power of the Congress did not require immediate institutional legitimation. The actions of the Committees of Correspondence, of the Sons of Liberty or of the spontaneously organized crowd were self-sufficient. Under the direction of the Association, the Congress established committees of inspection elected by the electors of the old legislature. The Association thus initiated a politics that challenged the forms and norms of political behaviour inherited from England. This experience presented a typical example of the constant interaction, neither foreseen nor foreseeable, of theory and practice which runs through American experience.

Although the conflict had reached the point of armed struggle in the interval between its two meetings, the Second Congress still sought reconciliation. It did not tell its troops to cease fire, for the English would have seen that as a sign of weakness. But, in the beginning of July 1775, it sent an 'Olive Branch Petition' to Parliament, which the latter firmly rejected. On 6 December, the Congress then formally disavowed its subordination to Parliament while still affirming its allegiance to the King. This was the final argument the colonists could make as colonists, supported here by Adams's *Novanglus* and by certain arguments drawn from Wilsons's *Considerations*. English history was invoked one more time, notably the famous *Calvin's Case* of 1608 where the court, via Coke, declared that in the case of Ireland (whose nobles were not represented in Parliament) a country could be subject to the King without being *ipso facto* subject to Parliament. But this (pre-modern) appeal to English history made no sense on the theoretical plane, given that *Calvin's Case* predates not only the Glorious Revolution but also the revolution of 1640! It is no surprise, then, that the King decreed that the colonies were in a state of rebellion, opening the October parliamentary session of 1775 with a bellicose statement accompanied by a legislative proposal stipulating that any American ship was subject to seizure, and erecting a blockade against American trade.

The news of the royal decisions reached the colonies in the winter. The formal Declaration of Independence came only in July 1776. In the meantime, organizing continued at the local level. Already, the First Congress had endorsed the Suffolk Resolves, a petition from a Massachusetts committee which, after a violently rhetorical preamble, explained that, in order to pursue the tactic of passive resistance, one had to disobey English institutions, disregard British justice, stop paying taxes and, finally, let the people elect officers to their own militia and learn as soon as possible the art of war. In June 1775 Massachusetts had asked the Second Congress for the authority to set up its own government since one of the Intolerable Acts had suspended its Charter and its institutions. With the assent of Congress a new Charter was drafted, which served as the basis for legitimizing its civil and military institutions until 1778, when a new Constitution was proposed. This decision by Congress followed the same pattern as those authorizing the creation of the Association committees. The Congress gave its authorization; the colonies – towns, committees, citizens – acted. Although there was much talk of Congress being manipulated by the Lee-Adams junto, and although it did in fact try to influence political decisions, the movement actually came from society. The Congress simply crowned these social initiatives *symbolically*. It did not act as a central power but rather drew its legitimacy and its authority from a popular political experience which had not yet been given theoretical form.

The colonies responded to the King's bellicose policy by drafting new constitutions, the first of which were those of New Hampshire and South Carolina. Rhode Island went it alone, following the colonial conception of the autonomy of the colonies, and declared itself independent in April 1776. Virginia had been in an uproar since the previous year, when Governor Dunmore had promised freedom to the slaves in exchange for their participation in the struggle against the armed insurrection that had led finally to the bombardment of Norfolk on 1 January 1776. This provocation led the Virginia Convention – which was strictly speaking illegal, since the legislature had been prorogued by Dunmore – on 10 May to instruct its representatives to Congress to demand independence. Richard Henry Lee made that proposal on 7 June 1776. The ground had been prepared by Congress itself on that same 10 May, when it had ordered every colony not possessing a legitimate government to create one. The Congress then decreed on 15 May, in the preamble of its instructions to the colonies, that they should abandon all allegiance to the Crown, proclaiming that all authority henceforth resided in the people. These two actions were aimed at allowing the committees implementing the Association's policy to replace recalcitrant or hesitant legislatures still controlled by the old establishment. Their success depended upon the relative strength of the opposing social forces in each colony. Emphasis was placed on the fact that authority resided in the people, and not in the Congress – which nevertheless authorized itself to vote measures applicable to all colonies. But beyond their practical consequences, these resolutions had an impact at the level of political theory; from then on, independence was only a formality. It remained to be established in reality and its consequences had still to be comprehended.

## INDEPENDENCE AND ITS DECLARATION

The resolution decreeing independence proposed on 7 June by Richard Henry Lee did not ask merely that ties with England be broken. It also proposed the formation of alliances with foreign powers and the preparation of a plan of confederation to be submitted to the colonies for their consideration and approval. It was in fact the need for alliances, and primarily one with France (which had been defeated in 1763 but was still ready to seize the opportunity for revenge), that had determined

Congress's decision to declare itself formally independent. Before this declaration, the 13 separate rebellious colonies could not count on serious aid from foreign powers. The Declaration therefore was merely the first and easiest of the decisions to be taken. Once the formal Declaration was prepared by Jefferson, only two days of debates were required to ratify it, whereas months would pass before agreement on the proposed terms for possible treaties with allies was obtained, and more than a year before a constitution, the Articles of Confederation, could be framed. Another four years were needed before the last colony rallied to that constitution.

The American Revolution, whose culmination was apparently the explicit declaration of independence, was a historic break, but it was not conceived as such. In a certain sense, it was a natural evolution, made necessary by the course of social events, a rational consequence rather than an act of the passions. It could be situated easily within the tradition of the Glorious Revolution. Violence did not play a key role; the battles of Lexington and Concord, in April 1775, did not as such lead to the break. Nor did independence create new institutions; the new nation, which called itself the United States of America, was still made up of 13 sovereign political entities whose social form of governance remained essentially unchanged even though the reference to the monarchy had been abandoned. In truth, one ought to speak of *united States* and not of a single unit named *The United States*. The new nation was not united around a single will; the foundation for its political sovereignty existed only in opposition to the old mother-country and in relation to the allies it sought. By its very form, Richard Henry Lee's resolution indicates that the document proclaiming independence was in no way a charter of government or the creation of a new political institution.

But if American independence is not based on a specifically political break, it is no less a *novum* in political theory. With respect to the final efforts of the colonists to remain within the Empire, the novelty of the Declaration is quite evident. In 1774 John Dickinson had tried once again to apply the distinction between commercial regulation and internal taxation. His *Essay on the Constitutional Power of Great Britain over the Colonies in America* ended, as one commentator puts it, by drowning itself in an ocean of footnotes. James Wilson's *Considerations* marks a theoretical turning point, although one part of his argument remained prisoner to a pre-modern conception of the nation. He opens a new path only when he highlights the idea that the foundation for every legitimate government resides in the fact that it pursues the happiness of its subjects. Jefferson went further in 1776.

The Declaration of Independence is a short document aimed at justifying legally and morally an action already undertaken. Thus, the first paragraph is formulated in the conditional: 'When in the course of human events, it becomes necessary for one people to dissolve the political bands which have connected them with another, and to assume among the powers of the earth, the separate and equal station to which the Laws of Nature and of Nature's God entitle them, a decent respect to the opinions of mankind requires that they should declare the causes which impel them to the separation'. The Americans are seeking once again to legitimate their political actions first of all on the social and theoretical plane. Their appeal to public opinion speaks of the ties of one people to another; and their self-justification is based on natural law. The second paragraph then outlines the implications for political theory of certain truths labelled 'self-evident', the liberty and equality of people. Government is instituted to protect and to secure these self-evident truths by giving them the form of rights. But this governmental power that gives a political form to pre-political truths depends, and is founded, upon the consent of the governed.[4] If government threatens or destroys the end for which it was instituted, the people have the right to alter it or to abolish it and to create a new one whose institutions will be capable of assuring their safety and happiness. Since it would not be prudent to change government for light or transient reasons, and since experience proves that people are more disposed to suffer than to abolish the forms to which they have become accustomed, the Declaration must demonstrate that a long series of abuses and usurpations, whose goal is always identical and whose strategy is consistently applied, aims at establishing a despotism. In this case, the people have the right to rebel against it and to establish a new government capable of assuring their safety and rights in the future. Thus, after these two first paragraphs, the Declaration presents a long indictment designed to demonstrate before 'a candid world' the justness of their decision to separate from England.

Although the argument presented in the body of the Declaration of Independence is developed in historical terms, the function of the Declaration distinguishes it from pre-independence modes of thought and struggle. It no longer is a matter of trying to reclaim the rights of an Englishman; nor is it any longer a matter of appealing to the clear interests of the home country; and it no longer is a question of moral obligations. It is no longer the Parliament or the Prime Minister but the King himself that stands accused. The ultimate authority appealed to is the people, the opinion of all mankind. As Jefferson had already suggested in his *Summary View*, it no longer is a matter of violations of the English Constitution and its Whig form but of renouncing a previous imperial contract between a king and a people endowed with its own social institutions that sees itself obliged to take back the liberty it had freely alienated but which now is endangered. The most noted commentator on the Declaration, Carl L. Becker, is correct in asserting that one does not invent a new philosophy in order to justify a revolution; but it does not follow that the argument invoked by the Declaration is based solely on Locke's contractualist theory, as both Becker and received opinion assume. The appeal to history that constitutes the body of the Declaration requires a theoretical reading, all the more so since the famous triad of liberal rights – life, liberty and property – is replaced in the opening theoretical paragraph with a reference to 'certain' inalienable rights whose triadic formulation thus makes no claim to establish an exhaustive or exclusive list. And more important still, the right to property, which both classical Whig theory as well as Locke justified as the condition for free political participation, is replaced here by the right to the pursuit of happiness. But this pursuit of happiness, which goes beyond the happiness invoked by Wilson in his *Considerations*, can only be subjective and is never attained once and for all. This implies, on the one hand, the legitimation of private interest in politics and, on the other hand, that the participation of the subject in the definition of the political can no longer be simply virtual.

The Declaration of Independence is not principally a theoretical document, and its consequences at the level of theory appear only in practice. The spirit of independence had already been attained when the Declaration sought to give it thematic form. The 'pursuit of happiness' must be understood first of all in this context. The Declaration does not say anything more about it; it is left to practice to delineate it and to politics to give it institutional form. The major part of the Declaration details the grievances of the colonies, which are said to manifest a pattern that begins with the deprivation of the colonies' right to self-government and the replacement of their institutions by agents of the King whose meddling has gone so far as to interfere in the administration of justice. An army maintained under conditions of peace has become independent of civil authorities; its existence has been used to justify the imposition of taxes and the abolition of judicial protections, which are summarized in a long paragraph which corresponds to the passage of the Intolerable Acts. The King is then accused of waging war against the colonies, threatening their trade and inciting the 'merciless Indian savages' against them. All these accusations form a pattern that is to be recognized by the 'candid world' before which the Declaration pleads its case. It is the overall pattern, and not this or that act, that authorizes the American people to renounce the political contract that had tied the colonies to the King and to England. It is Old Whig thought that recognizes this pattern, which is not the breaking of a Lockian governmental contract.

The historian will judge whether Jefferson's summary of the past 12 years of colonial history is exaggerated; the philosopher is struck by two apparent contradictions in the logic governing the Declaration of Independence. The two penultimate paragraphs explain first of all that the colonists have addressed humble petitions to the King, who, in responding with insults, has behaved like a tyrant unfit to govern a free people. The Declaration then explains that their English brethren had been warned of the misdeeds of their Parliament and that the colonists believed that their sense of justice and their ties of kinship could be counted on. But why hark back on the misdeeds of Parliament? Why impute wrongs to one's English brethren? Is this meant to imply that they might have helped, but that they have become corrupt, like the Empire, due to their power and wealth? Or is the suggestion that they in fact have political institutions like those being elaborated in the colonies, built on institutions of the type described in the second paragraph of the Declaration which affirmed the right to resistance? Or, finally, are the colonists claiming to be the last rampart of a form of liberty that once inhabited the British Isles?

The last paragraph of the Declaration of Independence contains an ambiguity that suggests an explanation of the real function of this document in the evolution of American independence and of its theoretical understanding. The independence being decreed is that of the colonies, considered individually, which are each constituted as a State independent from England but independent also from the other newly independent States. Thus, the Declaration grants the prerogatives of an independent nation to each of the States – namely, the power to make war and peace, to conclude alliances, to establish commercial relations, and such like. The Declaration had indicated the same thing in its title, which reads: 'A Declaration by the Representatives of the United States[5] of America, in General Congress Assembled'. But the Declaration was necessary for the (not yet politically constituted) Confederation to obtain the material assistance it required in order to defend itself against the political threat posed by England whose fleet had arrived in New York's harbour on 30 June. How can one reconcile the independence of the parts (of the States) with the independence of the whole (of the united nation)? Is this not a return to the theoretical problem of an *imperium in imperio* which had dominated the first phase of the debate over the Empire? The future Confederation would have to go beyond the contradictions that undermined the Empire. The Declaration of Independence does not indicate how to resolve the question, and tries even to ignore its very existence.[6]

To understand the Declaration of Independence as a theoretical reflection upon experience as it was lived since 1763, we must look once more at the role played by the Continental Congress. It had been the agent of *symbolic* unification and the guarantor for the *political* legitimacy of a self-organized social world to whose creation its concrete actions made no contribution. The *symbolic* presence of the Congress called forth this social creation; its symbolic role permitted these social institutions to assume a political dimension that transcended the immediate cause from which they had arisen. This *symbolic* role of the Congress explains why no one called attention to the contradiction between the rights of the 13 States and the right of the nation to unite around a single united will. The Declaration offers a precise expression of the American experience, but this experience itself had not yet drawn its own practical or theoretical conclusions. Thus, for example, in 1777 when John Dickinson undertook a draft for the Articles of Confederation, the only model he could think of was the Albany Plan, whose failure in 1754 might be said to mark the beginning of the Revolution. The political thought of the new American people therefore was still far from approaching modernity. It was to reach that point for the simple reason that, quite naïvely, it stuck close to reality.

# 4 History Rethought: The Revolution As Rupture?

## THE HISTORIOGRAPHY OF THE REVOLUTION

If historiography usually passes through the stage of hagiography before discovering the questions worth asking, the Americans have been lucky. Their historical debate began already during the time of the Revolution, and the institutions created and modified by the 13 free States gave rise to further questioning even before they were adopted. By the end of the War of Independence the Americans had learned the art of comparative constitutional principles, which imposed a historicist, but not relativist, perspective on their institutional history. An analysis of historical reflection on the first phase of the Revolution therefore sheds light on its structure. This recourse to historiography – and to philosophy – is necessary because, even if none of the texts which bear witness to the revolutionary experience has a legal or constitutional status, that experience has remained constitutive of the American political system. This continuous reformulation of the founding experience is the result of the open character of its development toward institutional forms that, in turn, have proved to be remarkably open.

Those who chose to remain faithful to the Crown were forced into silence, and often into exile, once the English army was no longer there to protect them. They did not produce a real counter-history of the events that led the colonies to the break with England. A few pamphlets appeared, of which the best known was written by the former governor of Massachusetts, Thomas Hutchinson, whose private reservations concerning the measures voted by Parliament, as we have seen, were accompanied publicly by a rigid execution of his instructions, which culminated in the Boston Tea Party. Hutchinson, who came from an old American family, sought above all to refute the historical arguments presented in the Declaration of Independence. He had nothing to say concerning the principles set forth there and the dilemmas confronting the Empire. As he had asserted repeatedly when he was in power in Massachusetts, Hutchinson saw only the machinations of demagogues, an easily manipulated crowd, and the avarice of certain merchants seeking to turn a profit from anarchy. Hutchinson did not understand the colonial critique of Parliament's 'corruption' by the Court; indeed, he had accepted and benefitted from this practice, erected into a system since Walpole, and insisted that the sovereignty of the Empire could only be absolute, and that it resided in Parliament. One could oppose the measures voted by Parliament, but only by appropriate ways and means – as he himself had tried to do several times during the period preceding the break. Years later, during his lonely exile, Hutchinson returned to this period of his public life in the third volume of his monumental *History of Massachusetts-Bay*, which was published by his grandson in 1828, but he did not deviate from his earlier position.

The historiography of the Revolution first found expression during the constitutional debates within each of the 13 new States. It was taken up again at the Constitutional Convention which drafted the new federal Constitution in 1787. The stakes were aptly summarized in 1909 in the previously cited phrase of the historian Carl L. Becker: 'Home rule, or who shall rule at home?' Constitutional questions, such as the extension of suffrage or the creation of a bicameral legislature or the power to be granted to the executive, were perceived as issues with material stakes – which, indeed, they were. Once the constitutional period ended, these stakes were to take on an institutional form. This was expressed in the creation of the first system of political parties, an institution that none of the constitutions had foreseen. The existence of political parties had no place in the political science of the era; traditionally, the presence of what were called 'factions' implied an imperfection, a division in the City. It therefore was necessary to invent a theory in order to provide an explanation of this novelty. The French Revolution occurred at just the right moment.[1] The differences between the parties of Jefferson and Adams could be explained by reference to a theory opposing the different principles of these two revolutions.[2] The agrarian virtue that served as the basis for the optimistic vision of the Jeffersonians was contrasted with the goal of a strong central government justified by the need to check the passions of the crowd while encouraging commerce and supporting the nascent industries of the young country. Each side of this practical struggle took the opportunity to claim the Revolution as its own and to accuse its competitor of betraying the principles of their common struggle.

Such political and partisan historiography continued until the political demise of Adams' party. If the disappearance of the Federalist party marks the end of the political divisions inherited from the Revolution, it also sheds light on a series of socio-economic and regional problems that culminated, 32 years later, in a civil war. While not claiming to establish a causal link, it is not surprising to see this era give birth to a strongly nationalist and unified historiography, of which George Bancroft is the best representative. Bancroft introduces the first volume of his monumental *History of the United States of America. From the Discovery of the Continent*, which appeared in 1834,[3] with a hymn to the glory of his country, which he concludes as follows: 'It is the object of the present work to explain how the change in the condition of our land has been brought about; and, as the fortunes of a nation are not under the control of blind destiny, to follow the steps by which a favoring Providence, calling our institutions into being, has conducted the country to its present happiness and glory'. And the first chapter of Bancroft's final volume, which appeared in 1882, explained that 'there was no revolt against the past, but a persistent and healthy progress'. The providential action of which the first Introduction spoke was that of the American will, both free and moral. Concerning this will, the last volume says further: 'History carries forward the study of ethics by following the footsteps of States from the earliest times of which there is a record . . . history imposes with evidence that tyranny and wrong lead inevitably to decay; that freedom and right, however hard may be the struggle, always prove resistless'. This optimism, which sees the Revolution as a moral necessity in which, in principle, all participated is confirmed in the short paragraph Bancroft added to the just-cited Introduction to the first volume, when he republished it a half-century later: 'The foregoing words, written nearly a half-century ago, are sufferred to remain, because the intervening years have justified their expression of confidence in the progress of our republic. The seed of disunion has perished; and universal freedom, reciprocal benefits, and cherished traditions bind its many States in the closest union'. The Revolution, in short, survived the Civil War; liberty and morality, of which Bancroft's work claims to be both the chronicle and the encomium, continue to reign.

Bancroft's thesis draws upon North America's geographical specificity, which gave the independent and united colonies a horizon that protected and encouraged their experience, that of a continuous and uninterrupted progress: 'There was no revolt against the past, but a persistent and healthy progress', he insisted at the beginning of the volume dealing with the Revolution. But this frontier horizon could not be conquered and pushed back indefinitely, it could not perpetually remain an incitement to further progress. Progress would one day be achieved, and an identity crisis would follow. This is precisely what a young historian from the University of Wisconsin, Frederick Jackson Turner, announced in 1893 in an essay on *The Significance of the*

*Frontier on American History*. Turner's celebrated thesis expresses succinctly the manner in which Americans, on the threshold of the 20th century, conceived their Revolution. Independence brought with it the end of monarchy and the creation of a *de facto* republic whose institutions remained to be determined. According to classical political theory, a republic must expand until its new wealth undermines its foundation, the austere virtue of its citizens. In other words, the republic is condemned to die in time. But the frontier allowed Americans to push back the effective expiration date; space did battle with time. The closing of the frontier thus challenged the nation's identity. The historian, like the political theorist, had to take this into account.

Two divergent approaches arose when America began to move beyond this identity crisis at the end of the 19th century. The first approach accepts without question that the country had become, in its own fashion, an empire. This was all the more evident as one of the responses to the conquest of the West was the pursuit of a new frontier in the Far East, symbolized in the 'open door' policy toward China. History, meanwhile, had entered the University; historians went to study *Wissenschaft* with Ranke and his emulators in a Germany that also was beginning to think of itself as an empire and whose historians were singing the praises of the *Primat der Aussenpolitik*. The result was the integration of American history, previously thought of as isolated, into the context of English and even European history. The study of history came to concentrate on English institutions and their transformation by the experience of Empire. Colonial history was now studied from the English point of view. The measures against which the colonists were protesting were legitimated by a detailed analysis of England's institutional and commercial policy, which appeared in the final analysis as moderate. Although some even blamed the rebellious colonists, the principal argument advanced by this thesis was that the Revolution was inevitable, given the differing conditions and needs of the two countries. All of this meant that the idealistic and idealized image painted by Bancroft had to be rejected; the Revolution was not just a simple and honest affirmation of liberty against big bad England with its tyrant king and its corrupt ministers.[4]

The other reaction to the psychological shock represented by the closing of the frontier was to try to preserve the ideal while ridding oneself of the idealization. The analyses of the so-called 'progressive' school stressed economic interests and the conflicts they engendered. Its analysis was concerned especially with the post-independence period. Its principal thesis aims at building up the generous goals of the Declaration of Independence at the expense of the type of thinking found in the Constitution of 1787, which, according to this view, represented the triumph of counter-revolution. For the period considered thus far, the analyses of the progressives were mostly empirical, studying for example cleavages within one colony, as in Carl L. Becker's account of the colony of New York. Another exemplary work published around this time and coming from the same political viewpoint is that of Arthur M. Schlesinger. In *The Colonial Merchants and the American Revolution, 1763-76* (1918), Schlesinger analysed the politics of the merchant class throughout the colonies in order to see how their perception of their real interests could be reconciled with their decision to participate in the struggle against England. Schlesinger was the first to show that their participation waned as they came to discover that the influence they had exercised over the crowd during the campaign against the Stamp Act could also escape their grasp. This had actually happened two years later during the movement against the Townshend Acts, when the Sons of Liberty undertook to organize layers of the population that had until then been rather passive if not 'deferential'. This progressive thesis was formulated in more theoretico-historical terms in J. Franklin Jameson's *The American Revolution Considered as a Social Movement* (1926), whose thesis is epitomized in the following famous phrase: 'The stream of revolution, once started, could not be confined within narrow banks, but spread abroad upon the land'. In sum, the progressive school treated independence in the context of a transformation of social relations whose further development in their own society this school desired.

This turn-of-the-century historiography remains quite empirical in orientation, guided as it was by a few very general principles that ultimately cannot be challenged because they determine the facts which are empirically brought to light. If both imperial and colonial interests are assumed to be legitimate, the only thing left to do is to describe their inevitable and fatal interaction. Similarly, if it is assumed that people really know and act on their interests, the patient work of the progressive detective will each day furnish new motives for the merchants to manipulate the masses and new explanations for these masses' own capacity to assert themselves despite everything. This thesis was carried to its extreme limit just before the Second World War, in John C. Miller's *Sam Adams, Pioneer in Propaganda*, which reduces the Revolution to the manipulation of public opinion. But this explains nothing about the Revolution in itself. At most it describes the *how*, but in no way the *why*.

A final school of historians, born after the Second World War, should also be mentioned here, by way of transition. This 'consensus' school, or school of 'American exceptionalism', built on Tocqueville's famous remark that the United States was 'born free'. These historians asked why the United States never had broad-based socialist movement. Tocqueville's argument suggests that America, not having known feudalism, did not experience reaction either; its revolution was thus a predestined and simple matter. Starting from this standpoint, American political history was described as a series of efforts destined to fail from their very inception; neither restoration nor political actions seeking to transform a fundamentally liberal society were possible. This method of relating all political analysis to a brute social fact may be criticized, above all on the empirical level.[5] But this analysis, even if that was not its goal, puts into question the very concept of Revolution. If the Revolution is only the continuation of a simple pre-given social state, it is in no way a revolution. Therefore the question itself must be put into question, and this task is none other than that of philosophy.


## PHILOSOPHY

The thought of John Locke is supposed to have determined the first phase of the American Revolution as that of Montesquieu is said to have dominated the drafting of the Constitution which was its culmination. Looked at more closely, this schema does not hold up. Locke's name is frequently cited, often in conjunction with that of Newton. But the Locke who was 'in the air' at the time is not the author of the second *Treatise* but rather the epistemologist and sometimes the educator or the author of the essay on tolerance. Locke wrote his *Treatise* between 1679 and 1681 in order to help Shaftesbury's party put into effect what became, nearly a decade later, the Glorious Revolution. The goal was to convince the Tory aristocracy that this change was legitimate; that is why the argument set forth in the *Treatise* is directed especially against Filmer's paternalism. It was necessary to give contractualist political theory a form that would not threaten the *social* order while still being able to transform *political* institutions. A century later, the colonists could take very little from this argument. Its theory of free consent is founded upon a tacit agreement and not on the kind of active participation that developed in the years 1763–76. If the attempt to apply Locke's contractualist theory to a concrete situation is made, the difficulty is that during the first years of the imperial debate the colonists based themselves on pre-modern ideas in order to justify what became only later the assertion of a modern politics. Locke's theory remains Whig in as much as it presupposes the existence of a power with which society can enter into a contract; but it is different to the extent that it treats society as pre-existing and independent of this power. This was the *dilemma*, not the solution, that the Americans encountered when they undertook to construct independent States.

Free citizens could, of course, employ the image of a contract in a rhetorical way to justify their refusal to pay taxes imposed by Parliament on non-represented political corporations. This argument could even legitimate the break after the fact, but it could not have motivated or guided the colonists in their struggles.[6] Can one really say that the Revolution was justified because England had broken a contract with the colonies? Or did the revolutionary argument have another resonance, one which pointed toward a future that it is itself worthy of analysis? So far, we have seen the conflict unfold primarily in the defensive terms of a colonial reaction against English measures. Nor were the positive institutions that developed under the aegis of the legitimating and the symbolical action of the Congress based on contractualist theory. Rather, they revived the old popular and pre-modern aspiration for a 'moral economy', which became political and modern due to the symbolic intervention of the Continental Congress. But a theoretical form capable of discerning the uniqueness of these new forms of political participation remained to be delineated. This further development called upon classical political thought.

Locke's influence is all the less important as his political philosophy is itself out of phase with the political theory of his time. J. G. A. Pocock's polemic against 'the myth of John Locke'[7] shows that practical questions of the day were discussed in reference to the 'ancient Constitution', the nature of feudalism and the permanence of government standing over against a changing society. We saw that, in the debate with England, the Americans had recourse to just such pre-modern arguments, whereas the English position was that of then-modern Whig theory. The founding of the Bank of England, the consolidation of the national debt and the building of a commercial empire raised questions that Locke's theory did not address: those of public virtue, which is supposed to exist in contradiction with private commerce, and those of the free personality, which was supposed to be founded upon the possession of real property but which was put in question by the appearance of new artificial or financial forms of wealth, themselves evaluated by their market value and dependent upon demand and therefore, in the last analysis, upon evanescent and changing public opinion. These questions are obviously those of classical theory, ones which the new socio-economic situation had made relevant again at the same time that they cast doubt on the pertinence of the traditional answers. The liberalism that will be born in America, and whose founder is supposed to be Locke, seems to have been indifferent to these political questions, notably that of the place of the free and virtuous individual in a political society. And yet, American liberalism took shape precisely around these classical political questions. To start from Locke would therefore be to avoid the question that became crucial for Americans when they finally became free: what is the relation between classical public virtue and that 'pursuit of happiness' of which the Declaration speaks? If happiness is only a private experience, what then will be the foundation of the Republic?

If one persists in searching for the roots of a liberalism that would explain the specificity of American institutions within the Revolution, a revival of the thesis of the 'two revolutions' and their respective fates can be useful. Jürgen Habermas proposes a redefinition of the argument, starting from the idea of natural law.[8] He distinguishes two different readings of this theory. According to the first, nature is good and just; it is only a matter of eliminating what interferes with its free functioning. Thus Americans like Tom Paine will seek a minimal government, a decentralization of power, and an economic policy founded upon *laissez-faire* principles. On the other hand, the reading that sees natural law as a norm to be realized suggests an attempt to impose a philosophy on a reality that may resist it. Thus the French will be Jacobin voluntarist centralizers who make every effort to determine the course of social change by the imposition of political projects. But this does not imply that the rejection of voluntaristic and Jacobin natural law theory re-establishes automatically the individualistic picture of the social contract attributed to Locke.[9] Indeed, that would be a return to pre-modern thought, which presupposed the real existence of natural law in some social form. Paine's solution does not hold up as an alternative, as independent Americans came to see when they attempted to draft a constitution. They had to resolve the questions of how society is to be politically represented, and of how the political is to be incarnated in a symbolic form of sovereignty.

The distinction between two revolutions is developed differently in Hannah Arendt's *On Revolution*.[10] According to Arendt, the American Revolution remained a political revolution whereas the French Revolution was forced to turn toward the social question. The political dimension relates to the universal; it allows particular questions to be symbolized or articulated in a form that removes their self-interested, private and divisive character. Social demands cannot be settled without dividing society against itself, thus destroying the political unity that holds citizens together and creating the conditions for civil war. On the other hand, the political question, that of the good life in the City, is that of unity. This does not mean that it denies the existence of social divisions; on the contrary, by starting from that question society becomes aware that there is a public interest that transcends – but does not eliminate – social divisions. But although Hannah Arendt reveals here an important aspect of the American Revolution, she does not explain how the colonists came to this miraculous discovery, which allowed them to establish and preserve the future of their Revolution. The conclusion to her book evokes the contemporary experience of 'workers' councils', whose lineage she traces from some of Thomas Jefferson's projects for local self-rule on through to the heroism of the Hungarian people in 1956. This continuity is fascinating, but one would like to know where this tradition comes from and upon what it is based.

The work of Bernard Bailyn, which has renewed the study of the American Revolution, furnishes the beginnings of an explanation of what Arendt calls this American political 'miracle'. Referring to Caroline Robbins' important study of *The Eighteenth-Century Commonwealthmen*,[11] Bailyn proposes a 'republican synthesis' on the basis of his rereading of the pamphlets of the revolutionary era. The type of thought called 'Commonwealth' or 'civic republicanism' or 'civic humanism' that we have summarized under the concept of 'Old Whig' thought had little influence in England after the establishment of Walpole's system. But its protagonists – Trenchard and Gordon's *Letters of Cato*, Catherine Macauley's essays, or Burgh, whose *Political Disquisitions* appeared in 1774 – influenced deeply the debate in the colonies.[12] They saw a fundamental and primary opposition between liberty and power. The latter is necessary to the existence of society, but it cannot help but seek to increase itself at the expense of liberty. The mixed constitution, which strikes a balance between political institutions and social structures, is conceived as a way of protecting liberty. But it is necessary to remain vigilant, for the danger remains inscribed in the nature of power, and in the sinful finite nature of man. This republican and civic style of thought explains the colonists' sensitivity – which some would label paranoid – to English measures that did not in themselves constitute grave political or economic injustices. Little by little, it seemed to them, the power that was England's was invading the province of colonial liberty – aided in this respect perhaps by the new economic prosperity of the colonies which made it less likely that they would make the sacrifices necessary for defending threatened liberties. They therefore had to act before it was too late. The long list of injustices recited in the Declaration permitted the rebels to justify themselves – to themselves and to the 'candid world'. This explains also why they criticized 'our English brethren' who had remained deaf to their appeals and who had failed to come to their aid, thus proving that after having come to their rescue in the 1760s, they had since become corrupted.[13] The colonists therefore had to make the break before the virus crossed the Atlantic.

This civic republicanism of the Old Whigs analyzed by Bailyn can explain the logic behind the colonists' interpretation of the English measures that led them to react; it does not yet explain their action itself, or the institutional form that it took. The interpretative grid may function as a negative ideology,[14] but it offers nothing positive, except perhaps a return to the *status quo ante*. This ideology therefore remains pre-modern. The preservation of liberty through the mechanism of an English-style mixed constitution was not an option in a society with neither king nor aristocracy. That institutional balance had been based upon the existence of three estates; its functioning depended on the virtues specific to each estate. Lacking such estates, the Americans could have returned to classical thought, taken up in the 18th century principally by Montesquieu (whose aristocratic prejudices they did not discern). The republic, on this view, is founded upon the virtue of the individual who sacrifices for the common good. But such classical thought was not made for a nation of merchants and artisans guided by their own private interests. In the course of the events leading to the break with England, the Americans sometimes believed that they possessed this virtue, but they were sometimes forced to admit that they were lacking in it. At times they tried even to impose it, speaking of the creation of a 'Christian Sparta', invoking agrarian land laws limiting private property, and proposing sumptuary laws or prohibiting theatrical performances. In the long run, those who continued to use the terms of republican thought slid toward a different interpretation of virtue, replacing its public form with a private virtue founded either upon religion or other private values such as education or the sacred character of the family. As a disillusioned patriot, Noah Webster, argued in 1788, in America, the reference to virtue found in Montesquieu's definition of the republic must be replaced by the concept of private property.

The 'republican synthesis', based on the work of Bailyn, has not garnered unanimous support from American historians, who do not appear to have appreciated its theoretical implications. An indirect attack was offered by Garry Wills, who agrees with the rejection of Locke's supposed influence but who seeks to replace it with the influence allegedly exercised by the Scottish philosophers, notably Hutcheson and Reid. We will not analyze here this rather philological plea for the Scottish influence that supposedly emerged openly in Jefferson's drafts of the Declaration of Independence.[15] The theoretical argument that underlies it boils down to a rejection of the idea of the primacy of abstract selfish individualism in the formation of the American character. Scottish thought – from which developed the economic theories of Ferguson and Smith – sees the primacy of society and community over the individual. It rejects the image of two isolated and abstractly free beings binding themselves together by means of an artificial contract in order to form a social unit. It also insists on the positive role of commerce, which replaces virtue as the motive force unifying society for the good of all. Its conception of a moral sense (the heart), differing from abstract reason (the head) and capable of deciding the ends man assigns himself, allows Wills to propose a quite evocative interpretation of the Declaration. But it does not explain the process that led the colonists to declare themselves independent. Nor does it explain in what respect the Revolution was a revolution.

To understand the unity of a process of which the Declaration is only a philosophical reflection, we must return to the role played by the Continental Congress in 1774 (and which the Stamp Act Congress had already assumed in a certain manner). This Congress had no real power nor any recognized political legitimacy *vis-à-vis* previously existing institutions. Nevertheless, it activated a political mechanism through which the 13 colonies asserted themselves as independent republics. The Congress was their unity, a unity whose reality they denied and to which they refused to grant any concrete power. But it existed, it occupied and structured a common intercolonial space. It therefore held a symbolic power; it was the public place wherein 13 independent colonies could meet, seek to understand each other and see themselves in and with the eyes of others. These 13 societies were, so to speak, the social; Congress represented the *political*. That this place for the political was a site without power is the key to the mystery of Independence as well as the Revolution. The colonists assumed that their unity was embodied in the Continental Congress in the same way that they had accepted their union with England, and that they had sought at any cost to remain within the Empire as long as their belonging to it seemed to them symbolic and political. *It is only when English power was displaced from the symbolic level to the real one that the colonists were forced to separate themselves from it.* In a word, American politics is founded from the outset on a representation of power as *an unoccupiable, an empty or symbolic place.* This interpretation fits both with Bailyn's thesis on civic republican thought and with the idea that Locke's contribution ought to be found somewhere in American institutions. Locke and his idea of consent enter into a republican form of thought from which its social foundations, the three estates, are absent. This new theoretical constellation gave birth to a new politics.

This analysis of independence as revolutionary returns in a certain sense to the starting point underlined by John Adams: James Otis' case against the Writs of Assistance. Otis' thought was pre-modern, first of all because it distinguished between governmental power and natural or divine law; it was pre-modern too in its rejection of the distinction between politics and morality. The symbolic power of the Congress had to confront very real problems, but within the symbolic structures of modernity. The existence of the Congress created that single, unified will that is the political. This single, unified will is separate from society, which is made homogeneous due to the fact that its divisions can henceforth be only quantitative since its previous qualitative distinctions depended upon political authority. What is the content of this political will? With independence it came to incarnate national sovereignty. For the English, such sovereignty is the constitution, that is to say, a mixed political society constituted by the King, the aristocracy and the Commons. But whereas England *is* a constitution, the United States had to endow itself with a Constitution that would found a *limited* government. But how then could it represent this single will, this sovereignty? The answer gave a modern form to James Otis' thesis on natural law. But this answer in its turn raised also the question that Otis had confronted between morality and the political. The solutions provided during the first period of institution-building during the Confederation left unresolved the problem of protecting the minorities who do not participate in the incarnation of this single, unified will that is the Constitution. *Symbolic authority in this case was treated as if it were real, or something realisable in fact.* It was left to the Federal Constitution of 1787 to resolve this final inheritance from James Otis and the revolution that inaugurates modern politics. But the historian has first to take up the threads of the story before the philosopher intervenes again.

# Part II
# Free Institutions:
# The Representation of the Common Good and the Individual

# 5    History Lived: The Birth of the United States

## THE REALITY OF INDEPENDENCE

Independence having been declared, it was now necessary to make it real: to win the war, of course, but above all to draw the consequences of the break with England. These consequences were social as well as political; they involved a theoretical (or ideological) re-examination of the premises that had brought about a state of independence that was not always desired and to which some were resigned for the lack of other real options. Some contemporaries, and later some historians, were of the opinion that the break would have come sooner or later, given the demographic and economic growth of the colonies; after all, an island should not govern a continent. This is undoubtedly true, and Tom Paine's *Common Sense* had made this idea vivid; but the break was now public and could be reflected upon; it was not simply an evolution but an authentic revolution. The word existed, but the political concept had not been theorized. The Glorious Revolution in England had sought only to restore a *status quo ante*; and although a king had been hanged in 1649, following six years of civil war, order had been re-established after the death of Cromwell and the fall of the 'fanatic and anarchic' republic he had directed for ten tumultuous years. The new United States could not be understood along the lines of the first model and did not wish to repeat the second. It was necessary to develop a new model for which there was no precedent.

The road that led to independence had both a practical and a theoretical side, just as the Declaration of Independence had offered two forms of legitimation, one historical and the other theoretical. The recitation of misdeeds imputed to England and its king in the Declaration was implicitly based upon Old Whig theory, which imagined a power that tends to grow constantly as the expense of a frail and ever corruptible human liberty. This description corresponded to the practical experience that was at the origin of the conflict. But the theoretical justification set forth in the first two paragraphs of the Declaration appeals to a contractual theory of natural law according to which the political contract binding two free societies had been broken *de facto* by the English measures subsequently denounced in the

81

Declaration. Does this imply that the other end of the road Americans began to travel in 1763 had to open onto a new form of political thought? This is what is suggested in a letter written in 1815 by ex-President John Adams, when he reconciled his differences with Thomas Jefferson after their bitter partisan conflict at the turn of the century. 'What do we mean by the Revolution? The war? That was no part of the Revolution; it was only an effect and a consequence of it. The Revolution was in the minds of the people, and this was effected, from 1760 to 1775, in the course of fifteen years before a drop of blood was shed at Lexington.' Adams' argument implies that the new political institutions of the independent States and their confederated union merely conformed to the eternal truths of political science, finally free to be put into practice. But John Adams was criticized as an Anglophile and aristocrat by the Jeffersonians because he admired the English constitution and praised its principles even though he criticized what he considered its practical drawbacks.[1]

John Adams' point of view was not the only one possible. A friend of Jefferson (who was abroad, as the American Ambassador to France at the time) proposed a radically different interpretation on the eve of the Constitutional Convention. The militant doctor Benjamin Rush affirmed that 'the war is over: but this is far from being the case with the American Revolution. On the contrary, nothing but the first act of the great drama is closed. It remains yet to establish and perfect our new forms of government, and to prepare the principles, morals and manners of our citizens for those forms of government after they are established and brought to perfection'. This statement corresponds more closely to the contractualist thought expressed in the first two paragraphs of the Declaration of Independence. It is as if the practical realization of liberty which Adams saw as achieved before the War of Independence opened not only onto a liberty of mind but also and especially onto a real liberty that was none other than that of men in the state of nature presupposed in the contractualist theory of natural law. Whereas the pessimistic puritan Adams staked his hopes on science to correct and rule human nature, Jefferson, the optimist imbued with Enlightenment principles, assumed that this human nature was capable not only of providing itself with institutions that would be suitable for its natural liberty but of criticizing, even reforming, such institutions.[2] In this sense, independence was only the prelude and the precondition for the Revolution that was beginning.

The two theoretical arguments – the Old Whig or republican, which Adams exemplifies in his own way, and that of contractualist natural law, on which the Jeffersonians based their views – are encountered not only in the founding document that is the Declaration of Independence; they were also part of the lived experience of the new Americans. The situation was fluid; it was necessary to make do with a few principles from which one tried to draw practical consequences. Did independence imply a dissolution of the previous government (while its social foundations remained intact), or did this break restore the pre-social state of nature? If there was a dissolution of government and a rupture of previous ties, were all social bonds dissolved or only the political ones? And if society continued to exist even though the government was dissolved, how could this society endow itself with new and legitimate political institutions? Since the conflict with England had turned on only specific grievances and since disobedience was therefore only selective, as the churches had taught, should one rebuild on the basis of the unaffected parts of the political edifice? And in that case, should one have recourse to the old political institutions, or ought one to start on the basis of the social relations that were not affected by the conflict in order to create a new political constitution? Or, was the struggle of a more radical character, such that neither existing institutions nor prevailing social interests could be presupposed? This last option would open wide the door to utopia, which abstracts from human nature and its history in order to imagine a purely political and transparent society. Finally, what was to be done with the new forms of popular organization that had developed at the beginning of the struggle against the Stamp Act and that had been legitimated by the congressional act decreeing the establishment of the Association? They were useful for a time, but as the conservative advocate of independence, Gouverneur Morris, noted, the mob was beginning 'to think and reason', which could be dangerous.

These questions are not abstract, as Morris' remark indicates; they were born with independence, both on the theoretical and practical planes. It would be wrong to think that one of the options is 'progressive' while the other is 'reactionary'. A brief sketch of the available choices makes clear the theoretical ambiguity confronting the Americans. According to Locke, the dissolution of government does not imply the disintegration of society. This suggests the possibility of retooling the old assembly and colonial charter simply by eliminating the reference to the English sovereign and his magistracy. The result would be a constitution dominated by the legislature (a unicameral one following this logic, although by reason of habit this was in fact only realized in Pennsylvania, and in that case it occurred for different reasons). The unbroken continuity of existing social ties implies, however, that the individual parties to the contract are already property owners and that they have interests to be represented, or at least to be protected, by a mixed government. Such a government would have to limit the power of the legislature by means of a strong executive and an upper chamber whose wisdom and freedom of action are guaranteed by their ownership of private property. In classical terms, the first of these constitutions would tend toward democracy, the second, while not necessarily monarchical, would be aristocratic in character. Both could take a republican form. But in the first case the political structure would dominate society by decreeing the common good to which private interests must be subordinated, whereas in the second political institutions presuppose the existence of social divisions that are a constant threat to the attainment of the public good. Finally, one can conceive of a third model in which a society not dissolved by the Revolution would be the outcome not of an English charter or pre-political social relations but of a compact among free persons who freely left the mother-country to establish themselves as citizens in a new world until then devoid of government and laws. This radical contractualism, in a world where the virgin lands to the west beckoned to the discontented and the ambitious, implies the permanent and uncontrollable danger that new contracts could create new political entities that would deprive the union of its most vital forces. All of these theoretical models were envisaged during the first decade of American liberty.

The Old Whig tendency seems to have the most radical implications. It implies the creation of purely republican institutions, whereas contractualist thought, which is founded upon private interests, does not necessarily imply a republican politics. The Old Whigs started from the idea of a radical break and of a return to a state of nature in which the individual enjoys total freedom. From this standpoint, the effort to reconstruct politics cannot make use of institutions inherited from the past; it must appeal to the entire people, assembled in conventions whose sole and unique function consists in framing new political institutions. Such institutions would then be approved (or rejected) by popular vote before being put into effect. The institutions proposed by a convention of individuals who possess only their own liberty are purely political in character; their only object is the promotion of the common good, which is none other than the *res publica*. The republic thus constituted appears as the incarnation of the interest of these free persons as equal citizens. The republic is defined thereby as a government of laws before which all are equal by law and right. But this republican equality raises several problems. It is a public form of equality, an equality among citizens. Either it would have to deny all private inequality as alien to political institutions or else it would have to recognize these inequalities but treat them as merely quantitative interests. In the first instance, unacknowledged social inequality threatens to distort or divert the public good; the republican form would then be merely an ideological veil. In the second instance, the problem is how to define an institutional form that allows people's interests to be expressed at the political level, to confront each other and to balance their differences, which have now become political and therefore qualitative. If there is a relatively broad-based suffrage, for example, how can one explain the equality of quantitatively unequal votes or the inequality of qualitatively equal citizens? A radically pure republic which abstracts from qualitative social differences rediscovers these differences either in the form of a levelling, but republican, democracy where the majority threatens a minority, or in the reality of a plutocracy where the public good becomes the property of an interested minority.

The practical choices of the new Americans, which provided a more or less coherent synthesis of this theoretical logic, were determined by the experience that had led to independence. The implications of what the Continental Congress named 'the Association' were particularly important. The Association took different forms in different regions and circumstances, developing the sense of the unity of the 13 colonies that had begun to be forged by the Committees of Correspondence and the Sons of Liberty. The political legitimation of this organizational form can be understood in terms of contractualist theory. Those who form an association in order to achieve a precise goal preserve all of their natural liberty, above all the liberty that enjoins them not to destroy the very foundation of this liberty. But what is this foundation? There are two possibilities: either the goal of the Association is in fact the *res publica* that founds the liberty of each, or society is divided – there is conflict – and each individual must defend his/her own interests. In the first case, where apparent or private interest is sacrificed to the public good – which is the ultimate foundation for that interest – one can speak of a virtuous choice whereby the citizens sacrifice the private sphere in order to assure a common public life. In the second case, those who seek to realize the goal of establishing the Association are obliged to take coercive measures against those who refuse to join with them. The majority (or what is supposed as such) imposes itself on a minority that will thus either be temporarily neutralized or forced into exile. Finally, tactical differences might make it necessary to create factions or sub-associations that would try to force each others' hands. This eventuality would transform those who have been neutralized into opponents within a system whose overall structure is nonetheless accepted by all. Divisions will no longer then be political but social, and therefore bearable.

The Association was a real popular presence that the artisans of the new institutions could not ignore. Committees functioned as a kind of self-government which took on an ever greater sphere of action. The Congress had decided to create committees in 'every county, city, and town, by those who are qualified to vote for representatives to the legislature'. The suffrage was quite extensive in towns where the artisan population was organized, sometimes within the framework of the committee, sometimes on its own. The Congress had assigned to these Association committees the task of supervising all importations of merchandize, overseeing its distribution, storage and eventual sale, and publishing the names of those who failed to comply with the decision to boycott British trade. Unlike in the 1760s, when voluntary non-importation had prevailed over the English, the 'Association' had explicit coercive powers (the effectiveness of which varied from colony to colony, the Congress itself not having such power). The Congress had recommended also the creation of a militia that would put itself on a war footing. Since this was only a recommendation, those who volunteered showed a certain egalitarianism seen in the election of officers and the constitution of representative soldiers' committees by the troops.

The various models developed in accordance with local circumstances. Instances of virtuous action were not rare, at least if one accepts the actors' rhetorical justifications. Religious factors played a part as well. Force was used both to realize the positive goals defined by resolutions of the Congress and to eliminate dissidence – by censoring publications, for example. There were reports of arrests of loyalists ('Tories' in the eyes of the Old Whigs), who were required to pay the expense of their involuntary confinement. Finally, one saw the birth of sub-associations, notably among artisans, which sought to influence the course of events. Their incorporation into overall political life can be seen, for example, in Philadelphia, where the committee first was called the Committee of Forty-Three, then the Committee of Sixty-Six, and finally the Committee of One-Hundred. The same method of enlargement by cooptation occurred at New York and in Charleston even before the Declaration of Independence was signed. This process of integrating radical opponents was repeated after independence in the case of those who had been neutralized.

The course of the war and its social effects are the final element that must be included in the premises of the scenario describing the first years of life in the new United States. The symbolic power of legitimation exercised by Congress had to confront not only the reality of the English army (and its Hessian troops, lent for the occasion by an obliging cousin to the Hanoverian king, George III), but also – and sometimes more than anything else! – the 13 States and their regional interests. The War of Independence was at the same time a civil war.[3] It disrupted the economy as well as institutional life. New opportunities were accompanied by new difficulties. Individual behaviour, one's self-conception and social role, one's hopes and fears, were upset. The theoretical, and even ideological, structures that emerged from the experience of conflict with England had to be given a concrete and practical form capable of assimilating so many innovations. After all, the ultimate legitimation of the newly independent power could only be its ability to use this power well, and to provide that 'happiness' which for Wilson was the end of government, and which the Declaration established the right to 'pursue'. The experience of the war was that of a people who, beyond having declared itself independent, claimed also to be republican. It did not matter what institutional form this republic took in this or that State or in the ideas of this or that politician; everyone postulated the existence of a common good, as a *res publica*, that unified them. During the war years, this unity existed *de facto* in the armed struggle. But things became complicated later on.


THE WAR

Six weeks after the declaration of Independence, the 20 000 men of the English army reached Long Island, where they easy defeated the weak colonial resistance in this rural region barely affected by the rebellion. The English did not pursue their advantage, preferring to enter Manhattan. The war was to last another five years before aid from France gave General Washington his decisive victory at Yorktown. And the Americans had to wait until 1783 and the defeat of the French in the Caribbean for the Treaty of Versailles to be signed. The clauses written into this treaty contained the germ of future conflicts, the threat of which weighed on the institutional forms of the now free nation.[4] The guarantees provided to loyalist emigrants, the recognition of the commercial debt owed to former English suppliers, the maintenance of British garrisons on the northwestern border (and on the border with

Canada, which had declined the Congress's invitation to join in the
struggle for independence) and Spain's position on the Mississippi did
not offer the prospect of permanent peace on a tranquil island. The
former conditions affected private interests, the latter went against
regional interests. The experience of the war years and the potential for
conflicts implied in the terms of the peace treaty could not but affect the
outlook of the politicians in the young republic.

The experience of the war was that of disunion in unity. George
Washington's national army was in principle under the command of the
Congress. But it was made up in large part of troops raised and paid for
by the States and directed by their own officers. The Americans expected
a brief war in which patriotic and republican virtue would soon triumph
over English conscripts (and 'the Hessians'). But things were not so
simple. It took two years for Washington to assure his authority over
other regional contenders. The difficulties came not only from personal
rivalries or from questions concerning the competency of other officers;
problems relating to regional differences among the States making up
the Confederation were also involved. Southern gentlemen did not
always get along with their more democratic comrades in arms from the
North, whose troops ill tolerated southern aristocratic behaviour,
preferring their own officers, often elected by the troops themselves.
Washington's army was like a conglomeration around a central core
(reinforced, after 1778, by the arrival of volunteers, especially French,
but also Poles like Kosciusko and Pulaski or Germans like von Steuben
and Kalb). The local militias entered into action when their territories
were at stake. They were better integrated, but their men often had
enrolled only for limited periods, and desertions were not the exception.
Important victories, like that of Saratoga in 1777 that sealed the alliance
with France, and others on the western frontier and in the South, were
the result of local initiatives taken in the field.

Financing of the war posed enormous problems for a Congress with
no constitutional authority over the citizens of the States or even over
these States themselves. Strictly speaking, Congress could not even raise
a loan, since it did not have the legal power to secure a steady income
that would guarantee repayment to the lenders. France, nevertheless,
began its aid even before the signature of a formal alliance, by means of a
commercial enterprise directed by Caron de Beaumarchais. Once the
formal French alliance was concluded, other lenders, especially Dutch,
contributed loans. But all this was not sufficient, and it became necessary
to print money. The resulting inflation helped to wipe out already
incurred debts whose real value fell rapidly, starting in 1779. Faced with

an impasse, Congress turned over its power to the army commissaries who somehow or other managed – as is their wont – to see to the immediate needs of the troops (as well as their own). Meanwhile, the States assumed responsibility for the operation of their own militias and for their own institutions. These material difficulties, of course, had political consequences. The most important of these was negative, due to the strictly symbolic character of the power held by Congress: at no time was there a question of appealing to *'la patrie en danger'* as a way of reinforcing the central authority.[5]

The support of the loyalist population, on which the English had been counting, did not meet their expectations. The English were sometimes aided in the West, but for reasons that related rather to the accumulated feelings of discontent toward the powers back East; some members of the local élite fraternized with the English when they occupied New York, Philadelphia or Charleston; and, of course, there was the celebrated case of failed treason by the former hero, General Benedict Arnold, who tried to turn over the fort at West Point. This relative absence of loyalist activity does not mean that the Americans were all united around the goals of achieving independence and establishing republican institutions, as the legend of a peaceful and legalistic revolution would have it. We have seen that the 'Association' for non-importation used violent and illegal means. These methods and the so-called committees of safety continued throughout the war era. Arbitrary arrests, summary punishment of deserters and impressment of young men into the army were not rare occurrences. When inflation heated up, these committees tried to control prices; if provisions were in short supply, they did their best to assure a fair distribution. In some cases, the committees printed paper money, negotiated with the Indians or prohibited the distillation of spirits under the pretext that grain had to be saved for food consumption. Faced with unemployment, the New York committee tried to create factories as a way of employing the poor. In order to evaluate the general level of violence accompanying the Revolution, Robert R. Palmer attempted to compare the 'revolutionary' nature of the American experience with that of France. As concerns the number of emigrés, he counts 60 000 from the United States and 129 000 in France, which meant 2.4 per cent of the population of the United States as against 0.5 per cent of France's much denser population. Concerning confiscations of private property, Palmer finds that France, ten times larger than the United States at the time, had confiscated only 12 times more goods (individual goods, for there was no Established Church to be expropriated in the United States). The great difference between the two revolutions at this level comes from the fact that the loyalists did not succeed in uniting in their struggle against the advocates of independence – in part because they shared common Whig principles while differing over how best to apply them.

Despite their divisions, which would soon surface, the Americans were unified from the outside by the war itself. The war furnished them with a shared experience, a tradition, a legend that could be grafted onto the classical and religious model of heroic, moral, and republican self-sacrifice. But the war also gave birth to a stratum of newly rich people who had profited from troubled times; and with this stratum was born also a sense of social resentment and jealousy which rejected all distinctions, whether merited or not, as well as a leveling tendency which some would call anarchic. New prospects were opening in a country liberated from the bonds of the Empire (and from its protections). But it was necessary now to make use of these prospects, which implied the creation of new productive and commercial relations. The inflation caused by the unregulated issuance of paper money favoured some while it helped to ruin established wealth and to eliminate the traditional idea of a 'fair price' for goods. New businessmen with national ambitions and adept at manipulating modern financial and banking arrangements emerged. The weakness of the Congress of the Confederation, forced by the vagaries of the war to sit in five different cities in the space of a year and a half, created a situation where the only personalities with a national standing were military figures, the most notable of whom had become the living incarnation of the myth of Cincinnatus when he returned home at the end of the war. The young military officers had a completely different experience of what was to become an independent country; their points of view were not limited to those of their particular States. These 'Young Men of the Revolution' had a 'nationalist' outlook that would transform the Confederation into a federal political system for which history offered no precedent. The success of that reflective project depended on the lived experience of unity in diversity offered by the war.[6]

## POLITICS

The Continental Congress had played a symbolic role of legitimation during the break with England. It was now necessary for it to assume real, effective power. There had been brief debates in 1775 about the institutional form of the Confederation. A new plan worked out by John

Dickinson, who had come finally to support independence, was discussed during the summer of 1776. But a new question emerged now that unanimity was no longer as urgent as it had been during the debates that led to independence. How can independent States be represented in a Congress whose decisions would influence politics or society within these States? This theoretical question differed from that of virtual representation – which had been resolved only in a negative way by the break. It brought with it practical consequences which revealed the divergent interests of the large and small States, those whose wealth came from real property and those whose wealth was based on movable (or slave) property, those whose populations were large and whose opening toward the western frontier still offered opportunities for expansion, and States with closed borders whose populations were becoming dense (and who were slaveless). The problem of a positive form of representation had been broached but never systematically thematized during the long debate with England (except by the Galloway Plan, which was rejected by the first Continental Congress); the war and its domestic impact gave it a new and urgently practical form.

Despite the constitutional legalism which had typified the pre-1776 colonial politics, the independent Americans did not rush to formulate a new confederal constitution. After the debate during the summer of 1776, they returned to the question only in May 1777, when the English occupation of Philadelphia had forced them to evacuate their capital, and when the onset of inflation began to require a systematic response. More important was the need to reach some sort of an understanding among themselves so that they might conclude an alliance with France. It is important to note that the Congress met behind closed doors and that its debates did not excite public interest, as evinced by the fact that there were no pamphlets dealing with this issue. It was the act of confederation and not its institutional form that concerned people. The theory developed during the long process of maturation leading to independence seemed to suffice for the practical necessities of the moment. Nonetheless, the final text – the Articles of Confederation – was not unanimously accepted by the 13 States, any more than were various of the propositions of law that emerged from its deliberations. Indeed, it was only a few months before the fighting ended that Maryland finally voted to join the Confederation. In other words, the war to achieve a state of independence – whose roots were nourished by a debate over constitutional legitimacy - was conducted by a people without constitutional legitimacy itself. Moreover, the constitution finally adopted in 1781 was modelled on a reality outdated by the necessities of war and the resulting social transformations.

The behaviour of politicians during these years of war and incertitude was marked by a naïve optimism that trusted in republican values and virtues. But contrary to the rapid theoretical development that had led to independence, this period experienced a rather simplistic and unreflective application of formulas borrowed from the dictionaries of republican theory. This is seen in the experience of drafting a constitution as well as in daily political practice. There was a refusal to recognize the need to adapt to new conditions and to the imperatives of a politics that seeks to relate particular interests and the supposedly general interest. The young James Madison, who was later to develop what some consider still a 'Machiavellian' theory of the role of private interest and ambition, was in no way atypical when he refused to conduct a political campaign to get himself elected to the Congress and was beaten by the owner of a local tavern. Such experiences might cause doubts in the minds of some, but such doubts built up only slowly and almost had to be forced on people before they began finally to reflect upon the institutional structures of the Republic and upon the form of daily political practice. For the time being, people lived in a world of 'as if . . .' while socio-economic problems accumulated and the war was bogged down. On the local level, people tried to manage as best they could – which, indeed, fitted perfectly well with their own sense of priorities.

The weakness of the Confederation and of the Congress is explained in part by the fact that the legislative aspect of government dominated all other functions. This is understandable in a people that had just freed itself from a monarchy whose executive was threatening to corrupt and to overwhelm the system. The principle of legislative dominance was the logical conclusion of Whig thought. Legislative omnipotence was one of the unanimously accepted principles of American republicanism. But the daily functioning of a legislating Congress proved arduous because it had to attend to everything, which meant overwork for its members and inconsistency between the decisions taken by the Congress and their execution by the member States of the Confederation. The rotation of the personnel of this Congress, decided by the States of which they were the representatives – or rather, the agents – aggravated the situation even more. It slowed down decision-making and increased confusion in debates, as it was often necessary to revise what had been decided in order to satisfy the local interests of each group of newcomers. The idea of creating an executive office was rejected on the basis of the Old Whig ideology which feared the establishment of an extra-congressional authority and the consequent corruption which would be involved in appointments to subordinate posts. Congress found itself confronted with a multitude of details; some let them slip by while others took advantage of the situation in order to promote their own interests. This could only contribute in the long run to a decline in Congress's reputation and legitimacy.[7]

## THE POST-WAR PERIOD

Congress's lack of real influence during the war, which had favoured (and made necessary) local initiative, became a serious difficulty in peacetime. Military victory eased the pressures that had held together divergent interest groups in a unity that could be thought of as republican in character because of the sacrifices imposed by the presence of the enemy. Historians, like its contemporaries, are unsure how they should designate the period from 1783 to 1787: Was it a 'critical period' in which the fate of the country was at stake?[8] The apparent ungovernability of society presented by the rejection of congressional authority, and sometimes that of the States as well, was perhaps only the continuation of the tradition of self-government inherited from colonial institutions and democratized during the pre-independence era when the masses who had been organized by the merchant élite achieved autonomy in the institutions of the 'Association'. After all, the crisis of the Confederation's political institutions affected directly only a minority whilst the great mass of people did not worry about the government unless it intervened in their affairs, as England had done during the decade previous to independence. But this image of a depoliticized public does not describe the state of mind of a people that had sacrificed for independence, not simply for economic gain. A crisis there was, but it concerned the self-representation of the republican spirit. Thus, when in 1785 the wealthy inhabitants of radical Boston, who had previously distinguished themselves by organizing the Tea Party, established a tea house called the *Sans souci*, their republican virtue was at its symbolic low point. In other words, the crisis was political and not simply economic and social.

It is true that an economic recession followed the war, but it was accompanied by the economic adaptations necessary to meet the new situation created by the establishment of peace and the victory over England. Its effects lasted for several years, but its end was in sight by 1786. The relatively self-reliant colonies absorbed the shock of the economic changes as new commercial ties were established, new manufacturing industries were born and the old ties with the Empire – and the restrictions that they had imposed – were rebuilt on new bases. Inflation, which had increased the overall mass of money in circulation, favoured the growth of economic activity. On the other hand, this inflation was the result of the enormous debt of both Congress and the individual States, and it weighed on the republican spirit of the Old Whigs. They remembered English history in which the creation of a national debt and of a national bank (which was also being discussed by Congress), had permitted the establishment of a permanent, peacetime army; the uncertain conditions left in place by the Treaty of Versailles, moreover, made it seem likely that the same thing might be forced on them. When they saw the *nouveaux riches* who had arisen during the war, often under dubious conditions where patriotism was combined with personal interest, they could not help but wonder about the health of their new republic. The new wealth was not traditional landed property, which, according to the classical theory, guaranteed the liberty of the citizen. That liberty might be destroyed or limited by inflation (which, on the other hand, corresponded to the wishes of indebted farmers). But the contraction of the money supply wished by some harmed others. This suggests that the economic crisis was not in itself a danger; rather it expressed the crisis of the republican spirit incapable of forging suitable political institutions and forced to question its own presuppositions about the nature of society and about the virtue of a citizen.[9]

One way of resolving the self-doubt experienced by American republicans was to return to the local level, to the States and to daily affairs. National politics was far off, its goals abstract, and its effects indirect. The Americans remained a colonial people; their experience was limited and their goals simple. After all, history had taught them that republics perish when they grow rich, expand and become diverted from public affairs to enjoy their wealth at the price of losing their soul.[10] But, the colonists had proved their ability to organize themselves into committees responsible for directing boycotts, setting price controls, conducting guerrilla warfare against a power that was trying to interfere with their liberties. It was necessary once again to put these liberties into practice in new forms of self-government. Some claim that this return to localism as a solution to their political problems masks its reactive character, which expresses the fear of provincials confronted by a modern world beyond their understanding.[11] Without being wrong, this does not take into account what the American public understood as its republican destiny. It is more useful to see this return to the local level and to the everyday as the result of a fundamental doubt over their ability to be republicans and their virtues as politicians. In order to better grasp this reaction, we must turn to the institutional structure established by the independent Americans.

The institutions giving concrete form to their republican conceptions made clear to the Americans the meaning of their lived history. The actual functioning of these institutions polarized and unified their experience around a central problem – representation – that the actors had not been fully conscious of but whose implicit logic had governed their actions. We will begin with the immediate political experience of the States before returning to the confederal structure by way of an examination of the radical constitutionof Pennsylvania, whose agitated battles led its critics to seek a solution at the national level. This return to the national level obliged both critics and defenders of the established system to turn away from the strictly political analyses that had until then dominated the debate. One might describe their experience retroactively as a belated discovery of *political sociology*, necessitated by the disappearance of the national political unity that had momentarily been realized in the struggle against a common enemy. But before leaping to conclusions, we must first follow the maturation of the crisis of the type of political theory that had been inherited from the past. Our passage by way of the States is imposed by the American mind and American morals; it was expressed, for example, in the fact that the legislatures of seven of the now free States felt obliged to vote for the Declaration of Independence themselves in order to legitimate it and make it binding on their own citizens. From such anecdotes, political theory grows.

# 6 History Conceived: Republican Institutions

## RADICAL CONSERVATIVES; MASSACHUSETTS AND VIRGINIA

With the proclamation of independence, republicanism became more an ideology than a theory of government. A republic meant simply a society without king or aristocracy. To this negative definition was added a vague idea that the *res publica* was – or ought to be – something held in common. These definitions obviously were not sufficient to sustain a political struggle. Thus the concept assumed a moral function, a utopian value, a regenerative mission. The virtue of the individual who sacrifices for the common good was to be the foundation of the institutions that would be established by independence. This ideology without fixed institutional content could play an even greater role because the advocates of independence had widened suffrage in order to assure popular support during the war. The lack of specific content of republican ideology allowed and even encouraged it to merge with the Old Whig theory that the colonists had used to understand the implications of English policy. This explains the institutional dynamism – seen by some as real or potential anarchy – present in the political life of the States. The image of a power that is in principle opposed to a free people and which tries to extend its control over a people seeking only to live by and for itself was pregnant with future conflicts. An ambiguity concerning the meaning of the individual liberty to which the theory pointed enriched the potential turbulence of political life while assuring its open-ended character. Is such liberty public and political, or private and self-interested; is it the liberty of man or that of the citizen? The theoretical question had practical consequences.

The practical difficulties that arose can be understood theoretically when it is seen that Whig thought is fundamentally opposed to the republican idea because it rejects the notion that any government based upon representation could be legitimate. The Whigs granted that power was necessary to the functioning of society. But power had to be controlled. The popular election of representatives or magistrates did not guarantee that these officeholders were more legitimate or any less susceptible to the corruption inherent in power. Once the executive authority of the government in London had been rejected, the Whig solution was to transform the magistrate into an executive without power. Jefferson, for example, simply labelled him 'administrator'.[1] This magistrate would have neither the power to declare war nor the authority to coin money, name judges, pardon criminals and, less still, the right to confer honours. He would be named by the legislature, which would also nominate judges and other State functionaries. What is radically new in this picture is that the old image of a legislature whose function is to control abuses of power in the name of the people is inverted. Power is no longer separated from a society (or from the legislature that represents it) which protects itself by the control it exercises over its representatives. In the new 'united States', power and society are identified; the task is now to represent power, no longer to defend society or the individual from it.

The transformation of the question of political representation might have been solved within the classical Whig heritage as theorized by Montesquieu's *Spirit of the Laws* or in the version worked out by Delolme, whose *Constitution of England* was often cited.[2] The classical Whig theory portrays a mixed constitution in which political institutions take into account the real, qualitative differences within the social organism. The resulting institutional organization must include checks and balances so as to protect the people's liberty. Legislative omnipotence, as suggested by the Old Whig approach, is therefore excluded. This explains the adoption of various measures – such as non-re-eligibility, rotation or annual election – which attempted to remedy the problem. A more radical solution was the apparently democratic idea of binding instructions for representatives. But that idea is not modern; it had been applied in the colonial era, and its origins lie in the first phase of the history of political representation, when the nobility sent delegates to negotiate with the King. The principle of binding instructions eliminates *de facto* the relationship between the representative and the represented as well as the role of the representative. As an inhabitant of Massachusetts put it during the selection of delegates to its 1780 Constitutional Convention, if the representative cannot exercise his own judgement, 'the greatest idiot may answer your purpose as well as the greatest man'. But this was no solution either. The Americans might have recalled that during the debate over virtual representation, Burke had emphasized that the principle of binding instructions transforms legislatures into meetings of ambassadors sent by hostile powers. Burke was defending the Empire, the Americans wanted to be republicans. The problem of representation revealed a contradiction latent in the first principle of republicanism: either there exists a common good, a *res publica*, that serves to guide the representatives' free deliberations, or else there exist only particular interests to be federated by compromises that are always subject to revision. This contradiction opposes the representation of a good common to all and that of the particular interests of each. The first standpoint expresses Old Whig republican politics, the other the standpoint of contractualism. The first confronts the dilemma of virtual representation, the second that of binding instructions. The liberty assured by institutions modelled on one or the other idea of representation is of a different and distinct nature, even if it is exercised within the framework of balanced or mixed political structures.

The idea of a mixed constitution was frequently invoked in the debates over the creation of new, free constitutions. Delegates often received instructions, especially those who were State delegates to the Congress of the Confederation. They were in effect veritable ambassadors, the representatives of independent political entities. This posed practical problems, which we will consider in the actual operation of the Confederation. Another difficulty arose at the state level. In establishing checks and balances, a socially mixed regime could also have the effect of inducing governmental paralysis since private individual liberty was preserved without protecting or encouraging that of the citizen. This paralysis resulted from an ambiguity in the theory, which was being applied under social conditions different from those of old Europe. Was it really a matter of balancing principles or political virtues embodied by certain citizens due to their specific social functions? That was the case in classical theory, which Montesquieu revived in order to defend an aristocracy threatened by the alliance of the King and the new bourgeoisie. But the newly free American republic did not include an aristocracy and it was out the question to create one. One might propose to replace this hereditary aristocracy by a natural aristocracy whose talents and virtues would be recognized by all citizens. The colonial legislatures had already thought of themselves in this way when they opposed the members of the Council as well as other magistrates named by their English governors. But could such an aristocracy be assured of recognition if the suffrage was sufficiently broad to allow for demagogy? Experience led to doubt on this score. The other option proposed to replace the principle of a mixed constitution by a structure founded upon individual interests from whose confrontation contractual compromises could emerge. But as soon as interest is privatized and all interests are qualitatively equal to one another, how can one determine which interests merit representation?

These theoretical questions found their solution in a practice guided by the need to legitimate actions already taken under pressure of necessity. Above all, a legal form had to be given to the local and sporadic initiatives that had issued from the committees. The Continental Congress's call for an 'Association' was one way of pursuing this. But since some States were so jealous of their independence that they judged it necessary to vote for the Declaration of Independence themselves, the solution had to come first at the State level. The now independent States had inherited different institutional forms. Some colonies already possessed charters guaranteeing them autonomy in domestic matters; in such cases, it sufficed merely to eliminate references to the King. Elsewhere, the task proved more difficult. The case of Massachusetts is typical. The Intolerable Acts had annulled its charter; it was governed since 1774 by a temporary congress, approved by the Continental Congress but lacking in formal legitimacy. The constitution this temporary congress proposed to the electorate in 1778 was rejected because, among other reasons, it was the work of an assembly that would itself direct the new institutions it was creating. This contradicted one of the fundamental republican principles invoked during the conflict with the English Parliament: a republic is a government of laws and not of men; one cannot be at the same time both judge and party to a suit. A specially elected convention was therefore called. The principal author of the constitution proposed in 1780 was John Adams, whose *Thoughts on Government*, written during the session of the Second Continental Congress, served as a general guide for the authors of most State constitutions. Adams' arguments can serve as an introduction to more concrete constitutional reflections without losing sight of the implications of the voters' rejection of the 1778 constitution which was an affirmation of the primacy of popular sovereignty.[3]

Adams' *Thoughts on Government* rest on two interrelated premises: that politics is a science and that the end of government is the happiness of society. That happiness depends entirely on the constitution, on which, in turn, depends the government. Adams therefore rejects Pope's celebrated couplet:

> For forms of government let fools contest
> That which is best administered is best.

This attitude is easily understood: Adams' social happiness is not private enjoyment. Adams remains a republican. His definition of political happiness combines, pell mell, Confucius, Zoroaster, Socrates, Mohammed; in a word, happiness is only another name for virtue, which Adams makes the principle and foundation of government. Virtue is described as a passion in the mind of the people; it stimulates government more effectively than fear of a monarch or even aristocratic honour. Adams does not cite references here, but they are easily found in the literature of classical political thought. The republican constitution founded upon and animated by virtue is defined further as 'an empire of laws and not of men'. Adams grants that the powers by which a society is constituted can be combined or distributed in innumerable ways, and he is willing to accept suggestions for changes in the details of his plan; this openness is possible because, for the modern republic, the full and impartial application of the laws alone counts. A government of universal laws applicable to all is a sort of machinery for regulating the public behaviour of citizens. Adams does not specifically ask himself, however, what motive force will set the machinery in motion. Classical virtue, the principle on which his system is founded, might play this role, but the difficulty lies in the fact that a modern republic cannot presuppose its existence. Virtue must be at the same time the presupposition and the product of political science. Adams remains a New England Puritan sharing the Old Whig fear of corruption; he cannot imagine people always being virtuous citizens and sacrificing private interest for the common good. This is what led him to take up his pen against the simplistic recipes of Tom Paine. The problem posed by his circular definition of the republic by virtue and of virtue by the republic is not new. We will meet it again, both in its pre-modern form and in its modern resolution.

When Adams describes the legislative process of making laws for the republic, he encounters, without realizing it, the difficulty faced by the Old Whigs who sought to be institutional republicans. In a large society, not everyone can participate directly in legislative activity; representatives therefore must be chosen. Adams does not feel obliged to specify either their number or their qualifications; what is of greater importance is that the legislative body be 'in miniature an exact portrait of the people at large. It should think, feel, reason, and act like them'. The virtues proper to the social situations that make up the republic ought therefore to be present in its assembled political body. The image is that of an organism whose qualitative differences are harmoniously integrated into a well functioning unit. But Adams also states that 'it should be an equal representation, or, in other words, equal interests among the people should have equal interests in it'. But the quantitative representation of interests is not the same thing as the qualitative representation of social situations, which embody different principles whose fusion creates an organically unified whole governed by the pursuit of the common good. Interests have a common nature; they are comparable to each other. A majority formed out of these common and comparable interests would be able to impose its will on a minority which must, therefore, be protected by a system of checks and balances. The political machinery Adams describes therefore replaces the mixed principles that had unified and protected the estates in the English system. The political structure protects the society in this model which is founded by the circle in which political institutions engender virtue while virtue was supposed to constitute the premise that makes a republican government of laws function.

Although Adams is unaware of the contradiction on which his system is based, its presence is seen in his difficulties in trying to justify a bicameral legislature and the prerogatives he wishes to grant the executive. Adams insists first of all on the importance of the separation of powers. Each branch must have the right to defend itself against possible pressures and incursions by the other branches. A unicameral legislature that would assume executive and judicial functions – as was the case with the government of the Confederation – is therefore ruled out. He rejects the idea of a single, purely legislative chamber, too, because such a structure would necessarily enter into conflict with the executive power, leaving only a judiciary ill equipped to maintain balance between them. Adams therefore proposes the creation of a Council elected by members of the legislature to function as a second legislative branch which would have veto power over the popularly-elected representatives. The members of the two chambers would then, in joint session, choose an executive officer. He, too, would have a right to a veto, which he would exercise after having heard the advice of a Privy Council chosen from among the members of the Council. The resulting institutional structure is dual. It starts from a direct form of representation to construct, by a series of mediations, an apparatus for filtering or refining this first mode of representation, all the while making it, nevertheless, the foundation and the motive force of the whole contrivance. Adams insists upon the Old Whig maxim, 'where annual elections end, there slavery begins'. According to him, these annual elections will teach whomever is elected 'the great political virtues of humility, patience, and moderation, without which every man in power becomes a ravenous beast of prey'. The difficulty comes from the fact that this process of refinement culminates in a institutional mechanism that is supposed to replace the classical mixed constitution, through whose political form society was to be organically and functionally

integrated and the common good was expressed. That mixed constitution is the 'miniature . . . portrait' of which Adams spoke at the
beginning of his *Thoughts on Government*. But the machinery erected to
filter representation is without any social foundation, in reality or even
in principle. It revives the institutional forms of the old model, but its
content is not the same; it represents interests and it is supposed to
protect minority ones against those of the oppressive majority. This
absence of social foundations explains why the final third of Adams'
short essay returns to the problem of how to form virtuous citizens.
Adams comes out in favour of establishing universal military service,
setting up a programme of general education for impoverished youth
and adopting sumptuary laws that would guarantee the simplicity and
frugality of republican mores. Adams is clearly searching for a type of
virtue capable of founding the Republic; but this method is, once again,
that of an institutional intervention without social foundation or
political legitimation.

   What is striking in this political contrivance – which was put into
operation, fairly much as is, in the Massachusetts Constitution of 1780 –
is the contradiction between the machinery of political science, on the
one hand, and, on the other hand, the virtue upon which institutions are
to rest. Virtue is supposed to be at once present in institutions and
flowing from them, just as the common good appears as the condition
and the product of the republic. Adams' science is at first conservative or
defensive in character. It seeks to institute checks and balances against
the dangers of an oft-proposed unicameralism – which, indeed, was
actually put into effect in Pennsylvania, as we shall see. This science is
mechanical and formal, integrating quantitative interests that are
comparable one to another. But it becomes interventionist in character
when it seeks to specify the measures intended to promote this virtue
that, according to Adams, embodies happiness. Virtue is supposed to
create the conditions for republican behaviour, which sacrifices individual and private interest to the common and public good. And this is also
the objective of the social measures by means of which Adams completes
his system. But republican virtue cannot be understood in terms of
interest. If the constitution had not followed the old model of a mixed
constitution, as the image of the 'miniature . . . portrait' suggests, it
would have had to opt for unicameralism, in conformity with the logic of
Old Whig republicanism and with the struggle against the English
monarchy that had given birth in the new States to regimes with weak
executives. Reasons of a social order have to be added to the mediated
character of the constitutional architecture in order to explain why that
solution was rejected.

The fact that John Adams' proposal to endow the executive with real power went against the current of contemporary republican political logic as well as of the experience of the conflict with England should not be surprising. His theory is in no way atypical; and it served as a model for other States than Massachusetts. These theoretical republicans dreaded the development of a democracy (founded upon interest) which would have set a poor majority, manipulated by demagogues, in opposition to well-off republicans – which many among them were. Barriers had to be erected against such an eventuality, which seemed to flow from the Americans' rejection of virtual representation.[4] After all, the experience of the conflict with England had shown that the masses can be galvanized, organized, directed; and they knew as well that these methods sometimes led to unforeseen results. Was it not they who, in 1766, had seen to the construction, in the chamber where the colonial assembly of Massachusetts met, of a balcony from which the public could watch debates with the royal government? Had not their committees shown that popular mobilization can triumph over a merchant community whose economic interests were opposed to the popular cause? The political system of John Adams does its best to preserve the dynamic of popular involvement through the representation of social interests while also seeking to weaken this mode of representation by means of a system of political filtration. The introduction of interest onto the political stage, however, contradicts the foundation for the legitimacy of this institutional apparatus. Over time, the machinery will reveal itself to be without foundation; the Council and the executive represent nothing – or they represent merely a greater quantity of interests, with wealth replacing aristocracy and its political virtue!

The dilemma faced by John Adams is expressed in another form in his correspondence with the Virginian Patrick Henry during this period. Henry complained of a 'strong aristocratic bias' in his State that had to be fought. Adams responded encouragingly and demanded that 'a more equal liberty than has prevailed in other parts of the earth must be established in America'. But this egalitarian demand does not figure in his *Thoughts on Government*. There was no place for it there because the recognition of real social equality would have at the same time led him to grant that the second chamber and the governor could only have the interests of the rich for their foundation. The Constitution of Virginia, like that of Massachusetts, instituted political structures whose justification came from the theory of a mixed constitution in an organically hierarchized society. The existence of a certain 'cavalier' aristocracy in Virginia gave these structures an apparent social legitimacy that was lacking in Massachusetts. But this appearance ought not to hide another reality visible not only to the retrospective glance of the historian but recognizable in the structure of Virginia's constitution. The underrepresented western regions of the State, which were coveted by speculators and were the scene of a conflict between a lifestyle that could be described as republican and a dynamic new ethos founded upon private interest, had to be taken into account by the authors of this constitution. They had to make place for a society that did not seem destined for a classical republican political life.

Virginia's constitution is original because it is explicitly founded on a Bill of Rights, voted 12 June 1776, that is, before the adoption of the constitution, which did not take place until 29 June. This Bill of Rights is defined as 'the basis and foundation of the government'. The first article declares all men 'equally free and independent' and affirms that they possess certain rights 'namely, the enjoyment of life and liberty, with the means of acquiring and possessing property, and pursuing and obtaining happiness and safety'. It is not real equality that is aimed at here (although the pursuit of happiness is supplemented by the right to obtain it) but only equal freedom and independence. To the rights set forth in the Declaration of Independence of the Continental Congress are added those of property and safety. As in the Declaration of Independence, popular sovereignty is then affirmed. The government serves the people, of which a majority 'hath an indubitable, unalienable and indefeasible right to reform, alter or abolish it, in such a manner as shall be judged most conducive to the public weal'. The separation of legislative, executive and judicial power is affirmed along with the frequent election of the first two branches. The suffrage is granted to everyone who pays taxes according to the principle formulated during the struggle against the English Parliament; those who have not explicitly consented, by means of the suffrage, to the payment of taxes have a right to refuse to pay them.[5] Other guarantees were also included, such as right to trial by jury, the right not to bear witness against oneself, the right to a speedy trial and to be confronted by witnesses for the prosecution. Freedom of the press was proclaimed, a militia authorized and the formation of a standing army in peacetime prohibited. The penultimate article then invokes republican virtue in a curious manner: '15. That no free government, or the blessings of liberty, can be preserved to any people, but by a firm adherence to justice, moderation, temperance, frugality and virtue, and by frequent recurrence to fundamental principles'. Finally, the last article guarantees the free exercise of religion and affirms 'that it is the mutual duty of all to practise

Christian forebearance, love, and charity towards each other'. The relation between Christian virtue and the classical republican form of Article 15 is not made clear. As elsewhere, this juxtaposition expresses the persistence of incompatible representations of what provides the foundation and legitimacy for the new republican government. Virginia's Bill of Rights is unique only because of the explicit role it plays in founding the constitution of this State. But who is this 'man' whose rights serve as the foundation for the aristocratic constitution of the Republic of Virginia? In rereading the enumeration of his rights, one is struck by the fact that these are not political rights but private rights. The Bill of Rights makes a point of proclaiming the rights of property, safety and happiness. The citizen's relation to the government is contractual in character. The provisions guaranteeing equal justice are concerned especially with private matters. Virtue is invoked only in the second-to-last article, and the fact that the last article calls for religious tolerance suggests that this virtue is again private. One may thus understand the disillusioned remark of the conservative Carter Braxton during the debates at the Virginia constitutional convention: public virtue requires sumptuary laws, but these run counter to American mores. We are far from the republican Puritanism of John Adams here! The respect for the private rights of others remains alien to the world of classical republican values. The integration of this new foundation, the private man, into constitutional life had to introduce political innovations if it were to succeed.

Built upon these theoretical premises, the constitution begins curiously with an historical recitation of the necessary and justified break with the Crown. The authors explain that in order to remedy the 'deplorable conditions' created by the Crown, they are proposing an 'adequate and regular mode of civil polity'. This model is that of Adams' bicameralism. But its justification is different, as may be gathered from various clauses written into the constitution. Plural office-holding is explicitly forbidden. This may be explained by the bad precedent offered by England. The same goes for the requirement to conduct regular censuses in order to avoid under- or over-representation (which implies in theory the representation of quantities, not qualities, and is in practice a concession to the West). In rejecting the English model, this constitution departs from the organic conception of the republic and its social foundation as elaborated by Montesquieu. This change is clearly apparent in the structure of the upper chamber (the Senate). The two chambers differ solely because a senator represents a larger and more populous district. Whereas Adams sought to filter the representation of the people and of its real interests, Virginia was bent on preserving popular ties. Thus, its executive is designated by the two chambers meeting in joint session. The executive and the Senate are at the same time closer to the popular base and less powerful than they are in Adams' model. Neither one has any veto power, and the Senate cannot initiate laws but only approve or reject bills already proposed. In a word, the constitution of the Virginia Cavaliers seems more democratic or popularly oriented than that of the egalitarian and tumultuous State of Massachusetts.

The inversion that is implicit in the institutions of Virginia evinces a transformation of the Whiggism underlying the logic of the *Thoughts on Government*. The popular foundation for Virginia's constitution poses a problem only when one questions the grounds of its bicameral legislature. The practical reasons, one suspects, are to be sought in the State's social structure, dominated as it was by these Southern gentlemen with their aristocratic pretensions. But this motive could not be admitted. This is why the Senate is defined as the representative of larger (and therefore richer) districts. But according to what principle is it legitimate to give numbers (or wealth) their own autonomous representation? Jefferson had proposed the election of senators to nine-year, non-renewable terms as a way of assuring their independence; Mason had proposed that they be chosen by electors specially chosen for this end. The majority insisted that popular election would give more independence to this Senate, which was intended as a counterbalance to the first, less reflective chamber. In the actual functioning of its institutions, this could not help but create problems in this State with an open western frontier. The choice of popular election to the Senate brought out the problems involved the Americans' attempt to be both Old Whig and republican in a New World society, without social orders, that tends to sanctify the representation of individual private interest. Republican thought is forced to have recourse to a contractualist theory of the relations between the individual and the government in order to provide a foundation for representation, since the image of an organic society can no longer be evoked. The institutional form of the contract replaces the machinery constructed to protect individual equality before a common set of laws. The sole justification offered for this choice was the argument that wisdom, virtue or honesty cannot be measured, whereas property and numbers easily lend themselves to this end. It remained to be determined whether the former or latter criteria would prevail. The answer came only with time; experience prior to the Constitution of 1787 offered no solution. For the moment, the radical premises of 1776 culminated in institutions whose functioning remained conservative.[6]

## A RADICAL CONSTITUTION: DEMOCRATIC PENNSYLVANIA

It is often said that the democratic forces of Pennsylvania drew the most radical conclusions from the principles stated in the Declaration of Independence. The convention that drafted its constitution had been elected following the Congress's call in May 1776 for all colonies to establish legitimate governments within their borders. This call was directed particularly at Pennsylvania, which, as a proprietary colony, did not depend on royal institutions. Its establishment, led by Joseph Galloway, held control of the assembly and used this power to slow the march toward independence. This policy of obstruction by the legislature and the establishment explains the radical nature of the Pennsylvanians' response to the new conditions brought about by independence. Like the leading citizens of the other colonies, those of Pennsylvania had long aspired to assert their autonomy. But whereas elsewhere the establishment was moving toward a break with the King's government, it seemed that the Pennsylvania Assembly first had to free itself from the control exercised by the Penn family in order then to assert its autonomy. Under the direction of Franklin and Galloway, the assembly therefore tried to play the King against the proprietor, thus complicating this colony's relations with the other colonies, which were increasingly turning their backs on the royal authorities. This peculiar situation explains why the assembly did not play the role of motive force or even sounding board for the popular movement, which had been developing since 1763. When independence was declared, the assembly, and its peculiar aspiration for autonomy, appeared anachronistic.

The constitution drafted by the State convention assembled in Philadelphia in 1776 has been compared to the Jacobin constitution of 1793. The convention that drew it up had no explicit mandate to do so; the call by the Congress to frame a constitution was supplemented merely by the needle of necessity. The hostility to the old leaders found in the text provoked their strong resistance. Along with the fact that Philadelphia was occupied during the war, this explains why the constitution was never submitted for popular approval (a deficiency which its enemies did not fail to use against it). The long resistance put up by the élite impeded the functioning of the government established by this constitution to such an extent that the viability of this radical democracy cannot be judged. Majority support for its institutions was probably never obtained; and opposition to these institutions grew steadily throughout their entire history, that is to say, until their replacement in 1790. More important, the provisions of this radical constitution served to sharpen the political debate in the other States.[7]. Because they were not able to gather the majority required to make revisions in this constitution, its enemies were forced to go over the heads of state officials and to obtain support from the national authorities, just as the State's radicals had done in 1776. The history of this unique radical constitution is therefore not unrelated to the attempt to revise the Articles of Confederation that took place in 1787.

The Pennsylvania Constitution includes three sections: an opening declaration, a bill of rights, and the plan of government. The opening declaration refrains from the usual historical catalogue of grievances against England. In its place appears an appeal to natural rights and to the right of the people to consent to the form of their government. The argument in favour of independence is thus formulated in contractualist terms. The title of the bill of rights explains that these rights belong to the 'inhabitants of the Commonwealth or state of Pennsylvania'. These rights are therefore political and not the abstract rights of man in general. Nonetheless, at first glance, the enumerated list of rights includes nothing surprising. It mentions the right of conscientious objectors not to bear arms (the Quakers were for a long time in the majority and it was necessary to rally them in support of the new institutions). More important is the addition of rights to free assembly, to petition for the redress of grievances and to demonstrate to present their complaints. These are political rights, guaranteed to people as citizens. But before concluding too hastily that the authors were challenging the abstract and individualistic foundations of social contract theory, we should note the presence in this enumeration of rights of another one which, at first sight, is rather curious. The inhabitants of Pennsylvania have the right to emigrate to another State or to 'such countries as they can purchase, whenever they think that thereby they may promote their own happiness'. This article of the declaration was aimed at protecting the Vandalia Company, which had interests in the territories of what are now the States of Kentucky and Tennessee. The contractualist republic and personal interests easily combined in this radical and democratic State of Pennsylvania. In contrast, we should add, an agrarian law that some wanted to insert into this enumeration of rights, did not obtain majority support.[8]

Since this Declaration of Rights can be read as a social contract,[9] we should examine the form of government that is to administer it. The plan of government, which follows the opening statement, is longer than other documents of the time, as if its architects sought to reply to the hostility that they knew would greet their radical innovations. The plan proposes a unicameral legislature, elected annually, whose 'president' is surrounded by a council of 12 persons elected in the cities and counties for a three-year term, renewable only after a four-year interim period so as to avoid the creation of a (political) aristocracy. This division of the presidency effectively rendered it quite weak. Moreover, political guarantees for the preservation of a space for public opinion are inscribed in the functioning of each branch of government. The doors of the legislative chamber had to remain open to all those 'who behave decently' unless the welfare of the public is at stake. No one could be a representative to the legislature for more than four years out of seven, and plural office-holding was prohibited as elsewhere. No one could represent the State in the Congress for more than two years in a row, a term that could be renewed only after an interval of three years. All laws had to be printed as public notices before being read for the last time in the legislature; and no law was to be ratified before the next session of this legislative body. Finally, the preamble to each law had 'fully and clearly' to lay out the rationale that had guided the legislator. As for the judiciary, judges were named by the council for seven-year, renewable terms and were remunerated 'with an adequate but moderate compensation for their services', which made them effectively dependent upon the public will. In addition to the right to a jury trial, imprisonment for non-payment of debts was prohibited (save in the case of fraud) and, more important still, specific provisions were made to assure that the inhabitants of the countryside and of the western part of the State would have fair access to the judicial system. Finally, sheriffs too were subject to rotation; they could not serve more than three years in a row and were not eligible for re-election for another four years.

On the institutional level, the Pennsylvania Constitution is remarkable first of all for the role it seeks to ensure for public participation. This attitude may be explained by the political situation of its authors, for whom popular support constituted their sole form of political legitimacy. This becomes evident when one reads the legal guarantees granted to inhabitants of rural and western frontier areas. The open-door policy relating to legislative deliberations, annual elections, and the lapse of a year between the introduction of a bill and a final vote on it appeal more to participation than to direct interests.[10] Likewise, the obligation that the legislator 'fully and clearly' explain the purposes of his bills sought to render the functions of government popular, comprehensible and controllable. The weakness of the executive officer and above all the system of rotation indicate once again that the authors of this constitution aimed not only at getting the inhabitants interested in the life of this republican State but also at getting them to participate in it. This effort was not necessarily implied by the constitution's contractualist principles. The theory of natural law evoked in the preamble could have been limited to the notion of tacit consent, expressed – as in Virginia – solely in the fact that one's voting signified at the same time one's consent to any taxes eventually voted upon. To understand better the political operation of this radical system, we must look in greater detail at its institutional structure, which was founded upon the political participation required to achieve popular support in the battle against the establishment and the old assembly.

This constitution, founded upon natural law, manifests the same preoccupation with virtue found in other States. This is no more surprizing than the fact that the State's institutions are expected to promote virtue as well as to safeguard it. Thus Article 45 provides that 'Laws for the encouragement of virtue and prevention of vice and immorality, shall be made and constantly kept in force, and provision shall be made for their due execution. . . .' This same preoccupation is evident in the pledges of allegiance that every State official had to swear ('or affirm', as the framers added, since they were also preoccupied with the issues of free religious expression and the rights of Quakers).[11] After having recommended a penal code less harsh in character and more suited to the crimes committed, the constitution, in Article 39, again exhibited its concern for virtue when it offered a method for dissuading criminal behaviour: 'To deter more effectually from the commission of crimes, by continued visible punishments of long duration, and to make sanguinary punishments less necessary; houses ought to be provided for punishing by hard labor, those who shall be convicted of crimes not capital; wherein the criminals shall be employed for the benefit of the public, or for reparation of injuries done to private persons: And all persons at proper times shall be admitted to see the prisoners at their labor'. The constitution also orders the creation of one or several schools in each county and of one or several universities in the State. Finally, the Declaration of Rights is explicitly attached to the body of the constitution. These measures designed to promote virtue would not have shocked John Adams. But why was there a need for them in a constitution founded upon natural law and which had laid out a set of participatory institutions? What did one expect of popular participation and why was this participation not considered capable of assuring on its own the virtue of the citizens?

The most radical innovation proposed by Pennsylvania was the Council of Censors, which was to play the role of a constitutional court in the broadest sense. It was to meet once every seven years to 'enquire whether the constitution has been preserved inviolate in every part; and whether the legislative and executive branches of government have performed their duty as guardians of the people, or assumed to themselves, or exercised other or greater powers than they are intended to by the constitution'. This is perhaps not very radical; the idea has its classical sources, like the Ephors of Sparta and the Censors of Rome; and Machiavelli had recommended this kind of a regular return to the founding principles of the Republic. The difficulty comes afterward: 'They are also to enquire whether the public taxes have been justly laid and collected in all parts of this commonwealth, in what manner the public monies have been disposed of, and whether the laws have been duly executed'. The very breadth of their task required extensive powers: 'For these purposes they shall have power to send for persons, papers, and records; they shall have authority to pass public censures, to order impeachments, and to recommend to the legislature the repealing of such laws as appear to them to have been enacted contrary to the principles of the constitution'. Finally, the Council of Censors could propose amendments to the constitution which would be submitted for approval to a convention specially elected for this purpose. (This never happened in Pennsylvania, but the procedure was put into use once in Vermont, in 1786.)

The Council of Censors met in 1783–84. In the meantime, the opponents of the constitution had changed their rhetoric significantly. Rather than be labelled anti-constitutionalists, they appropriated for themselves the name 'republicans' in opposition to the constitutionalists. They proposed radical revisions, modelled on the Massachusetts Constitution of 1780. They wanted to reduce the size of the legislature and to establish a Senate whose members would be elected for three-year terms. A single executive officer was to be elected by the people for the same term of office. The latter would have veto power and would nominate judges and other executive officers (who, according to the 1776 constitution, were subject to election). The Censors would be eliminated, and laws would no longer have to be submitted to the people before being voted on; the system of rotation would also be suppressed as contrary to the principle of electoral freedom. This last criticism of the 'anti-democratic' character of the 1776 constitution was developed further in an attack upon the tyranny of a unicameral legislature that was supposedly arrogating unto itself absolute rights just as the English Parliament had done. The election of an executive officer armed with veto power but dependent upon the people (and not on the assembly) and of a bicameral legislature from electoral districts whose boundaries were drawn without reference to size or wealth (as had been the case in the 1776 constitution) were also justified by the same appeal to popular sovereignty.

The constitutionalists responded to their opponents by accusing them of wanting to re-establish an aristocracy, even a monarchy; they emphasized the sociological fact that America had neither orders nor particular interests deserving special representation. The republicans' response was both practical and theoretical. It emphasized the chaos created by this assembly which concentrated within itself all executive, legislative and judicial power. The legislature had, indeed, become involved in just about everything: questions of equity, annulments of marriages, commercial issues, property title problems, and so on. And each new session of the legislature was allowed to re-examine the actions of the past session, so that society suffered from an inflation of laws. To this practical critique was added a theoretical claim: if you really believe in popular sovereignty, then convene a freely elected convention rather than settling your affairs in this Council of Censors where in effect you control a minority bloc capable of defeating proposed changes!

The minority bloc of constitutionalists held its own, and the Council of Censors did not succeed in reforming the constitution in any significant way. But the debate bore fruit on the theoretical level and in the comprehension of the political situation of the States. Its effects became clear when the confederal Constitution was revised. For the moment, it should be stressed that this radical constitution of Pennsylvania predated the formulation of the Articles of Confederation but was not considered as a suitable plan of government for the Confederation.[12] It was not conceived of as the beginning of a *social* revolution, although it did emerge from the (temporary) replacement of an élite by an alliance of urban artisans and frontier dwellers who demanded to be treated as citizens with equal rights. This radical solution took the form of a *political* constitution. If it is compared to the conservative-republican contradictions found in the constitutions of Massachusetts and Virginia, the Council of Censors appears as a sort of *popular senate* for counterbalancing a chamber ready to follow the passions of the moment. But this comparison was not made during the debates in

Pennsylvania; the republicans were too obsessed with their goal of retaking control of the State and the constitutionalists were still thinking in Old Whig terms (with some Saxon mythology thrown in for good measure). The idea of such a comparison came only after the experience of the Confederation and of its difficulties.

## THE CONFEDERATED STATE; ALLIANCE, LEAGUE, OR NATION?

The Confederation was, above all, a defensive alliance forced upon the newly free States that had to defend themselves against England. It began by endowing itself with autonomous institutions, which made it a league organized around a common policy; but it was neither institutionally nor politically the incarnation of a nation united by a unique will of its own. The Constitution uniting the newly autonomous American States was adopted by the Continental Congress only on 15 November 1777, years after the first military battles at Lexington and Concord. It went into effect only in March 1781, with its ratification by the small State of Maryland. The fact that the war could be conducted to a favourable conclusion in the absence of all legal governmental authority suggests the nature of the problem encountered in the framing and the operation of the new national institutions. This problem is clearly evident in the very terms of the Articles of Confederation. Indeed, the subject that gives itself a Constitution is defined in this document as the 'United States, in Congress assembled'. The Congress is thus a meeting of States, which are and ought to remain the foundation of all the authority of the nation and which give this nation a Constitution in order to assure their 'perpetual union'. The delegates to the Congress represent States (which are therefore the true members of this Congress); their mandates depend upon the legislatures of each of the States; and the decisions of the Congress apply to the States as such (and not to the individuals inhabiting these States). The Congress and the nation therefore have no will of their own; the republican idea of the common good does not apply to this Confederation, which nevertheless remains a State, endowed with a Constitution, that takes part in international political life. One might therefore expect the Constitution to be another political incarnation of Old Whig thinking, according to which Power is necessary but limited in order to assure the Liberty of its constituents – in this case, the States.

The problem to which the Articles of Confederation had to provide a solution is that the free States were not, as classical political theory would have it, entities organically and socially integrated in a whole defined along the lines of the model of the English mixed Constitution. These States were considered and they acted rather as equal political entities. And yet at the same time, by their physical size and character, they were unequal to each other. Thus, as early as 1774, when there arose what would become the interminable debate about the Confederation and the rock upon which it eventually was shipwrecked – namely, the question of the relationship between taxes and representation – Benjamin Franklin insisted: 'Let the smaller colonies have equal money and equal men and then have an equal vote. . . . If they have an equal vote without bearing equal burdens, a confederation upon such an iniquitous base will never last long'. But this quantitative inequality masked a qualitative inequality, as is shown in the answer Franklin received from John Witherspoon, president of the College of New Jersey at Princeton and delegate from his State to the Congress. Ought one to weight the suffrage according to the wealth, the population or the geographical size of the States? Certain States had a highly concentrated and already urbanized population; others were claiming lands to the West and could expect to grow larger; finally, the criterion of wealth would divide the merchant States from the agricultural ones. Looming larger for the future was the slavery question: ought slaves to be counted among the wealth of the various States or among their respective populations?[13] For lack of a better solution, it was necessary to resign oneself to the principle of equal representation for the States. The inherent injustice of this compromise, however, was felt by all sides. The existence of a league presupposed the existence of a common good, at least in the form of a common interest (which had been the case during the war against England, even if the temptation to conclude a separate peace had sometimes arisen[14]). But political institutions based upon a common good are different from those that allow the formation of a common interest. The former are republican in character whilst the form of the latter remained to be defined in a society in which the social estates of the mixed constitution and their corresponding political principles were absent.

The Articles of Confederation specify from the outset that each State retains all powers and all liberty not 'expressly delegated to the United States, in Congress assembled'. Their entry into this 'firm league of friendship with each other' takes place one by one, or 'severally'. The league's *raisons d'être* are the common defence of the States, the safeguarding of their liberties, and their mutual and general welfare.

These States promise to defend themselves or any one among them that might be attacked on account of religion or because of a threat to their sovereignty, trade or any other liberty. To this end, and the better to affirm their ties of friendship, they grant to each citizen of any other State (save for 'paupers, vagabonds, and fugitives from justice') all the rights enjoyed by their own citizens; and they promise to accept the decisions and acts of the other States (in the 'full faith and credit' clause, whose full importance became apparent only later). It would have been only a small step to create a common citizenship for all Americans, yet nothing is said about it, for the doctrine of the sovereignty of the States remains symbolically too great.[15] Rather than dwell on the political status of citizens, the Articles go directly to the elaboration of the constitutional powers of the Confederation. This institutional structure aims at protecting the autonomy of the States while assuring their defence, safety and welfare, the pursuit of which is the basis for their union. The powers that are described do not follow the English mixed model of three political powers, separate but organically tied by the connection between rights and duties; instead, they are quite simply functions in the service of a system whose end is the integration or rather the aggregation of interests for the purpose of preserving the private rights of each party.

The description of institutions does not begin with the affirmation of the omnipotence of the legislative branch, as had been the case in the State constitutions. On the contrary, in reading this somewhat confused document, one is struck not only by the dominant position granted to the interests of the States but also by the pragmatic and functionalist character of these institutions, which claim no theoretical justification.[16] The goal was merely to assure the independence of the States while delimiting the jurisdiction and powers that were to devolve upon the national authorities as a function of the requirements for coexistence among politically equal but really unequal States and the exigencies these States faced in the war for independence. The delegates to the Congress (who were not called 'representatives') were to be chosen by the legislatures of the various States, each in the manner they deemed best. The States were to remunerate their delegates as they saw fit. The terms of office for these delegates were not fixed; delegates could be recalled and replaced at the discretion of the State assemblies. The States were to send at least two delegates, but they could send up to seven. No delegate could serve for more than three years in every six, a restriction reminiscent of Pennsylvania's but found also in other places where the fear of the development of a new aristocracy remained strong. Plural office-holding was forbidden. Freedom of debate was assured by a clause protecting delegates against any arrest or interference while carrying out their functions (save in cases of treason, felony or other 'breach of the peace'). This freedom aimed at guaranteeing not the free speech of representatives but rather that of the States, which had the right to replace their delegates as they deemed fit, thus preserving control over their actions by means of what was in fact only an application of the principle of the binding instructions of representatives (which they had rejected in their own constitutions).

The long enumeration of powers of the 'United States, in Congress assembled' that follows deals especially with foreign affairs. It is noteworthy that in this sphere the powers of the States were limited. In the same way, concerted action by a group of States was forbidden. The goal was the avoidance of division, which explains why this same paragraph forbids Congress from granting titles of nobility and citizens from accepting them from a foreign power (but the Confederation does not forbid the States from issuing them). Other measures were aimed at preventing provocations by a single State which might on its own authority engage in hostilities that could implicate the entire Confederation. Each State was to maintain a militia, but the Confederation itself is not authorized to keep an army in time of peace. The league was thus united, but only against the world outside it.

Another provision carried the germ of a more solid unity. It prohibited the States from imposing customs duties that would contradict a treaty duly ratified by 'the United States, in Congress assembled'. The implications of this clause were felt later on, as were those of Article VIII, which stipulated that the costs of war consented to by 'the United States, in Congress assembled' would be paid from a common treasury supplied by taxes levied by each State, in proportion to the value of the lands in this State (this being 'estimated according to such mode as the United States in Congress assembled, shall from time to time direct and appoint'). These taxes, however, were to be collected by the State legislatures. This posed a practical problem which became, as we shall see, theoretical during the 1787 debates over the reform of the Articles. Another theoretical problem was already present. It concerned the idea of levying taxes according to the value of lands, which raised anew the question of equal representation for each State within the Congress, since taxation and representation had been connected in the American consciousness ever since the long polemic with the English Parliament.

The powers of 'the United States, in Congress assembled' are enumerated in an Article that is, by itself, almost as long as all the others put together. These powers included, of course, that of declaring war and concluding peace. A complicated procedure describes the judicial function assumed by the Congress in case of conflicts between the States, or between individuals who claim to hold Western lands according to grants made by the States.[17] No mention is made, however, of what powers might be exercised in order to carry any eventual judgements into effect. This implies that what was envisaged were negotiated settlements between allies rather than a process that would take into account shared national interests. The power to coin money (and to determine the value of money issued by the States) is granted to 'the United States, in Congress assembled' along with that of fixing the standards of weights and measures 'throughout the United States'.[18] To this modest prerogative was added the regulation of commerce and Indian affairs – except when this encroached on the rights exercised by the States within their own territories. The creation of a postal system reinforced the affirmation of national unity, as did a provision allowing 'A Committee of the States' to determine the 'necessary sums of money to be raised for the service of the United States' and to use this money to pay for services to this government. This same committee is also granted the right to borrow money in the name of the United States. But the States resume the exercise of their sovereign rights in another prerogative granted to this same committee, namely, the one requiring a State to levy and pay for troops 'in proportion to the number of white inhabitants in such State'. If a State finds that Congress's quota is beyond its means, it may provide only that number of men it deems itself capable of sending. But this clause, which was invoked frequently, and with potentially disastrous consequences during the war, did not pose major difficulties once peace was attained.

The Articles also established a committee of the States which was to sit when Congress was not in session. This was not a true executive branch. The legislative omnipotence typical of the state constitutions was instituted *de facto* in the confederal Constitution. But the dominant position of the national legislative branch was limited by the role granted to the sovereign confederated States. For example, the consent of nine States was required to declare war, conclude peace, approve treaties, coin money or borrow at the national level; moreover, unanimity was required for admission of new States into the Confederation and for the adoption of all amendments to the Articles. This amendment process took on crucial importance because of the introductory clause, which stated that 'Each state retains its sovereignty, freedom, and independence, and every power, jurisdiction, and right, which is not by this Confederation *expressly* delegated to the United States in Congress assembled' (emphasis added).[19] This restriction was increasingly resented by those who would soon be called nationalists and who called themselves – by a stroke of rhetorical genius – federalists.

What is striking to the reader of these Articles of Confederation is above all the omission of the lessons inherited from the long theoretico-political struggle against England. The rejection of parliamentary sovereignty was based upon near scholastic efforts to avoid the reproach of an *imperium in imperio*. But the Confederation was nothing but the establishment of such a solecism in the guise of a constitutional foundation. The government established by this Constitution was not a republic. It was an application of Old Whig thought, but without the invocation of virtue that had permitted that theory to avoid having to think in terms of institutions.

This government was neither the 'portrait in miniature' of which John Adams spoke nor the guarantor of social equality among its constituent members that Patrick Henry claimed to desire. It was constructed in order to articulate a politics based on the interests of its constituent members – a sort of contractualism at the inter-State level which foreshadowed the contractualism that prevailed in the constitutional practice of 'the United States, in Congress assembled'. The history of the functioning of the government of this Confederation, to which we now turn, bears witness to this devolution from republican thought.[20]

# 7  History Reflected: The Institutional Functioning of the Free Nation

## EVERYDAY PROBLEMS

The most important institutional fact for understanding the political life of the Confederation is that Congress held both the executive and judicial powers without having the legislative power that would have allowed it to take urgent decisions. Although much of the economy was based on self-subsistence, the break with England accelerated growth and investment which made possible and even necessary some form of interdependence. But the inhabitants of the colonies were interested in national politics only when events forced their hand. These people can be called 'democrats' protecting the local power they exercised; but this label says nothing about either the content or the form democracy assumed in their eyes. During the war, the institutional reality of politics at the confederal level remained remote. Those who were concerned with public affairs were usually active on the local or State level.[1] The politics of the delegates to the Congress was determined by the interests of their States. Yet at the same time and no matter what they thought about political theory, they had to take charge of a country at war, conduct diplomacy, and in general put to the test that virtue on which the advocates of independence, sure of the threat posed by the English Empire, had counted. In a word, the political theories guiding colonial practice had to be transformed into institutions capable of administrating – or governing – the country. If the Articles of Confederation did not allow for the creation of an effective government, could they at least assure the administration of the Confederation?

The Congress was ineffective as a legislative body for several reasons. The rotation of its member-delegates and their role as ambassadors of their respective States rendered compromise difficult. These men, whose horizons were often limited to their States' boundaries, lacked experience. Not all had the requisite competence on fiscal or military matters, yet each felt obliged to participate in all the debates in order to protect the liberty of their State from any injury. Under these conditions

119

they treated each other as potential adversaries, spent much time on petty details, and often lost sight of the larger implications of the point under discussion. Rumours and rivalries also played a significant role. All this is perhaps normal – or not too abnormal – in a legislature. But this confederal Congress also had to realize a new politics, and this in a time of war. Political observers and those who read accounts of their proceedings – which, however, were held behind closed doors, preventing genuine public debate – had little reason to admire this institution and less inclination to participate in it. Such disrespect for the Congress of the Confederation could not help but lessen its effectiveness. This difficulty was felt first at the level of military and diplomatic affairs.[2] The negative impression drawn by military men and diplomats when they were called upon to testify before the Congress was one factor that led them later on to insist upon the need for reform of the Confederation.

Congress's efforts to combat inflation were an expression of the difficulties arising from the dual role of Congress, as both executive and legislative in character. This institutional structure was in contradiction with the theory of the separation of powers as well as that of checks and balances to which so many Americans adhered. And the theory turned out to be right in practice. At the end of 1777, the Congress took measures to restrain the circulation of money and demanded at the same time that the States levy taxes in order to finance their own expenditures without having to issue paper money. The Congress also asked for $5 million in taxes from the States in order to provide for its own needs. Some States refused outright; and even those which wanted to co-operate did not always succeed in finding the funds requested; or they found it necessary for political reasons to spend the money at home. The idea of price controls (which had already been put into practice by some of the committees of the Association) was proposed the same year but abandoned the following year. What was possible on the local level was not realizable for the weak government of the Confederation. The situation worsened, inflation accelerated, and the Congress ended up deciding that it should lower its expectations. Army commissaries were appointed to carry out what Congress itself was incapable of accomplishing. Finally, when this expedient ran into difficulty at the end of 1779, the Congress had to ask the States to assume on their own the burden of financing the war. This request could be seen as motivated by material weakness; more important is the fact that it manifests the Old Whig fear of an invasion of the political into the social sphere. Rather than reinforce the central authority – which might have been justified by the fact that there was, after all, a war going on – it was preferable to leave it to the social to take care of itself. The Congress therefore rejected in practice the conflation of legislative and executive power, even though this was inscribed in the Constitution of the Confederation. At the same time, the choice of deferring to the States put to the test the principles of state sovereignty at the foundation of the confederal system.

Congress's rejection of the centralist, 'Jacobin' option was not only the product of a theoretical attitude; it was the result of a *de facto* situation which allowed the States to attack the central power. This may be seen in the experience of the leader of the nationalist and centralist faction, Robert Morris, who became for a time the virtual prime minister. Morris was named superintendent of finances in February 1781 when the Congress became aware of the problems imposed upon it by its dual role of legislative and executive branch. Finances, Foreign Affairs, the Navy and War were made separate administrative departments. Morris wanted Congress to propose that the States grant it the right to impose a tax on the importation of foreign goods (called the 'impost'). More than the immediate income it would bring to the Confederation, this measure was needed to assure potential lenders of its solidity and fiscal responsibility. Moreover, Morris wanted to consolidate the debt in order to create a stable currency that would further investment, which inflation made risky and scarce. Some have interpreted these proposals as a political manoeuvre in disguise, for Morris was also one of the leaders of the 'republican' faction that sought to reform Pennsylvania's radical constitution. Others saw in it only an effort aimed at putting the Articles of Confederation to full use. The debate was violent and the results were close. Morris ended up winning a victory without any real content. He obtained approval from Congress, despite his rather heavy-handed methods of managing his department. But, despite the backing of Tom Paine's pen and even an incitement to rebellion from some army officers who had not been paid, he failed to convince the States of the necessity of his single unified tax plan. The Articles had provided only for taxes assessed in proportion to the value of the lands of each State. Morris's taxation proposals aroused the fears of small States, like Maryland (which had only just joined the Confederation) or Rhode Island, as well as of large commercial States like New York. The signing of the Treaty of Versailles in 1783 sealed the defeat of Morris's plan by eliminating the pretext provided by the urgency of the war.

With peace, the Confederation was able to continue to live from compromise to compromise without being exposed to more than the threat of bankruptcy. A large step was made in 1786, when the States, led by Virginia, ceded to the Congress their claims to the western lands. This brought potential income to the Congress, although it had a hard time agreeing on how these lands would be used. Morris's proposals had aimed at consolidating all war debts in the hands of Congress. It was feared (rightly, as time would show) that this would be used as a pretext for levying taxes paid directly to the Congress, whose political autonomy would thereby be enhanced. Nevertheless, the transfer of these lands represented an important symbol of union which reassured the small States and those with fixed boundaries concerning their future in the Confederation. The passage of laws regulating the colonization of these territories constitutes one of the remarkable successes of the Confederation. Under Jefferson's leadership, a committee proposed that these lands be divided into territories for habitation. The Northwest Ordinance of 1787 provided for the establishment of temporary governments ruled by Congress, guaranteeing a republican form of government, freedom of religion, public aid to education, the right to trial by jury, and the prohibition of slavery.[3] When these territories acquired a population of 60 000, they were given the right to become full-fledged States of the Confederation. This promise is a political innovation by the Confederation which develops the theoretical implications of the struggle against England. The old colonies would not become, in their turn, an empire founded upon political inequality. This political innovation is worth underlining from the point of view of theory.

Peace brought with it neither a state of tranquil liberty nor the collective search for a common good recognized by all. The Treaty of Versailles contained the seeds of future conflicts. The Confederation was threatened by the Spanish on the Mississippi; the refusal by certain States to compensate for the loses borne by loyalists served to justify England's maintenance of troops on the northwestern frontier; and finally, piracy continued to disturb American commerce which had to find new paths outside of the old empire. These difficulties united the country against the outside and demonstrated the need for a unified commercial policy. At the same time, however, this implied that economic interests would finally be granted legitimate entry into political discussion. Postwar economic changes led the South to adopt more intensive methods of cultivation than those used in an agricultural economy based upon tobacco and indigo; New England agriculture suffered as a result, but its trade and commerce profited from new outlets and from the diversification required by the closing of the Caribbean (which France had not been able to recapture from the English, who had delayed the signing of the peace treaty until after the French naval defeat in the Caribbean in 1782). With the mercantilist strictures of the English Empire no longer in effect, new businesses were being created. New forms of business enterprises – corporations, interstate commerce, public works – were being developed or were changing in character. The depression following the war was of relatively short duration. When business picked up again, there came an increase in imports from countries seeking to gain a foothold in the former preserves of the English. New fortunes increased domestic consumption while others kept in step with fashion by going into debt. One might well fear that austere republican virtue would suffer in this new environment. Under these circumstances, the imperfect functioning of the institutions of the Confederation was not reassuring.

## PROBLEMS OF POLITICAL THEORY: THE RETURN TO THE STATES

Once independence was finally won, the Americans found themselves free within a political structure built on the principle of an *imperium in imperio* which they had fought against while a part of the British Empire. Their dearly won liberty once again seemed threatened, undermined from within both by the institutional functioning of the Confederation and by the new economic interests that were influencing both politics and the behaviour of its citizens. In 1763, no one was republican; now everybody was. But the optimism that came with victory concealed the theoretical problem we have already noted, and which threatened to arise again during peacetime. Was the republic founded upon virtue or was it limited to creating institutions capable of producing virtue? As an ideology, republicanism carried a regenerative charge; as political science, it bore a more sober message. Experience seemed to lead to a doubly pessimistic conclusion: Americans were lacking in virtue, and their institutions were not capable of producing it. The religious component of the Old Whig ideology could resurface here, finding an ally in political science and its theory of political cycles. The regeneration promised by the Revolution would be followed by a fall, and liberty would give way to anarchy before leading to a resurgence of tyranny. The fragile structure of the Confederation, founded upon the solecism of a dual sovereignty, offered no bulwark against this foreseeable fall. The crisis was not economic or social: it was ideological and deep-seated.

The combination of the legislative and executive powers in the institutions of the Confederation embodied another of the principles against which the colonists had rebelled. But the doctrine of the separation of powers coming from the English Constitution was ambiguous. Was it a matter of separating socio-political functions, where each function represented a constitutive element of the organic whole of rights and duties that is an organized society? This image is that of the 'miniature . . . portrait' of which John Adams was the theoretician. From this point of view, individual liberty had been imperiled because the measures taken by the English were destroying the social unity that was its foundation. But the separation of powers could also be justified by reference to a political science inspired by Newton. A strict delimitation of the domains of action proper to each power then appeared necessary in order to assure that the governmental machinery would be able to discover and implement the common good. From this point of view, individual liberty was threatened by the degeneration of republican institutions. But, when reality opened their eyes to the contradictory structure of their new confederal institutions, the Americans discovered that their individual liberty was not so simple a matter. This liberty was present in the form of divergent interests; it affirmed rights without giving a place for duties. The image of an organic society endowing itself with a republican form of representation was no longer tenable. Social unity gave way to competition between individuals, States, regions; egotistical atomism was destroying the illusory reality of a *res publica*. If the confederal institutions had some coherence, it had to be sought on the side of the States making up this Confederation. Perhaps their autonomous existence would guarantee individual liberty. The presumed vice of the Articles of Confederation would be in fact a virtue; the Confederation would be only an executive power whose legislative impotence preserves liberty.

The prospect of a degeneration of the republic raised the fear that democracy, which was more or less being practised in all the States, was only the prelude to anarchy.[4] The Americans did not distinguish very carefully between the two concepts, although that of the Republic was by far the most frequently used. We have already seen how the ease in directing and controlling the crowd during the pre-revolutionary struggle had inspired some leaders to adopt the idea that broader participation in public life did not necessarily lead to anarchy. The extension of such participation, however, was not always envisioned without apprehension. The Declaration of Independence, the success of the rebellion, the war and the rise of new institutions marked the end of the old patterns of authority and obedience among Americans. Rebellious individualism, critical of authority and sure of its rights, raised the problem of how to legitimize authority in the social and especially in the political sphere. Independence brought not only the end of an order founded upon a tacit code of deferential conduct where each knew his place and the behaviour expected of him. The free American did not see why he had to obey laws in whose writing he had neither participated nor consented. Had not the slogan *No taxation without represention* been repeated often enough since the protests against the Stamp Act began? But what kind of representation was at issue here? The distinction between active participation and tacit consent to legitimate authority corresponds to the distinction between democratic and republican forms. If the Articles of Confederation had founded a divided and disfunctional republic, perhaps democracy could preserve liberty and found political legitimacy in the States.

The problem of legitimating the political authority that is supposed to represent liberty poses another of the questions already debated during the break with England. The colonists had asked themselves how they could be represented in a Parliament that was situated in London and unfamiliar with their local circumstances. They had rejected the doctrine of 'virtual representation' which was based upon the idea that a common good shared by the whole Empire actually existed and that the Parliament was responsible both for determining and for implementing this common good. They had been tempted at one time to recognize Parliament's right to regulate external trade, leaving internal taxes the responsibility of the colonies. This distinction, made most strongly by John Dickinson's *Farmer*, was later rejected. Similarly, the newly independent States refused Congress, Robert Morris, and his administration the right to regulate commerce by the establishment of a set of common customs duties; like the Townshend Acts, these proposed duties were perceived as a pretext for Congress to procure funds for itself and therefore to exercise control over the States. Since this was a matter of State authority over the individual, certain parallels to the earlier struggle could not help but resurface in people's minds. Virtual legitimation being unacceptable, real representation had to be implemented. It remained to be seen whether the free individual would participate as a man and a democrat or as a citizen and a republican. This implied not only the suffrage question but also, and above all, the question of the role to be played by self-interest, whose social reality could no longer be denied. How was *social* interest to be represented as *political*?

The long theoretical and political debate with England provided the concepts for formulating a democratic and participatory theory which seems capable of surmounting this difficulty. When they declared themselves independent by breaking the political tie that establishes authority, the Americans found themselves in a theoretical state of nature whose conceptual definition remained ambiguous but whose emotional charge was quite strong. We have seen that, for the Declaration of Independence, this political break did not dissolve the social contract uniting the colonists with each other; the Constitution of the Confederation was conceived as a (Lockian) political contract concluded between already constituted and independent social States. But another reading of this experience was possible. If the political break with England dissolved all ties of authority, as the voters of Massachusetts, for example, had asserted when they rejected the Constitution of 1778 on the grounds that it was not the work of a Convention elected expressly for this purpose, then the legitimacy of laws required another justification. This justification appeared at first in the principle of legislative omnipotence present in all the State constitutions. The legislature is taken as the representative of the will of its constituent members, who give themselves the laws they think best through this intermediary. The individual is obligated by these laws to the extent that he participates in the election of this legislative body. But this is a private individual, a pre-political individual. Its liberty is a private form of liberty, that of pursuing its own interests – or its happiness, as the Declaration puts it. But the authority of law comes from the fact that it is public, applicable to all as citizens of a republic governed by laws and not by the whims of (private) men. The private individual thus finds himself in the same relationship to the State that the States have *vis-à-vis* the Confederation. The democratic solution therefore does not resolve the problem of political representation.

Pennsylvania's constitution sought to overcome this dilemma of representation by recourse to an active democracy, the key to which was the Council of Censors, meeting once every seven years in order to revise laws or to propose constitutional changes. From the point of view of the science of checks and balances, this council played the role exercised elsewhere by the Senate. But whereas the latter is supposed to embody another principle than that of the popular will, the Council of Censors constitutes a popular check upon the *vox populi*. It is in this respect that the Pennsylvania constitution can be called democratic. What the censors actually did in practice when they met in 1784 illustrates, however, the difficulty involved with this democratic solution. Faced with the issue of deciding the legality of a legislative act annulling the charter an earlier legislature had granted to the University of Pennsylvania, the censors had invoked the doctrine that forbids *imperii in imperio*, concluding that corporations (as the University was) could not claim to be autonomous 'governments' within the State and that this State alone, through its legislature, had the right to legislate on general questions. The retrospective repeal of the charter was therefore held by the censors to be valid.

This practical decision by the Censors of Pennsylvania is a good example of the theoretical dilemma posed by the Articles of Confederation. The States, constituted out of the nothingness of the state of nature, had no other foundation than the popular will. This will, being constituted in terms of private interests, could not assume a legitimate and therefore universally valid institutional form without putting into question the individual will that it was to embody. The mediation between the public and the private, the universal and the particular, failed. The result, on the practical plane, was a permanent state of instability that affected the functioning of the Confederation and especially the functioning of the States' institutions. Laws passed or charters granted in one session could be revoked in the next. This latter instability, more than the difficulties of the Confederation, made Americans aware of the need for political reforms that would change their representation of the political sphere. Because of the primacy of the States within the confederal system, the return to the State level revealed the need for reforms whose import would go beyond the local boundaries of the States. The general problems raised by the struggle against England had found their first theoretical solution in the States' constitutions. This time the movement proceeded in the opposite direction.

The theoretical difficulty which dominated institutional life during the Confederation era turns on the question of representation. For a long time, the royal authorities or else the common good of the Empire had legitimized English laws. Old Whigs and republicans were in agreement on the need for laws, but divided on how they were to be founded. The Old Whigs, allied with participatory democrats, insisted upon limiting the authority of the laws so as to protect a form of liberty they conceived of as including both a public dimension and a private one in which interest was legitimate. Little by little they came to doubt the existence of the virtue that was supposed to be the foundation of public liberty. But the private or self-interested foundation that remained generated legislative instability which compromised the effective operation of institutions. Thus, for example, no one would make investments if the legislature was not able to give assurances that conditions agreed upon today would remain valid tomorrow. The republicans, on the other hand, proposed to stabilize institutions based on their representativeness. But their image of representation was only negative; representation was a makeshift compromise in view of the fact that not everyone can directly participate in everything and that chaos results when they try to do so. The positive foundation – the objective and the criterion for representation organized along republican lines – had yet to be defined. For some, it was the public liberty of the individual *qua* citizen that mattered most. For others, it was the liberty of the States. For others still, it was a matter of the social equality underlying the concept of a republic which its institutions were to express 'in miniature'. Confronted by the question of representation, the authors of the Articles of Confederation had adopted a compromise position; they established equal representation between States for political decisions while proposing that taxes be assessed in proportion to the value of the lands under cultivation in each State. This solution could not be a lasting one, but recourse to the amount of population, the value of landed wealth or a combination of several factors did not resolve the dilemma any better.

# 8 History Rethought: Revolution and Counter-revolution

## THE HISTORIOGRAPHY OF INDEPENDENCE: THE VIEW OF THE VANQUISHED

It is often a good historiographical method to start from the view of the vanquished in order to avoid succumbing to the self-satisfaction of the victors, who are too often inclined to explain their victory in terms of (moral or material) historical necessity or by reference to a heroism that has triumphed in spite of all obstacles. As we have already seen, the loyalists did not work out a historical apology capable of competing with the interpretation offered by the advocates of independence because both sides shared a political philosophy in terms of which the basis for the break was a theoretico-political error rather than the result of a social evolution. To the colonists' thesis of a royal plot they opposed that of a plot by the advocates of independence. The observations of loyalists in exile who saw in the Revolution the end of a society and a way of life are of more interest. They criticize the 'new men' born of the Revolution who were vulgar, obsessed with money, polyglot, and so on. The society that resulted from the new politics was characterized by alienation and anomie and animated by the unending pursuit of monetary and financial wealth. This new society appeared to the loyalists as *anti-political*, privileging the private over the public, self-interest over virtue, anarchy over order, and the particular over the universal. How, they asked, can one presume that the inferior could command, or even pretend to elect or designate, the superior? How can one allow a free, all-powerful and subjective sort of criticism to replace the deference due to one's betters? The troubled life of the Confederation seemed to offer an ample confirmation of the loyalists' arguments, which found its echo in the republican opposition in Pennsylvania and elsewhere.

However, the vanquished of the Confederation were not the loyalists, although one can see in Beard's celebrated thesis a confirmation of their fears. According to Beard and the so-called 'progressive' interpretation, the transition from the Articles of Confederation to the Constitution of 1787 represents an anti-democratic constitutional counter-revolution. Beard suggests the resolution of the famous question posed by Carl L. Becker, who asked whether independence should be understood as a struggle for self-government or governmental power ('Home rule, or who shall rule at home?'). The argument was presented by Beard in 1913 in a book whose title, *An Economic Interpretation of the Constitution*, indicates that he is not claiming to establish a theoretical dogma. Beard is offering *an* interpretation, not 'the' definitive solution. As Stanley M. Elkins and Eric McKitrick show,[1] Beard's analysis belongs to a type of historical interpretation that appeared in the United States around 1888. Fiske's celebrated book, *The Critical Period in American History*, which elaborates on the interpretation of the Confederation era as a period of crisis, anticipates this current. But the 'crisis' that underlies this interpretive style was the one the United States was undergoing at the time of Beard's writing. To understand their own time, authors like the jurist Pound, the philosopher Dewey, the sociologist Veblen and the historian Beard tried to get beyond formal or surface appearances to uncover the 'true' motive forces of society. They sought to unmask the role of interest, above all that of economic interest. This did not result in a theory of social classes, and still less in a theory of their inevitable conflict. These progessive Americans were animated by an unshakeable faith in the basic goodness of the people; their research was aimed at understanding how this people could have let itself be misled; and their assumption was that, once its eyes were opened, the people would act accordingly. The progressives had applied what Elkins and McKitrick call 'the "reality" technique', which proceeds from the principle that what is important is that which cannot be seen; what is hidden is the conspiracy that must be brought into broad daylight. From this point of view, the fact that Beard's title puts the emphasis on the indefinite article, *An*, indicates the absence of grand theoretical pretensions on his part.

Beard analyzed the socio-economic composition of the Constitutional Convention of 1787. He discovered among its members lawyers, city-dwellers or people from the Eastern seaboard, and people who had a financial interest in the outcome of their labours. These people held or had speculatively invested in the debts incurred by Congress or the States during the war, or they were speculators in the western lands; or, as creditors, they could not live with the inflationary effects of paper money not backed by a stable government. Also present at the Convention were merchants and manufacturers who had profited from the new opportunities offered by independence. Finally, there were those whose fortunes depended upon legalized slavery. Nevertheless, Beard insisted, these men were not 'doctrinaires like those of the 1848 Frankfurt Assembly'; they were practical men constructing a constitutional edifice on a strictly practical basis: that of economic interest. Small farmers and artisans were nowhere to be seen; debtors in need of ready cash and inhabitants of the western frontier were also absent. Although it adopted the name of a 'convention', a form that democratically-minded Americans had often employed in the past to ensure political legitimacy, Beard stressed its illegitimate relation to the Articles of Confederation as well as the fact that its members were not democractically elected. This is why the new Constitution affirmed (along with Locke and contractualist theory) that private property is a right antecedent to both constitution and all government. No democratic majority has the power to revoke this right, by legislative action or as in Pennsylvania's 1784 meeting of the Censors.[2] The new Constitution was therefore neither the work of the entire people nor the result of a decision of the States; according to Beard, it was created by 'a consolidated group whose interests knew no state boundaries and were truly national in their scope'. Their recourse to national institutions was aimed at breaking the popular will and setting obstacles in the way of popular power on the State level.

　　Beard's thesis rests on a distinction between the democracy of the Articles of Confederation and the representative republic that conservative forces sought to found. A series of studies by Merrill Jensen, beginning with *The Articles of Confederation* (1940), seek to show that these conservatives were already present and active during the debate over independence. They based their arguments upon an interpretation – which we have called 'pre-modern' – of the English Constitution and of the colonial charters, while the democrats appealed to the theory of natural law. After independence, these conservative elements continued to promote their material and political interests throughout the Confederation period. At the height of their influence, they dominated Congress through their use of administrative policy as directed by Robert Morris; and the fact that Morris did not hesitate to call upon discontented army officers for help (this is what Jensen calls 'the attempted *coup d'Etat* of 1783') illustrates their determination. The goal of this conservative group, however, was neither to make use of the institutions of the Confederation to promote their interests nor to take over parts of its machinery. Their objective was quite simply to take power. In Jensen's words: 'The battle of Yorktown in the fall of 1781 and the peace negotiations under way gave no joy to the nationalists. Their arguments for centralisation and the supposed efficiency and economy that would result depended heavily on the continuance of the war, and they knew it'. They did not abandon their efforts with the close of the war, but they had to take into account the fact that they would need more time to attain their goal.

Beard's thesis, which dominated the debate until the end of the Second World War, was criticized in the 1950s. Robert E. Brown, in his *Charles Beard and the Constitution* (1956), parses Beard's text line by line to refute it in a host of details while also demonstrating its theoretical circularity. But in trying to prove too much, Brown simply reminds us that everyone agrees that people's interests have an influence on political decisions. Bancroft, the Whig idealist and great historian of the last century, had already emphasized this fact, following the lead of members of the Convention themselves. But what kinds of interests are we talking about here? Forrest McDonald offers a first interpretation in *We the People: The Economic Origins of the Constitution* (1958). He notes that a third of the debts were the responsibility of the States and that the Constitution did not stipulate that the new government should take charge of them.[3] McDonald seeks to show the existence of a pluralistic coalition in which regional interests and those of particular States were intertwined. This politico-economic reality can thus replace the conspiracy Beard believed he had detected. Similarly, Jackson Turner Main, in *The Antifederalists: Critics of the Constitution* (1961), analyzes the interests of creditors threatened by the inflation resulting from the States' uncontrolled printing of money before emphasizing the distinction between those regions whose economies relied on commerce and those that were self-sufficient. This interpretation, which denies the existence of class interests, is presented in a slightly different light by Lee Benson in his *Turner and Beard: American Historical Writing Reconsidered* (1960), which offers a social interpretation, starting from a cleavage between the advocates of an agrarian society and those who saw the future in terms of their own commercial interests. Likewise, another book by McDonald, *E Pluribus Unum: The Formation of the American Republic, 1776 – 90* (1965) returns to the question of the western territories to explain the policy of the nationalists. Revising Benson's thesis, McDonald argues that the distinction between 'broad-minded' and 'narrow-minded' people is more important than that between commercial and agricultural interests. At this point, the terms of analysis have become rather fuzzy, and it is better to stop here and recall simply that Beard's thesis dominated American historiography for a period of 40 years. That interpretation in terms of conflict was replaced during the 1950s by the school of 'consensus' or 'American exceptionalism', which replaced the stress on conflicts of interest by the notion of an underlying ideological-democratic unity. This school, like Beard himself, had the merit of posing the question of the theoretical nature of the Revolution itself.

The Confederation, however, did not truly become an object of historical reflection. The picture to be sketched would be at once too vast – covering 13 States plus the Confederation, war and peace, the public sphere and the birth of the private – and, paradoxically, of too little interest in its rather monotone variety. One can attempt, like Merrill Jensen, to demonstrate the viability of the confederal institutions; and yet, the proof can never be definitive, for the Confederation was replaced. One can, like Eric Foner, depict the experience through social biography[4] in order to bring out both its ruptures and its self-understanding. One can, like certain New Left historians, try to retrace this history from the standpoint of the popular classes. But none of these approaches is entirely successful; this period of 'crisis' seems to defy explanation – unless it is in and through the actions of those who resolved it in 1787. Analyzed from that point of view, historiography becomes sociology. Nevertheless, this is not the only option. We have seen that the 'crisis' was above all ideological, that it put into question the self-understanding of the newly free Americans. The evolution of this crisis during the Confederation era must be grasped as it was lived: starting from political philosophy.

## SOCIOLOGY OR POLITICAL PHILOSOPHY?

Beard's argument is not only based upon vague economic notions; it rests upon an unclear distinction between the alleged democracy of the Articles of Confederation and the Republic founded by the Constitution of 1787. If the independence declared in 1776 and implemented by the various State constitutions had genuinely been of democratic inspiration, with the legislative assemblies as its reflection, why would these same assemblies have appointed delegates to a Constitutional Convention whose aims were anti-democratic? The document drafted in Philadelphia in 1787 was sent to 'the United States in Congress assembled' with the recommendation that it be submitted to a convention appointed for this end in each State, a procedure that was in perfect agreement with the tradition that had developed since 1776. If one defines democracy in terms of popular suffrage, it is the government of the Articles of Confederation that is not democratic. Each State possessed a single vote, whatever its size or population. The delegates to its Congress were named by the State legislatures and could be recalled by them. One State could, all by itself, block the operation of the entire governmental machinery, as was seen with the impost proposed by Robert Morris (which was blocked by Rhode Island, the tiniest of the States) or with final ratification of the Articles (blocked until 1781 by little Maryland). Finally, if one still insists on the non-democratic character of the Philadelphia Convention it should be noted that it was set up exactly like the Continental Congress, which had declared independence and drafted the Articles of Confederation. As for the non-democratic character of the republic established in 1787, we will have to wait for the description of its institutions before making a judgement.

What is certain is that the Constitution of 1787 created a new and united nation. Its backers had the brilliant idea of taking the name 'Federalists' in the debate over ratification, but their goal is better defined by the term 'nationalist'. We have tried to understand the difficulties with the functioning of the Confederation in the conceptual terms of the political theory to which the Americans ascribed. But it is well known that institutions can continue to function for a long time before some external necessity or a new awareness on the part of the citizens leads to their reform or replacement. Theoretical inconsistency in the old institutions does not explain, by itself, the new nationalist policy or its success. Sociological explanation, which is midway between political theory and the '"reality" technique' employed by Beard and the progressives, furnishes the beginnings of an answer. After their critique of the progressive interpretation, Elkins and McKitrick offer their own analysis, centred on the new politicians whom they call the 'Young Men of the Revolution'. They note that the Federalists were on the average 10 to 12 years younger than those who had declared independence. Their experience was marked by the war and by national politics. As a consequence, they did not have local bases of support, and local matters were not their principle concern. Many had served in the army, others in the Congress. Their political careers were tied to the creation of institutions that would allow them to play a role that was national in scope. Their polemics with their anti-federalist opponents turned above all on the national/local distinction, not around that between democracy and republicanism. Their idea of what political authorities could and should do reflected their experience and their national ambitions.

Finally, to come back to the central theoretical question of the age – that of representation – these 'young men' wanted to represent neither wealth nor numbers nor, of course, the federal State: it was the *nation*, whose sovereignty had been declared in 1776, that was to receive its proper representation in their new political institutions.

The new national politics thus returned to the old republican problem of the nature of the *res publica* and of the political means capable of determining it. Before examining the political institutions envisaged in the new Constitution, it should be stressed that the political style of the Philadelphia Convention changed the signification of those institutions away from the form in which they were conceived by Beard and the progressive school. For the sociology of Elkins and McKitrick, the democracy/republic distinction is simply not pertinent. This is even clearer in another sociological approach, which claims to be more political and which refuses to distinguish between these concepts at all. This latter argument is not without interest for those who are seeking to understand the general relation between theory and practice in the American politics whose framework is the new Constitution. John P. Roche, who was an advisor to President Kennedy when he wrote his essay, highlights a continuity in the style of American politics, of which he makes himself the apostle. The sociologist does his best here to demystify the image of the men of 1787. Their ideology matters little; they are for him only archetypes of the politician and not 'metaphysicians, disembodied conservatives or Agents of History'. In a word, he says, he wants to lower them from the status of immortals to that of mortals in order to be able to learn from their lesson. According to him, their democractically-inspired politics is aimed simply at pursuing consensus; and the 'revolution' carried out in 1787 was a plot of the same kind as that of John F. Kennedy who, between 1956 and 1960, 'plotted' to become President![5]

The 'democratic' politics described by Roche flows from the national aims of individuals frustrated by the egotistical and narrow behaviour of the States and confronted with a population that had, for the most part, withdrawn into themselves and were little preoccupied with political questions. They had four advantages in their efforts to mobilize the people: the support of George Washington, Father of his Country; energetic leaders connected through a communication network formed during the war; an aptitude for defining problems in a pre-emptive fashion so as to circumvent localist indifference; and the existence of a latent nationalism based on the idea, inherited from the war, that the country had a collective destiny. The text convoking the 1787 Convention was astutely formulated; after all, no one could be opposed to debate, all the more so since the States remained the final arbiters of any decisions taken or proposals offered. Moreover, since they had called for the Convention, they could manage to ensure that people from their side would be nominated. Once the Convention met, they imposed secrecy on the debates in order to facilitate their manoeuvres as well as the possibility of compromises; and they helped to set the agenda by proposing a complete plan of government so as to avoid interminable parliamentary discussion. Roche retraces the process through which the initial plan proposed by Virginia was progressively transformed. Underlining the various compromises reached, Roche defines democracy as an *art of compromise* aimed at establishing consensus. During the initial debates, the nationalists were in the majority, but they were well aware, as one of the delegates had put it, that 'Our object is not such a government as may be best in itself, but such a one as our Constituents have authorised us to prepare, and as they will approve'. The last clause was decisive. This same idea was voiced repeatedly during the debates. The result is described by Roche as a 'patchwork', or as a 'makeshift', masking real problems behind ambiguous formulations and leaving it to pragmatic good sense, the inspirer of compromise, to resolve these problems in the future.

Roche's interpretation of the drafting of the Constitution and the political practice that guided this process presents the national interest, the *res publica*, as the simple product of compromises worked out by the representatives of various private interests. He describes a pluralist democracy from which classical and republican political ideas and aspirations are absent. The individual is free to pursue private interests; and the plurality of interests protects the very individualism that is the foundation of these interests. Such an individualism poses the problem of the existence and of the nature of the social community that founds the political unity within which they exist, for such a pluralism presupposes the absence of national goals. This sociological interpretation of the birth of the politics of pluralistic American liberalism is plausible only if the theoretical debates that constituted the path of the Revolution since 1763 are ignored. Roche is aware of this limitation, but he does not draw out its consequences. He notes that once the compromises were achieved, Madison and Hamilton set out in *The Federalist* to defend theoretically the new institutions that resulted from these compromises. These two men, each in their own way, were henceforth supporting a political system that they had criticized in the course of the closed-door Convention debates. For Roche, this is simply the proof of 'Madison's devotion to the art of politics', for the argument he developed in *The Federalist* contradicts 'his basic convictions about the true course the Convention should have taken'. But this conclusion is too simplistic, too functionalist, too rationalistic. We will have to examine more closely the drafting and the theoretical justification of the Constitution before we can define the nature of this democratic republic of united States whose politics presupposes *nolens volens* a national will and a common good to be represented.

The sociological interpretation moves directly from the question of the crisis to the nature of the response without suspecting that the interpretation of the latter determines how much value will be placed on the former. The crucial fact of the Confederation era is the predominant position of the legislative assembly in every State and its impotence on the confederal level. This legislative domination was the natural result of the conflict with the English monarchy; what is more, the new republic was first and foremost a society with neither king nor aristocracy. But the practical difficulties inherent in this institutional structure could not help but instigate a new theoretical reflection. On the State level, the problem stemmed from the passage of too many laws affecting all aspects of private as well as public life. Inversely, the Congress of the Confederation was incapable of fulfilling its mission because of the autonomy granted to its constituent members, the States. In the first case, the problem was that of frantic lawmaking, meddlesome and erratic in character and discredited even in the eyes of those who benefited from its occasional measures of support. In the other case, governmental paralysis prevented any response to the economic recession that came with the end of the war. It seemed that to remedy the situation one would have to return to the State level, but this solution would only weigh down state institutions even more. One could understand paralysis on the confederal level – whether this was cause for satisfaction or reason for regret; but the institutional muddle that seemed to reign among the States, and notably in Pennsylvania, had to make one reflect. Whose fault was it? The people, and the people alone, were sovereign. There were no more scapegoats.

This theoretical reflection, conducted on the State level, has been studied in greatest depth in Gordon Wood's *The Creation of the American Republic, 1776 – 87*, which analyzes the debates that were to give birth to a new politics free from the presuppositions of inherited classical political thought. A single example will serve to illustrate the implications of Wood's analysis, for it goes to the heart of the question of the 'crisis' of the Confederation years. If a sovereign people must express itself through its legislative assembly because it is materially impossible to meet as a direct democracy, what is the nature of the delegated responsibility granted to the representative? The multitude of responses to this question are well known, from binding instructions to the principle of virtual representation, passing through notions of express or tacit consent. A second-level question can then be posed: what kind of legitimacy do laws voted by the legislative assembly enjoy before they are implemented by the executive power or the judge? Given the deliberate impotence of the executive authority and the fears of judicial arbitrariness, the legislative assembly had to take responsibility for everything. But what then remains of the generality of law in a republic that claims to govern by laws and not by men once the legislative assembly begins constantly to intervene in particular cases? Is there a limit to legislative competence, as James Otis and colonists faced with the omnipotence of the English Parliament had claimed at the beginning of the movement for independence and sovereignty? This series of questions, raised and repeated in case after case, in the South as in the North, gave birth to a major innovation in political theory: the independence of the constitutional judiciary, recognized as a distinct branch of government equal in value to the other powers of government. We will return to this theoretical innovation, but it is worth underlining here that it had its origins in practice: the incessant intervention of the omnipotent legislative assembly in daily life led people to recognize the need to create a *limited* government. The Republic will henceforth not only be a government of laws; it will also be, by means of the judiciary and by means of the Constitution, a *doubly limited* government.

But the first result of theoretical reflection on the question of representation still does not explain the crisis. The practical solution that occurred to Americans goes further. If the legislative assembly abused its authority, it had to be restrained either by adding a second house or by increasing the powers of the executive – or else by applying both solutions at once. This is already what John Adams counselled in his *Thoughts on Government* in response to Tom Paine's optimistic unicameralism. We need not return to the difficulties raised by this constitutional structure. The important thing, on this level, is that a new justification for this traditional institutional structure now appears. Confronted with practical problems, the Americans passed progressively from political theory to concrete sociology. They learned to recognize the role of interest and to integrate it into their political theory. The Senate was no longer seen as the incarnation of the principle of wisdom or as the aristocratic custodian of political virtue; and the executive was no longer seen as a principle of energy and order embodying the honour of the nation. Recognizing finally that this classical and pre-modern representation of the political was ill suited to the conditions of the new world, the Americans had to forge a new conception of the representative nature of republican politics. To appeal simply to interests in general did not suffice; the common good could not be likened to a quantitative agglomeration. How can one compare commercial wealth, a modest farm, artisanal skill, speculative investment and the frontier outlook? And what can be said about experience, wisdom, honesty – not to mention virtue – which remain the basis of political institutions?

This 'crisis', whose economic, political, sociological or moral manifestations can be analyzed in detail, has to be understood in terms of the question of the representative nature of the political. It is necessary to speak of '*the political*' here (and not simply of 'politics'), for it is not only the legislative assembly and its functioning that are at issue. The magistrate and the judge, the law and the duty of the citizen, the local and the national – and even the distinction between the political and the moral which had surprised James Otis so much – must be grasped from the standpoint of the relations of representation. Who represents me and how does he represent me? Is the judge representative in the same way as is the legislator? How can the law impose an obligation upon me as a citizen, an author of this law, if at the same time it contradicts my interests and I find myself in the minority at voting time? What allows a small State like Rhode Island to reject taxation and thus paralyze the Confederation? Although the historian does not draw this conclusion, all of these dilemmas are based upon a simple philosophical error that had already been recognized by Rousseau and Kant[6]: the Americans still thought of representation as something real and realized. They wanted to see and even to feel the incarnation of their wills in their institutions. They did not perceive the constitutive difference between the representative and the represented, so that, unless they had recourse to binding instructions (which ends up paralyzing the system, as was seen at the confederal level), they could only end up feeling dissatisfied and frustrated.

The root of the Confederation's dilemma can be found already in the role of *symbolic legitimation* assumed by the Continental Congress at the time of the Declaration of Independence. The people declared themselves sovereign, but the institutions they had endowed themselves with were built on another model. These institutions were articulated in order to protect the people from a Power that was always inclined to grow at the people's expense. The positive form of the new institutions was therefore to be the expression of real freedom. But this was an error: the only power that now existed was the power of the people; they therefore did not have to protect themselves from it. Institutions modelled on Whig or Old Whig precepts could only mask the real relations existing within society. On the other hand, if popular power *really* sought to embody itself in political institutions, it would have found itself in the difficulty that confronted the French Revolution soon afterward. The search for a real identity, for an incarnation of the popular will in a republic, would tend to eliminate the representative relation from the political sphere. This tendency, strongly present during the Confederation period, explains the frustration that is palpable in all the socio-cultural experiences of the era; it explains the general ambiance, dominated as it was by a sense of 'crisis' that no one had succeeded in defining.[7]

American political experience since the beginning of the debate with England was dominated by the question of representation. The new conception of the political that was born out of the 'crisis' deepened this concept even more, both in its object and its form. The causes of the 'crisis' cannot be circumscribed by sociology any more than they can be described by the historian. It is a question of political thought, of political philosophy. But, as was their habit, the Americans got there by way of practice.

# Part III
# From Republican Politics to Liberal Sociology

# 9   History Lived: Bankruptcy of the Confederation?

## TOWARD PHILADELPHIA: MATURATION THROUGH PRACTICE

The impotence of the confederal Congress can be explained differently depending upon whether one emphasizes sociological, institutional or political factors. Except in the exceptional case of Pennsylvania, the old élite generally maintained its power in the newly independent States by co-opting new talent, just as it had always done. Its predominant position was nevertheless threatened by the new economic situation, which favoured the creation of new fortunes and opened the way for new talents. It was also challenged by the forms of political action invented during the period of resistance against the English and by the independence of spirit which had surfaced in a society that had just won its political independence. Under these circumstances, the élite could first of all seek to take advantage of the independence of the States guaranteed by the confederal institutions in order to preserve its power. But if local politics presented a challenge to its rule, as was the case in Pennsylvania, it had to turn toward institutions at the national level, which were more isolated from the social forces directly threatening the order it had established.

The attention that began to be focused on national institutions was not inspired solely by narrow political concerns. The new strategy resulted also from a twin evolution which implied the need to rethink the bases of a republican theory that we have seen elevated into an ideology whose rational foundation had not yet been shaken by events. On the one hand, a coherent commercial policy capable of creating the legal structures for a unified economy had to be conceptualized. To the recognition of the independence of the political and economic that this implied was added, on the other hand, the evident fact of the coexistence of divergent interests, even within each State. The political power of these interests, which threatened the old élite, had not been foreseen by republican ideology. Tom Paine's disillusioned statement during the

143

debate over the creation of a State bank in Pennsylvania is not atypical: 'My idea of a single legislature was always founded on a hope, that whatever personal parties there might be in a state, they would all unite and agree in the general principles of good government . . . and that the general good, or the good of the whole, would be the governing principle of the legislature'. The fact that Paine speaks here of 'personal parties' that should unite reveals the pre-modern character of his republican theory. The parties or factions that appeared almost everywhere in the Confederation were founded in fact on the defence of interests, their foundation being the socio-economic order. Political theory could not ignore this new reality.

The end of the war showed that these persistent difficulties were not accidental or temporary. Feelings of mutual distrust among the States had never disappeared. The realization of their dearly won independence presupposed the elaboration of a policy, even if only a minimal one, on the national level. To the active assertion of interests within each State was added the existence of differing regional interests among groups of States. What is more, if some States showed that they were aware of the benefits to be gained from the confederal association, others, in contrast, placed their own interests ahead of those of the nation. We have already seen how the States reacted to two clauses written into the Treaty of Versailles. Reparations for loyalists and the return of lands confiscated from them depended upon the good will of the various State legislatures. These assemblies showed little enthusiasm to vote legislation in support of decisions approved by the Confederation, even though this failure might serve as the pretext for the English to resume the offensive against their former colonies. The other possibility could be clearly seen in the treaty negotiated with Spain in 1786, which temporarily prevented American access to the Mississippi in exchange for favourable trade concessions granted to the New England States. The Southern States, which were planning to commercialize the river way and to colonize the region, obviously felt betrayed. The issue, therefore, was not simply one of granting the political existence of interests of a socio-economic character but also of interests related to structural differences within the confederated nation. If it was easy to believe that the former type of interests did not stand in the way of national coexistence, it was, on the other hand, more difficult for republican theory to accommodate the existence of interests of the latter type. Did not classical theory, expressed so well by Montesquieu, argue that a republic was for this reason impossible on an extended territory?

The sociological, institutional or political explanations for the failure of the Confederation take on their full sense only when related to what we have analyzed as a dialectic between practice and theory. The Congress of the Confederation occupied the symbolic seat of power that the colonists had granted to England in pre-independence days. The powers necessary for conducting war and diplomacy and for organizing commercial relations were considered legitimate in as much as they concerned only foreign policy and in as much as domestic policy in the colonies remained the province of those affected by such matters. But we have seen that this distinction between internal and external taxes, formulated by Dickinson's *Farmer* among others, was quickly overtaken by events after the Townshend Acts. It presupposed that one could differentiate between matters relating to the administration of the Empire that concerned the good of all and legislative activity that concerned particular ends. The accord of colonial and English interests, which had been the implicit definition of legitimate representation, could no longer be taken for granted. The question of the representativeness of Parliament and of the legitimacy of its acts had to be posed. The Congress of the Confederation was now to travel down the same road, for it found itself the heir to Parliament's symbolic political role. The confederal structure seemed to prevent a harmonious reconciliation. As early as 1777, Thomas Burke, a delegate from North Carolina, had declared vehemently that the Congress was only a 'deliberating Executive Assembly' without any powers of its own; ten years later, in his summa on American institutions, *The Defence of the Constitutions of Government of the United States*, John Adams described the Congress as a 'diplomatic assembly' with strictly executive powers. But these concepts contradict the Old Whig principles that were at the basis of this institutional structure.[1] According to these principles, the executive ought to be limited and controlled by the legislative power. But the Congress was at one and the same time a legislative and an executive assembly, thus introducing a contradiction the theory had not foreseen. To establish checks on the executive power was at the same time to limit the legislative power. The Congress found itself doubly impotent. Although this impotence was felt by all, once again it had to be conceptualized before it could be remedied.

Although the thesis has often been asserted, reform of the Confederation should not be seen merely as a response to the contradiction between State independence and national independence. And nothing proves that the Confederation might not have been able to function for many more years before hitting upon political compromises that would allow for a reform of the system. We have seen that two types of reform were being proposed. One kind attempted to improve the executive operations of the Congress by creating, as Morris had done, departments and executive committees; the other kind of reform envisaged an increase in the Congress's legislative power by giving it the fiscal authority to exercise the commercial powers that it possessed already in principle, thus freeing it in part from State influence. Some people went further, hoping to see the States themselves abolished, or at least reformed in such a way that would assign them a strictly administrative role after a rational reapportionment of their territory. These reformers could invoke the principle that assigning to a political authority a certain jurisdiction implies endowing it with the necessary means for exercising responsibility in this area – but they still had to define these means and, more importantly, to win political acceptance for them. The dilemma therefore was theoretical in the sense that a political integration of these new realities that were comprised of economic and regional interests had to be invented; and it was also a practical problem, since reforms not only had to be proposed but agreement upon their necessity had also to be obtained.

If the contradiction between the two sovereign authorities of the American nation does not by itself explain why the Confederation was reformed, this structure nevertheless suggests that the initiative for reform had to come from below, that is to say, from the States. The States had a minority veto power over all suggestion of reform; to get beyond this barrier, some sort of support within the States themselves was necessary. It is often said that the convocation of the Philadelphia Convention can be attributed to the fear and panic that followed the revolt organized by Daniel Shays in western Massachusetts. At the origins of these events we find the altogether typical problem of small debtors demanding that the legislature print paper money. The fact that Massachusetts sought quickly to repay its war debts readily explains the lack of available cash as well as the deflationary pressures to which Shays' fellow countrymen fell victim. The taxes levied to repay the debt by a government situated in the eastern part of the State and dominated by the powerful commercial interests of that region made it unpopular in the West. The rebellion could have been avoided by relaxing the laws providing for the repayment of the war debts and for the prosecution of small debtors. That, we saw, was the course taken in Pennsylvania. The unsatisfactory consequences that followed from the political structures that permitted this second orientation explain the national repercussions of Shays' Rebellion. In every State there were citizens who found themselves in the same situation as the Shaysites, and the political élite had reason to fear that radical demands along the lines of Pennsylvania's democratic unicameralism would become increasingly popular. Shays' rebellion lasted several months before being subdued in February 1787 by troops sent by the governor. In reality, however, this was only a beginning.

The effect of Shays' Rebellion was to make the need for a reform in the States even more evident. In fact, Shays' action was unique only in one respect: its armed resistance to the government, which had made this local uprising into a national political concern. In other States, similar popular movements succeeded in swaying legislatures (as indeed happened in Massachusetts, too, after the revolt was put down). Various measures were taken: printing money, legislative overrides of judicial decisions, laws protecting debtors and overturning legal provisions voted by previous sessions of legislatures. In Vermont, the Council of Censors called upon the people to hold a popular convention, which ended up by amending the Constitution. The problems that confronted the Pennsylvania Censors were therefore in no way unique. The political developments that ensued may be explained by the prevailing socioeconomic conditions or by the logic of the political situation. These revolts broke out most often in the West. The interests of small pioneer farmers were set against those of big eastern speculators (or sometimes companies of land speculators from several States or even from foreign countries, who were rich enough to pay large bribes). Such explanations, however, are only one step away from endorsing the theory of a conservative 'coup d'Etat' developed by the followers of Charles Beard. This explanation is insufficient. For reform to occur, the idea of reform still had to be popular, and it had to appear compatible with that republic for which the people had fought.

Precisely because Shays' Rebellion could be explained so easily by economic conditions, it influenced the spirit of the times. The birth of interest-group politics, the recognition of regional differences and the institutional contradictions that ensued, and the new economic and political institutions born of independence were problems for which neither the political theory of 1763 nor that of the post-1776 era were prepared. A sort of malaise developed which the Americans, so taken by political thought, were unable to bring to conceptual expression. At best, the rebellion in the West seemed to confirm the ancient wisdom according to which democracy inevitably degenerates into anarchy before turning into despotism . . . unless a new outburst, a *ricorso*, intervenes in time. George Washington's reaction is typical in this respect. In a letter of 26 December 1786 to his ex-comrade-in-arms

General Knox, Washington indignantly writes: 'Who, besides a Tory, could have foreseen, or a Briton predicted' these events? Under such circumstances, was one not justified in having mocked the supposed virtue upon which the Americans had wanted to erect their new republic, asked Washington? After having expressed this theoretical doubt, Washington mentioned in more concrete terms the English threat on the northwestern frontier and the ways in which the English might exploit American divisions for their own ends. Most importantly, he then asked his former military colleague why his State had not participated in the recent interstate meeting at Annapolis and whether it was going to participate in the one to be held in Philadelphia in May 1787. The practical threat posed by the enemy without was thus added to the theoretical doubts already undermining the Confederation from within.

Behind Shays' Rebellion and similar revolts loomed a new political problem of which people were beginning to become aware. If people constitute themselves as a society on the basis of their natural liberty before giving themselves institutions and laws, what is there to prevent them from returning to this state of nature in order to reconstitute society *and* government whenever the latter's acts no longer please them and the 'pursuit of happiness' loses its way? After all, the actions of the 'people out of doors', popular participation and/or open revolt had often been successful during the Revolution. The States' legislative assemblies were largely popular in composition, their senates and executive branches relatively impotent, being capable, at best – as in the epic battle in Maryland in 1786 or in Rhode Island at the time of the Philadelphia Convention – of blocking temporarily expressions of the popular will. We have already seen that in Pennsylvania republicans of the old élite, led by Robert Morris and James Wilson, had rejected their State's constitution. The same movement was beginning to appear elsewhere. A mechanical system of checks and balances was supposed to protect liberty. But liberty could be conceived only in connection with property, which was seen as the condition for its existence. The overturning of judicial sentences, the protection of debtors, the inflationary pressures stemming from the issuance of paper money and endangering the interests of creditors seemed, therefore, to put liberty itself into question. The expression 'tyranny of the majority' – whose terms would have been contradictory for Old Whig republicans – began to be heard. Another related but distinct idea, accompanied it: that of the importance of protecting minorities – this time against the arbitrariness not of an executive or of a king-tyrant, but against the voice of the people as expressed through the legislative assembly.[2] But it is one thing to criticize a democracy in the process of destroying itself and another to reform it before it commits suicide.

The practical steps to reform came slowly. The tax proposed by Morris, which remained for a long time on Congress's agenda, was finally rejected as the result of a veto by New York State. Morris then proposed seven amendments to the Articles of Confederation. These would have given Congress the power to regulate interstate and international commerce. To offset this loss of authority, the revenue earned from this regulation of trade was to be paid back to the States. Moreover, Congress was to be given the power to act against States that would not pay their taxes. Adoption of changes in the confederal tax system would henceforth require only a majority of 11 States instead of unanimity. Finally, the creation of a court whose jurisdiction would include matters pertaining to the Confederation was proposed; it would be able to act as a court of appeal in cases involving interstate commerce, international law and foreign relations. But the States rejected these proposals which came to them from above and which they felt were a threat to their sovereignty.

If the States were jealous and hostile to reform coming from the Congress, this was not necessarily because they were opposed to change itself. They had already made a small step in this direction during the meeting at Annapolis to which Washington had alluded in his letter to Knox. This meeting was held in September 1786, after the success, in 1785, of direct mediation talks over a frontier dispute between Virginia and Maryland. The States thus showed themselves capable of acting beyond their borders without intervention by the Congress. James Madison, one of the representatives from Virginia, took this success as a pretext for calling a general meeting, short-circuiting the authorities of the Confederation as the 1785 negotiations already had done. Madison had sat in the Congress of the Confederation for three years (that is to say, the maximum length of time authorized by the Articles of Confederation) before returning to local politics in his native Virginia. He was well aware of the distrust the States felt toward the initiatives of the Congress as well as of the latter's weakness. The practical gamble of the Annapolis meeting was to exhibit a national will without thereby injuring the States' sensibilities. Success depended upon elaborating a theory that could take into account newly arisen interests in such a way that it would transform the States' self-understanding and allow them to accept a new role without feeling robbed of their previous position.

Although nine States had in principle accepted the invitation to the Annapolis meeting, only five of them sent a delegate to the September meeting. The New England States chose not to be represented, on the grounds that the Virginia delegates, not being commercial experts, were certainly hatching some kind of political plot. Connecticut justified its refusal by the observation that this kind of extralegal convention had already served elsewhere to foment a spirit of rebellion. In order to avoid the impression of failure and to maintain the nationalist movement, one of the New York delegates at Annapolis, Alexander Hamilton, used a clause in the instructions of the New Jersey delegates permitting them 'to consider how far a uniform system in their commercial regulation and *other important matters*, might be necessary to the common interest and permanent harmony of the several States' (emphasis in the original document). That the delegate from New York had to make himself the interpreter of the instructions of the New Jersey delegates shows the difficulty of the situation. Hamilton staked his all. He proposed a meeting nine months later, at Philadelphia, in order 'to devise such further provisions as shall appear to them necessary to render the constitution of the federal government adequate to the exigencies of the Union'. Hamilton's proposal, formulated in very legalistic terms, declined to spell out these 'exigencies of the union', indicating simply that they were well known and had been discussed by everyone and that the situation of the United States was generally recognized as 'delicate and critical'. These proposals were approved by the delegates and sent directly to the state legislatures (a copy being transmitted to the Congress simply 'from motives of respect'). Reform would thus come from the States themselves.

Shay's Rebellion, Virginia's resentment over the Mississippi affair, New York's internal political situation and above all experience itself, which had put into question the very foundations of American political theory, had done their work. Only Rhode Island, whose domestic conflicts prevented it from sending delegates, was not represented at Philadelphia.[3] The combination of domestic uncertainties and pressures due to foreign and commercial policy questions therefore had ultimately made political change possible. The motive forces for this transformation, one might say, were the economic interests of a minority. But this statement does not suffice. What means did these interests have at their disposal? We have seen an initial difficulty due to the cohabitation within Congress of a legislative and an executive power. In order to control the latter, it was necessary to limit the former. This meant, however, that it was necessary to limit the legislative power of the States while at the same time increasing their executive power of control over their citizens. The establishment of such a direct relation between the citizenry and the national government could be considered as more democratic than the Articles of Confederation, which had never been ratified by a popular vote and which granted a powerful role to those apparently superfluous intermediary bodies that were the States. But once again, this idea remained without practical consequences. It was the States that were asked to send delegates; and they would nominate them and give them their instructions; they were not going to co-operate in an effort to put themselves to sleep! In other words, political theory, at least not in the usual and familiar sense the term had in American discourse, was not useful. It was necessary to find another language, that of interests.

## TOWARD A NEW MODE OF POLITICAL THOUGHT

During the months preceding the Convention, James Madison, the pragmatic nationalist who is considered the 'Father of the Constitution', devoted himself to the study of classical political theory and its contemporary applications. This preparation allowed him to dominate the discussion, whose overall goal went far beyond the terms of the political debate of the confederal period. Previous debate had remained prisoner of an abstract theory that prevented its participants from becoming aware of the specific and specifiable interests of the States and of private individuals. What Madison discovered in the classics was a radical break from the principal conceptual schemata of the constitutional period that followed the Declaration of Independence. His rereading highlighted in particular the vigilance or acuity that permits the politician to discover the particular interest behind the motives and acts by which universals such as the common good or natural law claim to be inspired.[4] This particular interest was analyzed both in detail and from the point of view of the general principle of action that it exhibited. Indeed, the search for constants in the history of political passions demanded that the analyst neglect neither sociological conflict between particular interests *nor* the generality of the theory that seeks to explain and control these particular interests. Madison applied this dual outlook to the context of the 'crisis' of the Confederation. The system that the Convention was to propose challenged not only the Articles of Confederation but also the political structure of the States, whose weakness and contradictions had been revealed by Shays' Rebellion and by the threat of the 'tyranny of the majority'. The political experience of the States had given birth to certain questions that were now seeking a solution on the confederal level, thus inverting the process followed at the time of the Declaration of Independence. The nationalist constitution responds, paradoxically, to the dilemmas of local politics within the States; and it does so, equally paradoxically, by finding the particulars which nonetheless can claim the kind of universal validity that political theory has always demanded. What was at issue was not a simple reform of the Congress of the Confederation and of its powers; the question concerns the republican experience of the United States – of the nation, and of the States that the nation united.[5]

At the same time that he was reading and rereading his classics, Madison wrote a short text on 'The Vices of the Political System of the United States'. This document can serve as a summary of the American political situation on the eve of the Philadelphia meeting.[6] Madison's argument begins with the concrete and immediate situation, about which he says he is certain that he will find unanimous agreement. He knows how important it is that his arguments find an echo on the local level in the States. He analyzes meticulously first of all the presuppositions that led to the present state of crisis before coming, then, to the theoretical and sociological premises of republican politics. His essay concludes with what he will call in *The Federalist* a 'republican remedy for the diseases most incident to republican government'. This essay on 'The Vices of the Political System of the United States' thus anticipates already the defence Madison will offer for the constitutional compromise that emerged from the Philadelphia Convention. That laborious compromise was not the solution Madison would have preferred, and he had expressed his true hopes for a solution at the beginning of the Convention in the proposals submitted in the name of Virginia. The principles expressed in this short work by Madison explain, however, why the final compromise appeared acceptable to him. For that reason, Madison's preliminary study should be analyzed before turning to the work of the Convention itself.

Madison begins his essay with five criticisms of the States' attitude toward the confederal government. The details of these criticisms are already familiar. Madison attacks the States' chronic inability to fulfil the constitutionally legitimate demands of the Congress. The States are then accused of encroaching on federal authority each time it seems to serve their own interests. Similarly, they violate the people's rights as well as treaties ratified by Congress, a practice which Madison explains by 'the sphere of life from which most of their members are taken, and the circumstances under which their legislative business is carried out'. This is not the fault of this or that person; it is due rather to the structural vice present at the very foundation of the Confederation which favours the recruitment of individuals with a short-term view for positions of State authority. Foreign powers have not yet taken advantage of the pretexts for conflict the States have provided, continues Madison, but this situation threatens the future peace and security of the nation – as Washington had already noted in his letter to Knox. Finally, the States violate each other's rights, as is evinced not only by the passage of laws aimed at favouring their own trade or at hampering that of others but also by the issuance of money with inflationary effects unfavourable to (State or private) creditors. Along these same lines, Madison criticizes the lack of consultation among States in the areas where such co-operation would be useful. The problem, quite simply, is that the self-interest of the parts takes precedence over that of the whole. Madison then cites other examples, such as the lack of uniform laws concerning the naturalization of immigrants or literary copyrights; he also mentions the absence of uniform rules governing the creation of commercial enterprises, especially those whose mission is in the public interest, such as the construction of canals, which can be delayed for this reason. In a word, local politics is harmful to the goal of national expansion – which, if it were to occur, would be more helpful to the States than anything they could undertake on their own. In fact, for Madison the Confederation is not a State; it is incapable of doing what a true modern government must do.

Madison then proceeds to an analysis of the Confederation from a standpoint that is already implicit in his criticisms. The Confederation is founded on the republican idea that law and power belong to the majority and that law and power are synonymous. This theoretical equation does not correspond to the reality with which Madison, the practical politician, was familiar. 'According to fact and experience', he explains, 'a minority of one third can succeed in dominating the other two thirds once it has the military might and the financial resources to do so; the same is true when the suffrage is granted to the poor, who will, 'for obvious reasons', join the ranks of sedition; finally, 'where slavery exists the republican Theory becomes still more fallacious'.[7] This argument is aimed at convincing the States that they would be better protected within a genuine nation where power and law would not be united in one assembly. Separating them would have two effects. On the one hand, those who might come to dominate the legislative assembly would not be able to pass laws endangering popular power. On the other hand, the popular power would be responsible for putting just laws into effect. For, continues Madison, on the level of theory as well as on that of practice, a law without sanctions is an empty and meaningless idea, as is a government without coercion. Madison explains the difficulties of the Confederation on this level by the 'mistaken confidence that the justice, the good faith, the honor, the sound policy, of the several legislative assemblies would render superfluous any appeal to the ordinary motives by which the laws secure the obedience of individuals'. He also pays tribute to the enthusiastic faith in human virtue expressed here while denouncing the practical inexperience that underlies that faith. The crucial point is that Madison no longer seeks to found institutions on the classical virtue so dear to the Americans of 1763 and those of 1776.

Madison breaks the vicious circle in which the State constitutions found themselves trapped. His political psychology is based on interests rather than on a virtue that is presupposed or to be created by a constitution. After all, he explains, action at the national level affects each State differently; and in each State there will always be politicians who will seek to exaggerate inequalities resulting from these effects in order to win public support. To this is added each State's fear that the others will not comply, with the result that none will obey. Finally, an additional source of weakness of the Confederation resides in the fact that it has not been ratified by the people, the ultimate source of power and the origin of the law. In some States, the Articles of Confederation are an integral part of the State constitution; in others, they were ratified only by legislative action. It follows that every time a State finds it in its interest not to respect the Articles, it can justify itself by reference to the primacy of its own constitution over that of the Confederation. Moreover, in so far as the Articles bind sovereign States, these Articles are in fact only a treaty whose violation by one of the 13 signatories frees the others from their obligation to comply with its provisions. A national Constitution must therefore be set on a firmer foundation. The question is: do material interests suffice?

These criticisms of the Confederation are based on a view that Madison clarifies in the final section of his essay. He attacks the inconstancy of laws passed by the States, which may vary with the will of succeeding legislatures, thus making even the most popular of laws unjust. Madison also explains the useless profusion of laws by the fear of the arbitrary power of the executive in applying laws that are too general. This fear is certainly justified, but the remedy offered by the States goes too far in the other direction, for the profusion of laws can become a positive nuisance. Madison therefore recommends a reduction of legal codes to a tenth of their present size. The fact that State laws are so often subject to change is another consequence of legislative inflation; above all, it obstructs commerce, 'not only of our citizens but also that of foreigners'. But this latter criticism from the standpoint of interests does not suffice. Madison returns to the problem of the unjustness of laws and to the challenge to the foundations of republican government that it fosters. This unjustness has two causes, according to him: the structure of representative bodies and the people themselves. Representatives seek election because of ambition and the pursuit of personal interest or in order to contribute to the common good. In the present situation, it seems, the first two motives predominate. Whence the question: how often and for how long will the public allow this to happen? To this question Madison adds another, more subversive one, namely: how long will the honest legislator let himself be deluded by self-interested leaders who hide behind sophisms? Rather than develop the institutional aspect of this question, Madison proceeds to an analysis of the people themselves. He recognizes that it does not suffice to have cast doubt upon the representative structures of the Confederation. Reform will have to come from the people, as it must in a republic.

Madison begins by stating a hypothesis that is not only radical but apparently contradictory to republican principles – namely, that every civilized society is divided into interest groups and factions. He proposes a broad and open-ended sociological description of these factions and interests: there are, of course, creditors and debtors, rich and poor, husbandmen, merchants and manufacturers; but Madison also includes here members of different religious sects and the partisans of various political leaders, the inhabitants of different districts and the holders of various forms of property. For a republican government, the dilemma stems from the fact that the majority, however it is composed, dictates the law. Under these circumstances, nothing forbids this majority from violating the rights and interests of the minority. Madison analyzes three motivations that might in principle prevent this kind of oppression. One may have faith in the prudence which makes people realize that their own good and that of the community are inseparable. But experience shows that this consideration is of little weight in reality. Second, respect for others, which is sometimes exhibited in relations between individuals, will be quickly overwhelmed by the passions that agitate public opinion – which is, moreover, easily manipulated by politicians. Public opinion is not governed by the same psychology as the individual. As for the third factor, religion, Madison notes that it arouses passions that are not easily controllable and are susceptible of becoming motivations for the oppression of others.[8] For Madison, there is only one realistic solution to the problem of protecting minorities: enlarge the political sphere in order to reduce the risk of creating a permanent majority with an interest in oppressing minority interests. But this idea remains ambiguous. Is it a matter of diluting private interest in the political sphere in order to prevent it from harming the political? Or is it a matter of public interests, like those of the States, for instance, which would compete with other equally public interests? And what can be said of private interests which claim to be justified by their public utility?

Madison's sociological definition of factions and interests seems to indicate that he is seeking to integrate and to protect the private sphere within an enlarged republic. But he knows quite well that, by definition, the *res publica* excludes the private. At the same time, he is convinced of the necessity – which had become manifest under the Confederation – of protecting minorities. Madison therefore changes strategy, as James Wilson had done before in his *Considerations*. But the proposal he now makes is new. He poses the question of what goals any government must pursue. The government, he asserts, must be a neutral arbiter between the various interests and factions that make up society in order that no faction usurp the rights of another. At the same time, the government itself must be sufficiently controlled so as not to become an interest on its own, an end in itself opposed to that of society. This new definition of Madison's transforms the image of government; it is no longer that of a sovereign power as described in classical theory. In an absolute monarchy, the Prince is neutral toward his subjects, but he may sacrifice their happiness to his ambition or to his avarice. In small republics, the sovereign people will not sacrifice the common good, but they are not neutral enough toward their constituent parts. Thus, just as a limited monarchy avoids the temptations of an absolute monarchy, an enlarged republic will check the dangers of a small republic. The size of the country limits the power of the faction or factions that run the government. That is to say, the admission of private interests into the political sphere requires a transformation of the concept of government. The classical models no longer suffice. As if he was aware of this shift away from the familiar tradition that had served the Americans so well, Madison makes one last remark, explaining that the republican form would undoubtedly be improved by an electoral process favouring the selection of noble and upright persons. This conclusion seems to express some doubt about the idea that republican virtue can be replaced by the salutary, because neutralizing, effect of the size of the republic. Madison thus glimpses the conceptual revolution required by the American experience, but he still does not succeed in stating what practice seems to impose upon the new republicans of America.

Leaving aside the virtue dear to classical political theory, Madison also abandons here the idea of the real or possible existence of a common good, a *res publica*, animating the republican politics he recommends. Government is no longer limited by an appeal to natural law, as it was for Otis, nor is it limited by the idea of popular sovereignty and its recourse to the right of resistance. Rather, government is limited *de facto* by the opposition of multiple interests and factions, whose very variety is supposed to serve as an obstacle to oppression. From this point of view, the criticisms of the Confederation are reduced to a single one. The State-republics were too small for the dilution of private interests to be able fully to play its role. Although Madison's logic challenges the classical conceptions on which American political thought was based, it still had to take the political reality of the country into consideration. Since independence, the problem facing Americans had been that of legitimating the authority of laws and of government once the reference to England had been eliminated. A national will guaranteeing this legitimate authority had to be instituted. Madison's logic boils down to saying that this quest was vitiated by the anachronistic political theory that had guided the Americans in erecting their new institutions. The new principle of interest could appeal to what remained of Old Whig thought, which sought a political structure capable of protecting liberty – a liberty, we have seen, that could be defined as either private or public according to circumstances. The liberal politics that is founded on the sociology of the self-interested individual could find a basis of support here. But other problems, ones that we have already broached (those of sovereignty and representation) also had to be resolved in the new constitutional edifice.

'The Vices of the Political System of the United States' does not draw out the implicit conclusions of its last part. Nor could Madison formulate them within the context of a Convention whose mission was to propose a plan of reform capable of garnering the support of the sovereign States. One cannot be certain that Madison would have accepted all the implications of his political sociology. Nevertheless, the replacement of the public by the private, of virtue by interest, of natural law by mere geography as the artificial limit to abuses of power, were part of the lived experience of the American people. Limited government and the primacy of interests, which remain characteristic of the American system, are rooted not in theoretical choices but in a lived reality that is given thematic form in the 1787 Constitution. But this lived reality is expressed there in a language, and according to principles, dictated by the practical need to win approval for reform of the Confederation in the absence of a united will. The result is the paradox of the effort we are now going to examine: the reform sought to create a strong State capable of confronting not only issues relating to foreign affairs but above all the centrifugal tendencies exhibited by the confederated States. Could a government of interests assume this role?

# 10 History Conceived: Toward the Constitution

## THE VIRGINIA PLAN

The Convention, which was to begin on 14 May 1787, did not obtain a quorum until 24 May. At that point Washington was unanimously elected president. Procedural questions were quickly settled. It was decided that the Convention would be held behind closed doors in order to permit everyone to express his thoughts fully and freely. The issues under debate were to be neither published nor communicated outside the meeting. The city of Philadelphia was obliging enough to spread dirt over the paving stones adjacent to the meeting room so as to eliminate noise from passing carriages during the deliberations. An official secretary, William Jackson, was designated, but his notes on the debates are less comprehensive than those kept by Madison.[1] Finally, on 29 May, the Convention got down to business. Edmund Randolph, Governor of Virginia, took the floor and presented, on behalf of his State, a plan whose principal author was Madison. Randolph asserted from the outset that the confederal system established by the Articles of Confederation had to be revised. It was necessary to create a government capable of protecting the States against foreign threats, against other States and against eventual revolts by their own citizens. To this end, the United States had to form a truly national government whose Constitution would have priority over those of the States. Randolph justified these radical proposals by summarizing the well-known difficulties of the Confederation and the dangers threatening it from within. Finally, so as not to frighten his listeners too much, Randolph stated what was to become the *leitmotiv* of the debates: the end dictates the means, but, in an America which insisted on preserving its liberty, these means must be founded on the republican principle. But the crisis of the Confederation had put into doubt the very meaning of this republican principle, and a long series of debates would be required before coming to a redefinition of the Republic that could serve as the means to the national ends sought by the delegates meeting in Philadelphia. In the process, the American understanding of the Republic was transformed.

The republican solution offered by Randolph dominated the first few

159

weeks of debates. The 15 articles included in his plan were premised on the need, expressed but not realized in the Articles of Confederation, to provide for the 'common defence, security of liberty and general welfare'. A national assembly was to be established; it would include two houses whose members would be elected from the States in proportion either to their financial contributions or to the number of free inhabitants. For the moment, the choice between these two criteria mattered less than the establishment of a national legislative body, which would effectively put an end to the idea of a confederation based upon the autonomy of and equality among the States. A choice between these two options concerning representation could not be made until after a prolonged discussion.

Although the final clause in this first article of Randolph's Plan opened the way for a solution to the problem of representation, this question was not crucial for the moment. Randolph suggested that proportional representation according to financial or demographic considerations could be applied 'as the one or the other rule may seem best in different cases'. This idea had already been proposed to the Congress of the Confederation; its origins go back to the debate with the English Parliament. It implied a change in the principle of majority rule in certain cases so as to take into account particular affected interests. Fiscal measures undertaken by a central government, for example, could have an effect on particular interests. Declarations of war or the elaboration of a commercial policy[2] could affect the rights of the States. Randolph did not explain in what way this clause allowed for the defence of a minority whose interests should not be sacrificed to a simple numerical majority. That clarification was achieved only later in the debates when the delegates, still imbued with the political thought developed between 1763 and 1776, began to take note of the evident political role of interests. The important thing for the moment was the affirmation of the national principle, which put a *de facto* end to the principle of the Confederation. The question of representation could be adjourned for the moment until agreement was reached on this crucial point.

The Randolph Plan proposed a two-house legislative assembly, the members of the second house being chosen by those of the first from a list drawn up by the State legislatures. This kind of filtering of representation recalls the one that we encountered in the Massachusetts and Virginia constitutions; it differs from them only by the way in which it takes into consideration the interests of the States, which, after all, had to be convinced to accept this transformation of their Confederation into a national government. The first house was to be elected by popular suffrage in each of the States (which thus retained an administrative role in the expression of political choices). This first house was the popular chamber; it would be independent, in principle, from the state politicians and their legislative quarrels, which had paralyzed the Congress of the Confederation simply by changing the composition of their delegations or the instructions given to their delegates. Randolph's proposals did not specify the length of their term of office; he stipulated simply that these national representatives would not be able to hold both national office and state office at the same time and that they would not be able to exercise state functions again until a certain, as yet unspecified, time period had passed. They could be recalled at any time and could not be re-elected before a certain, yet to be determined, lapse of time.

The goal of these clauses was to separate national interests from those of the States. This is why they applied also to the members of the second house. As for these latter members, the plan specifies that they would have to 'hold offices for a term sufficient to ensure their independency', implying that they would serve for a longer period of time than the members of the first house. These proposed measures suggest that the second house was to constitute a counterweight to the popular impulsiveness of the first. Nevertheless, either house had the right to initiate laws. More important than these provisions for separating the national from the local was the fact that, beyond the powers granted to the Congress of the Confederation, the national legislative assembly was also given the responsibility of intervening in cases where the States were not competent to rule or when the harmony of the United States was threatened by the actions of one or another of the States. More important still, the national legislature was to have veto power over every law within a State that seemed to it contrary to the national Constitution, thus conferring upon it a judicial function (comparable to that of the English Parliament over the colonies!). Finally, it could call upon the armed forces against any State that did not obey a federal law, guaranteeing in this way respect for its legislative or judicial actions. This plan was clearly more than a simple reform of the Articles of Confederation.

Despite the extended powers granted to this national legislature, the Randolph Plan also proposed an executive and a judiciary distinct from this body, thus bringing back the principle of checks and balances as a means to protect liberty. The executive, whose term of office also remained to be determined, was not re-eligible for office. His authority was not specified beyond the fact that he was to possess the prerogatives the Confederation had granted to its Congress as an executive power. The immediate purpose of this transfer of responsibilities was to avoid the confusion and overloading of which the Congress had suffered. But the concern to check the legislative power is present also in the idea of a Council of revision, within which the executive would collaborate with members of the judiciary in order to determine the validity of all acts of the legislature, including its vetoes of State laws. And yet the vetoes of this council were not to be absolute; the national legislature could override them on a second reading, thus balancing the check on it. However, vetoes of state laws were to be absolute so as to ensure the primacy of national goals. For the same reason, the establishment of a national judicial authority to settle jurisdictional conflicts between national and local authorities was proposed. The national Court was to have an exclusive jurisdiction, as yet undefined, and would be able to rule also in cases involving accusations against national officials.

The concluding provisions of the Randolph Plan were, in appearance, quite ordinary. They were designed to allow for the admission of new States as well as to guarantee that each new State or territory would be republican in character. We have seen that identical measures had been voted by the Congress of the Confederation in its law on the northwest territories. This enabled Randolph to assert that his plan was, despite its changes, an application of the lessons learned from the experience of the Confederation. In the same way the transitional measures leading to the adoption of the new constitution provided for the Congress of the Confederation to retain all its jurisdictional powers until its acceptance. On the other hand, Randolph emphasized that the procedure for amending the new Constitution was in no case to involve the Congress: it was well established by colonial experience and state constitution-making that one could not be both judge and party in the same affair. This is why the Congress of the Confederation was to submit the new Constitution to conventions specially designated by the people and not by the State assemblies. Its ratification would therefore be the expression of the popular and sovereign will of the nation. All these measures, which apparently confirmed the attainments of the Confederation as well as the political and administrative role of the States in the selection of the members of the two houses of the legislative assembly, were aimed in fact at abrogating the principle of State sovereignty on which the republican Confederation was founded. It is here, with respect to this theoretical question of sovereignty, that the radical nature of Randolph's Virginia proposals is situated.

Virginia's proposals were debated until 13 June. Discussion first followed their order of presentation, some speakers raising various difficulties, others emphasizing the advantages of the proposed plan. The enlargement of the sphere of responsibility of the national government appeared to some to mean the abolition of the States. No, responded Randolph; it is simply a matter of a form of government that would replace an impotent Congress. And the States would not be abolished; their political representation would be modified, but nothing more. Butler granted that the concentration of national power, to which he was nonetheless opposed, was more acceptable with the separation of the three powers and the division of their fields of action. Gouverneur Morris insisted that every community ought to have a single supreme power. But this seemed to hark back to the argument formerly used in favour of the omnipotence of the English Parliament. Mason noted, however, that the national authority could effectively exercise its power within the framework of the proposed plan because the government acted not only on the States but directly on individuals. But, objected Sherman, this change is too radical; the States will never accept it. This practical argument would be repeated frequently. The first proposal was nevertheless accepted by a margin of six States against one, New York being divided.[3] This vote of approval implied agreement on the principle of modifying radically the American system of government. The few arguments that we have just mentioned (each being a different reading of Randolph's plan) do not clearly communicate this radical decision, which remained implicit for the moment. Explicit unity was yet to be achieved.

Other parts of the discussion did not go so easily. Direct and equal representation for the States in the Confederation had been decided upon for practical reasons; to abolish it, a sufficiently forceful theoretical justification was needed (or a practical one, if this could be found). The choice between proportional representation based on fiscal contributions and proportional representation based on population was discussed as if these were mutually exclusive options. Madison declared himself in favour of the first solution, but King pointed out that it was not easy to determine the fiscal contribution of each State and that, moreover, it would change from year to year. Madison granted this problem, but he emphasized that, no matter what the alternative, it was undesirable to return to the system of equal representation for the States as provided in the Articles of Confederation. A more equitable form of representation would have to be found. Equal voting rights for the States had been justified within the theoretical framework of a league of independent States; the principle of the creation of a national government, however, made that practice both obsolete and ineffective. But not all the delegates viewed the new government in the same manner. Read, the delegate from the small State of Delaware, pointed out that his instructions forbade him from accepting a change in the Confederation's voting rules; if such was the objective of the Convention, he would have to leave. The Convention responded to this threat, which would not be the last, by deferring the debate over representation. The majority of the delegates were in favour of the creation of a truly national government, but they had yet to find the means for winning acceptance of this principle.

The principle of a bicameral assembly was accepted, with the sole objection of Pennsylvania, represented in this debate by the venerable Dr Franklin. This was not surprising in as much as the principle was already applied in the other States. But this unanimity prevented theoretical debate over the principle of bicameralism, a debate which would occur later and which showed that this brand of bicameralism was not the same as the one that had inspired the authors of the State constitutions. This agreement, too easily achieved for practical reasons, thus concealed the theoretical stakes. What was needed was a new theory justifying a national government in order to defeat the resistance of the States. The Convention had still a long road to travel before the implications of the confederal experience became clear.

The principle of popular election of the first house posed greater problems. Sherman and Gerry noted that the difficulties of the Confederation came from an excess of democracy that had allowed demagogues like Shays to lead astray a virtuous but easily duped people. Gerry attacked the levelling spirit whose passion for cheap government had reduced the salaries – and therefore the qualifications – of the servants of the people. Mason replied that this first house would be comparable to the English Commons. He was aware, of course, of the social differences between America and England; he criticized the upper classes who failed to realize that, within a generation, their descendants might well end up at the bottom of the social scale, for, he emphasized, there is not and there will not be a hereditary aristocracy in the American republic. But Mason did not think that this sociological criticism contradicted his political analogy with the House of Commons. In the same sense, Wilson compared America to a pyramid, whose base had to be as broad as possible because the stability and legitimacy of a republic rests on the confidence of the people. He added that popular election made the legislative body independent of the States, which was all the more desirable as the opposition to the measures voted by Congress had come from the State legislatures rather than from their populations. Finally, Madison added that popular election was a first stage in the process of selecting the best in a republic without a pre-existing hierarchy. Popular election, he added, would create the requisite feelings of mutual sympathy between the government and the people. None of these arguments convinced Gerry, who insisted on the lessons learned from the experience of direct democracy as practiced on the State level. Gerry therefore proposed as an alternative that the people select from a list of candidates which the legislative assembly of each State would designate. The initial proposal, direct and popular election, was finally adopted by six votes against two, two States remaining divided.[4]

The method of election to the upper house posed even greater problems. An amendment proposed that its members be chosen by the States. But proportional representation by population would then have implied an extremely large house, were Delaware, for example, to have even just one representative. The amendment was therefore withdrawn. Wilson pointed out that a second house chosen by the first one, as was foreseen under the Randolph Plan, would lack independence. He proposed the adoption of a system similar to that of New York (or Virginia, which we have analyzed above) where the creation of large districts had allowed for popular election of the upper house while ensuring that this house would embody a different political principle than that of the first one. A proposal by Pinckney, which was opposed to Randolph's, would have allowed the first house to choose the members of the second house from a list prepared by the States; this proposal was rejected by a vote of nine against two. But the original proposal by Randolph was also defeated, by seven votes against two.

The issue of the upper house was suspended in order to move to that of the powers of the national assembly. Deciding on the nature and extent of these powers might provide convincing arguments for those delegates who were still hesitant about the mode of selection for this assembly. Unanimity was rapidly achieved on the issue of the power to originate laws. More difficult, on the other hand, was the question of defining what matters the States were *not* competent to handle. Here again was one of the problems faced by the Articles of Confederation, which had strictly delimited the powers of the Congress. It is therefore not surprising that the Convention agreed with Madison's argument that an explicit enumeration of powers might create problems for some future government confronted with an unforeseen situation. The proposal granting supremacy to the national assembly was thus adopted in its general form. As to the question of its coercive powers, Madison, granting the difficulty of the issue, proposed to put off a decision, as it would depend upon the form the institutions themselves would take.

The debate over the executive revived the old fear of monarchy.[5] According to Pinckney, making the executive office an elective post was the most threatening option. According to some, what was needed was an active and energetic executive; others, true to the American tradition, wanted to leave the designation and description of his powers to the legislative body whose servant he would be. Another proposal suggested the addition of a council to the executive branch in order to give it more weight over against the legislature and to assure the people that there would be adequate control against instances of arbitrariness. Randolph himself was opposed to the principle of a single executive officer, seeing in it 'the foetus of monarchy'. Wilson replied that only a single executive officer could oppose the tyranny of the majority, but his motion was postponed at Madison's suggestion. Madison explained that, as with election to the upper house, it was better to define first the power of the executive branch before deciding on its form. The selection of the executive could be left to the people or to the legislature depending on whether one thought it necessary to preserve his independence or, on the contrary, saw this branch as a potential source of tyranny. This question as well as that of the length of the executive's term of office were debated further and then put off until later.[6] In a long speech, Dickinson defended his proposal that an executive could be impeached with the consent or at the suggestion of a majority of the States. He affirmed the need for a balance between the legislature and the executive, *and* between the national government and the States, the latter playing the role of an aristocratic chamber which was unable to take root in America. This idea, which preserved an important role for the States, would be taken up again later; the Convention, for the time being imbued with strictly nationalist aims, rejected it unanimously, with the sole exception of Delaware. National objectives still held sway over institutional questions, which nevertheless would resurface later.

The question of the make-up of the executive was re-examined from the standpoint of its practical implications. According to Wilson, those who advocated a plural executive feared that the people might think that they were seeking to restore monarchy. However, he noted, all the States had adopted a single executive, even if the power they had granted him varied from State to State. A triumvirate threatened to awaken animosities and struggles between those who held power, thus dividing the government. Sherman countered that every State had added councils to this executive in order to serve as a counterweight to him. But Gerry's comparison between a triple executive and a three-headed general won over a majority, which rallied to the idea of a single executive. Next, the question of the 'Council of revision' proposed in the Randolph Plan had to be settled. This led to a debate over absolute versus suspensive vetoes, which in turn brought up again the question of a singular or multiple executive. An absolute veto threatened to make the executive a monarch, creating a new form of tyranny, the elected monarch. On the other hand, the experience of the inconstancy of democratic rule argued in favour of some sort of veto power. It was therefore decided to give the executive the right to a suspensive veto, which could be overridden by a majority of two thirds of each of the two houses.

The succeeding debates on the judiciary, the amendment process and the procedure through which the new Constitution would take effect, issues which one might have imagined could take place without excessive complications, revealed the difficulties the Convention encountered on the practical level. The idea of executive nomination and legislative confirmation of judges was easy to understand for those familiar with the science of checks and balances, with history, and with politics. Nomination by the legislature would open the door to backroom manoeuvres; simple nomination by the executive power would concentrate too much authority in the hands of a single person. Moreover, the idea that the process of amendment should not depend on the legislative will alone was designed to facilitate the orderly adoption of necessary changes while preserving the republican idea of a government of laws in which one cannot be at the same time both judge and party in an affair. But debate on this question was postponed along with that on the oath state officials ought to take. The debate over how to call conventions to ratify the proposed new Constitution finally revealed the main problem: the need to win approval from the States. After a long discussion, Butler proposed that 'We must follow the example of Solon who gave the Athenians not the best Government he could devise; but the best they would receive'.[7] Political theory, too, had to be pragmatic.

The debate over practical matters returned to the questions that had previously been settled on the theoretical plane. Pinckney calculated that election of the members of the first house by the legislative assemblies of the States would guarantee their acceptance of the new Constitution. Gerry returned to his idea of nomination by the people and final selection by the assemblies of each State. Wilson opposed Gerry's suggestion with Adams' idea of a representation 'in miniature' of the entire society, adding to it Madison's idea about the advantage to be drawn from broader electoral districts. Mason contrasted the

168     *From Republican Politics to Liberal Sociology*

Confederation, in which the States were both subjects and objects of governmental action, to the new Constitution based on the people, who were conceived of as a set of individuals whose members should therefore elect their representatives.

At this point, Madison could use the arguments from his essay on 'The Vices of the Political System of the United States' concerning society's tendency to divide into interest groups that threaten to unite against a minority. He added references to Greek and Roman history, but also to English oppression and to slavery based on 'the mere distinction of colour'. His solution, as we have seen, was to enlarge the sphere of government. 'Divide the community into so great a number of interests and parties, that in the first place a majority will not be likely at the same moment to have a common interest separate from that of the whole or of the minority; and in the second place, that in case they should have such an interest, they may not be apt to unite in the pursuit of it'. But the Convention would not abandon inherited political theory so quickly. Dickinson distinguished between the fact that in a republic it is 'essential' for one legislative chamber to be based directly on the people, whereas it is only 'expedient' to let the other one be chosen by the States. He concluded that this combined method is 'as politic as it was unavoidable'. Pierce emphasized a theoretical implication of such a compromise, namely, that it permitted representation of the citizens of the various States both individually and collectively. Read's objection that the creation of a 'national' government would sooner or later eliminate the States found no support. Pinckney's proposal on the election of the first house by the States was defeated, but the theoretical foundation for its rejection was not understood in the same way by everyone. The problem would certainly arise again.

The nomination of the second house by the States, suggested by Dickinson, had the disadvantage of creating a large chamber if representation by population was adopted. Madison opposed this proposal by referring to the example of the Roman tribunes, whose numbers had increased at the same time that their influence declined. 'The more the representatives of the people were multiplied, the more they partook of the infirmities of their constituents, the more liable they became to be divided among themselves either from their own indiscretions or the artifices of the opposite faction, and of course the less capable of fulfilling their trust'. Gerry frankly objected to the idea of popular election of both houses on the grounds that two crucial social interests, those of commerce and of finance, risked losing everything. Curiously, no one seconded him. Dickinson brought up his proposal again, introducing this time the image of the solar system to explain the role he wanted to grant to the States, which were to be like planets around the sun, freely following their orbits. Too much centripetal force, or the absence of centrifugal forces, would destroy the proper functioning of the system. But Dickinson was all the more opposed to Madison with regard to the increased number of representatives, in that he wished to see the gradual creation of an equivalent of the English aristocracy. Wilson replied that the English model could not be applied in America, where the conditions for its existence were lacking. He did not wish the planets to be plunged into darkness, but neither did he think that it was they that heated the sun or provided it with light. As for Gerry's fears, he pointed out that the State legislatures were already oppressing those interests about which Gerry had expressed his concern. Mason came back to the idea that the States were to play the role of counterbalances in the system. Their role in the selection of the upper house would be precisely that. Dickinson's proposal to have the States choose the members of the upper house was therefore finally adopted. This was a defeat for those who wished for a national government, but they had to accept it as a lesser evil given the practical need for unanimity. Its theoretical implications, as suggested in the metaphor of the solar system, were yet to be defined. In the interim, the question of representation along demographic lines or according to the value of tax contributions, also remained in suspense.

Pinckney returned to the question of the national legislature's right to veto State laws. This was needed in order to put an end to the practice of indirect vetoes by the States which had done so much harm to the Confederation. Pinckney wanted to extend this veto right to cover all state laws and all state actions. Madison seconded him, again drawing his arguments from his essay on 'The Vices of the Political System of the United States'. A constitutional check such as veto power would convince the States of the uselessness of resistance and would obviate the need for coercive powers, an issue that had been briefly discussed during the debates before being postponed like so many other issues. According to the metaphor of the planetary system, the veto would allow the national government to assert control over the centrifugal tendencies of the States, preventing the States from leaving their orbits and destroying the harmony of the political system. But, asked Gerry, would such a practice really be conceivable in a society like that of the United States. Would the States accept being thus subjected?

Wilson replied with a comparison between the liberty of the States and that of individuals: the latter sacrifice their liberty by entering into society, even though abuses are always possible; the States must agree to make the same sacrifice. They did it, said Wilson, when the first Continental Congress affirmed that Virginia, Massachusetts and the other States no longer existed as *corporate* powers. But once State governments became established, jealousy, egotism and self-interest took over; the Confederation became impotent. Wilson did not think that there was a danger that the whole would sacrifice a part if this were not absolutely necessary; but, he insisted on the other hand, the whole ought not to be dependent on the part and on its particular interests. But the logic of these arguments for a national legislative veto power over the States did not succeed in convincing the delegates; the proposal was rejected by eight votes against four. It may be said that this vote marks a turning point in the debates.

The logic of the nationalist view now collided with the interests of the small States, as was clearly demonstrated the next day in the speeches of Paterson and Brearly. They returned to the issue of representation, which in the proposal under consideration would have granted 16 representatives to Virginia and a single one to Georgia. But neither was equal representation for all the States a just solution; and Brearly's proposal to redraw State boundaries was politically unthinkable, and not taken seriously. Yet no one was ready for compromises either. Paterson then put into question the whole discussion by challenging the Convention's authority: no one had envisaged a national government, and the people did not seem to him ready to accept it. Moreover, Paterson recalled, the Galloway Plan, which attempted to win representation in Parliament for the colonies, had been rejected by the Continental Congress. If this idea was rejected in 1774 because it was obvious that British domination would remain unchanged, why impose it now on the small States? Paterson warned the delegates that New Jersey as well as he personally would oppose such a proposal. Wilson's counter-argument that it was not clear why 150 inhabitants from Pennsylvania should be represented by the same number of representatives as 50 from New Jersey did not sway Paterson. Nor did a compromise proposal offered the next day by Sherman, which would have allowed for proportional representation in the lower house and equal representation of the States in the upper one, find an echo in the divisive atmosphere characterized by the defensive behaviour of the small States. Rutledge returned to an idea suggested at the beginning of the debates that would have allowed one house to be based upon representation by population and the other to have its representation formula based upon fiscal contributions. But the practical difficulties involved made this proposal impossible to implement. After a series of procedural manoeuvres, representation by State was rejected by the votes of six States against five. The narrowness of this victory implied that another solution would have to be found if the smaller States were to be satisfied and unity preserved.

## THE NEW JERSEY PLAN

The Randolph Plan, reworked by the Convention, was discussed in its final form on 13 June. The next day, at Paterson's request and on behalf of New Jersey and the other delegations from the small States, a one-day adjournment was allowed for them to draft a counterplan. The New Jersey Plan was presented by Paterson on 15 June and debated the following day. Explicitly taking the Articles of Confederation as its basis, it proposed to add to the powers already granted to the 'United States, in Congress assembled' the right 'to pass acts for raising a revenue, by levying a duty or duties on all goods or merchandises of foreign growth or manufacture, imported into any part of the United States'. The proceeds from a stamp duty – a Stamp Tax! – and the revenue from the postal system were to go to Congress, which would be able to spend this money as it saw fit. This plan also granted to Congress the right to regulate both international and interstate commerce, but punishment for infractions was to be imposed by the judicial systems of the States in which the infraction had taken place (with the opportunity to appeal errors of law and fact to the 'Judiciary of the States').

In the crucial question of the relationship between taxation and representation, Paterson proposed that the former be based upon population (with the three-fifths rule used for counting the slave population, as was already the case under the Confederation). If there was active or passive opposition on the part of the States, Congress was to be given the responsibility for assuring the collection of taxes, if it received the support of an as yet undetermined number of States. In as much as Paterson was proposing only a reform of the Confederation, and in as much as the Confederation already applied the principle of representative equality between the States, the plan did not deal with the question of representation. The legislature was to remain unicameral. A non-re-eligible executive, the number of whose members and the length of whose term of office also remained to be determined, was also proposed. This executive, which was to be the servant of the Congress, would be responsible for nominating certain federal officials and overseeing military operations, but it would not have the power to direct them. The members of the judiciary were to be appointed by the executive and to serve 'during good behaviour'. As a lower court, its jurisdiction comprised all cases involving accusations against government officials; as an appellate court, it could hear cases involving the violation of treaties and commercial agreements as well as tax collection issues. The system of checks and balances in this plan were therefore rather weak; the bulk of power was concentrated in the unicameral assembly.

Paterson concluded as he had begun, affirming the need to increase the powers of the national government. The laws passed by Congress and the treaties it ratified were considered as 'the supreme law of the respective States' even if they contradicted previously passed State laws. Individuals or States disobeying national law would be subject to punishment by 'the power of the Confederated States'. After a brief statement about the admission of new States (for which a republican form of government was not explicitly guaranteed), the plan concluded by affirming the existence of a common citizenship and a principle of judicial reciprocity which recognized that a crime committed in a State by a citizen of another State is still considered a crime. Nonetheless, although it proposed a reform of the Confederation, this plan did not challenge its political foundation – State sovereignty. It simply expressed the dilemma in which the Convention found itself caught: between the advocates of a truly national system and the adversaries of any attack upon the sovereignty of their States. Because it recognized the existence of a common citizenship and affirmed the superiority of the laws of the Congress and of its treaties, the Paterson Plan might have created a government capable of dealing directly with the most important and pressing matters facing the Confederation; but the States' continued domination of the single national legislative body offered the prospect of further conflicts among the States. Moreover, the nationalists viewed the organization of the judiciary system in terms of the authority of the States and the weakness of the executive as reasons why such a system would make it impossible to establish long-run harmony, even if it could be achieved in the short term. After two weeks of debates, which increasingly seemed to go round in circles, Franklin pointed out that, unlike the sessions of the Continental Congress that led to the Declaration of Independence, the Convention had not once opened its meetings with a daily prayer. His proposal to that effect was discussed briefly, being supported by some and criticized by others, until a parliamentary manoeuvre permitted the day's session to be adjourned.

The debates seemed to have reached the point of deadlock. Divine intervention itself had been adjourned!

Some of the differences between the Randolph and Paterson plans suggest the direction in which a final compromise (ultimately proposed by Sherman on behalf of Connecticut and now known as the 'Connecticut Compromise') would take shape. This compromise established neither a national system nor a reinforcement of the confederal one, but a new political form, liberal federalism. In this political structure, sovereignty resides neither in the States nor in a singular national will but with the people in their plurality, who exercise this sovereignty through a system of representation in which the representative and the represented can never coincide or be identical. The differences between the first two plans are first of all theoretical. Paterson, returning in his own way to Butler's comparison between the work of drafting the Constitution and Solon's effort, emphasized that it was not a question of perfecting the best regime but only the one desired by their constituents, that is to say, the States. Wilson, in contrast, declared his support for the Randolph Plan, pointing out that the Convention was only making proposals; the true constituents, the free and sovereign people, were left free to decide. Paterson then insisted that unanimity was required for any reform of the Confederation, basing his argument on the contractual character of a treaty between those legally autonomous entities, the States. Once a new treaty were unanimously signed, he would be ready to accept other States' right to exercise coercive powers as a last resort against a signatory State that failed to respect expressly signed convenants. Randolph, for his part, wanted to avoid the need for such use of coercive power; he therefore emphasized that the authority of the national government was to be exercised directly upon the individuals of which it is representative. This kind of representation of the people – and not of the States, as in the Congress of the Confederation – would guarantee the legitimacy of the national authority and allow it to avoid having to have recourse to force. In other words, Paterson remained within the framework of Old Whig thought, which aimed at controlling power, whereas Randolph sought to create a republican structure within which power is channelled by the structure of its institutions. Neither one resolved the problem posed by the replacement of the classical image of the public and virtuous man by the private and self-interested one. Nevertheless, Randolph's argument, which placed the emphasis on legitimacy and the direct relationship between the government and the citizen, had an important consequence that remains to be explained: a legitimate power does not exercise a form of coercion; rather, *power is transformed into authority* in a way that shows the Old Whig presupposition to be anachronistic. But this implication was not drawn out during these rather pragmatic discussions. We will encounter it only in the reflection on these events.

The first of the concrete differences between the two plans is the contrast between a unicameral assembly and institutions structured by checks and balances so as to counteract what Wilson called the legislative despotism exercised by an assembly possessing total sovereignty. This contrast concerns first of all the form of representation foreseen by the two plans: proportional for one, equality among the States for the other. The latter type of representation creates in fact a measure of inequality from the standpoint of population as well as from that of the wealth of the disparate States. In such a system it is possible for a minority (from the standpoint of demography or wealth) to dictate its will to a majority. In contrast, proportional representation permits a greater centralization of power and a broader jurisdiction as well as justifying the exercise of a veto power over State laws. Indeed, the Paterson Plan did not guarantee a single executive officer, and it tried to control the power of the executive branch by allowing a recall vote to be decided by a majority of the States. Although the Randolph Plan was vague about the functions of the executive branch, its advocates made a point of emphasizing the potential for corruption and disharmony that would come with a plural executive. Some found advantages in assigning this role to a single occupant of the executive office, particularly with regard to the efficacy of its action, but others on the contrary saw in it the danger of monarchy. Debate on this issue had been postponed in order to determine first the objectives to be assigned to this office before deciding what form it would take. This method, however, was ineffectual in as much as the definition of the executive's functions would depend ultimately on the structure of representation in the legislature. In the Randolph Plan, the executive was, in effect, an integral part of the system of checks and balances and opposed to the legislative branch's attempts to monopolize power; it was not to be a simple agent for executing the latter's directives. Indeed, the use of the term 'executive' to designate this function within the new federal political organization no longer corresponded to reality.[8] The contrast between the two proposed forms of legislative representation in the Virginia and New Jersey plans consequently entailed two different conceptions of the nature and functioning of the executive branch. The eventual resolution of the problem of the executive depended therefore on a new analysis which, in turn, would permit a new interpretation of the nature of representation.

The advocates of Randolph's plan now began an attack on the Paterson Plan. Hamilton summarized the criticism, familiar since the debate with England, against an *imperium in imperio* and then asked what useful role States could play in a continental government.[9] Madison, in turn, resorted to threats. Would the small States really be viable if they remained alone or joined in miniconfederations? King rejected the idea of applying the concept of 'sovereign' to the States since, as he said, they make neither peace nor war and vote on neither alliances nor treaties. As political entities, they are mute, for they do not speak to other sovereign entities and remain deaf to their entreaties; moreover, they lack the organs necessary either to defend themselves or to attack others. Thus, King concluded, the States have already abandoned *de facto* the essential part of their sovereignty. In his response, Martin defended the proposition that separation from England had recreated a state of nature among the States, which then confederated on an equal footing. Wilson and Hamilton rejected this thesis, whose foundations and ambiguities we have already noted. Wilson reread the Declaration of Independence to show that it was together, and not one by one or individually, that the States had declared themselves independent; their independence and their unity arose simultaneously. The rights the States eventually obtained therefore depended solely on the united and independent nation. Hamilton then took the floor again to assuage the fears of the small States by pointing out that the existence of common regional interests guaranteed that the three large States – Virginia, Massachusetts, and Pennsylvania – would not unite against the small ones. This statement of reassurance, however, no more succeeded in quieting the minds of the delegates from the small States than did the threats.[10] The potential role of regional interests mentioned by Hamilton was not understood on the theoretical plane but only in terms of political strategy.

In their response, the small States attacked the proposed nature of the upper house which, by its form and often by the arguments invoked in its favour, reminded them of English institutions. But their critique was not purely formal. Pinckney's long speech on 25 June established a few fundamental points. Yes, the English Constitution is the best in the world; but no, we cannot introduce it here. Looking closely at social conditions in America, one hardly finds distinctions based on fortune, and still less those founded on social rank; each possesses the same rights; 'a very moderate share of property', he explained, entitles people 'to the possession of all the honours and privileges the public can bestow'. And this state of equality will continue, given that so much undeveloped land is still available to immigrants and that urban labourers will be generously remunerated for this very reason. Moreover, the balance between the Crown and the people cannot be reproduced in a society without privileges; and the absence of a powerful executive means that there is no need to create balances to offset potential abuses of power on his part. Pinckney then asked where this wealth of which a Senate is supposed to be the protector is to be found? Landed wealth is well divided and not greatly productive; those with monetary and financial wealth are few in number; and everyone knows that commerce has never given birth to a nobility. The Convention is fooling itself by trying to model its institutions on a non-existent society; it is fooling itself, too, by setting as its objective the creation of a government whose authority will be respected by foreign powers. Pinckney simply wanted what he calls a modest government appropriate to modest American conditions. He saw a society made up of three classes – professional, commercial and propertied – who depend upon each other within a unified whole. These classes are not estates or antagonistic orders, as in England; if one insists on using the English model, they would all be comparable to strata represented within the Commons. One must therefore not seek to create a tripartite government because two of the three institutions supposedly necessary to that structure have nothing specific to represent. One ought, on the contrary, to maintain the role of the States in a simple, unicameral system.

This sociological analysis in which Pinckney defended the position of the small States could claim to reconcile the Old Whig outlook of the States with a republican structure founded on the existence of a *res publica* common to the entire society. And yet at the same time, it conceals a contradiction that suggests the direction in which the eventual compromise would move. Pinckney's sociology revealed the lack of *social* foundations for the classical *political* principles that served to justify the Old Whig and the republican outlooks. It is not possible to adhere simultaneously to sociological analysis and to classical politics. Since the first shows the absence of foundations for the second, one must find new political principles compatible with this new sociology (the old politics having already failed). Pinckney did not develop his analysis, which was aimed basically at refuting the arguments of the nationalists. Indeed, his own premises limited the import of his sociology in as much as the relationship between his three classes was conceived along the lines of the organicist and harmonic model inherited from classical political thought.

Wilson's and Madison's responses to Pinckney stressed the specific nature of the upper house. Wilson emphasized the representative character of the institutions of the States and of those of the nation. Representation is the basis of the republic. It therefore ought to be similar in both houses, which excludes the idea of having the state assemblies choose the nation's representatives. The upper house does not differ from the first except in the political – and not social – function it is responsible for fulfilling. But Wilson failed to specify here what this political function is. His proposal to have the second house designated by electors chosen for this purpose by the people was not seconded. Madison then took up the discussion in terms of a variation on the state of nature theme. A people seeks to endow itself with institutions in order to protect itself both against those who govern it and against the temporary passions that can seize hold of the people itself. This image was obviously drawn from the confederal experience: protecting oneself from those who govern corresponds to Old Whig thought; protecting oneself from one's own passions recalls the crisis lived through at that time. Although the analysis of that crisis belongs to the new political sociology and although Madison also granted, along with Pinckney, the absence of hereditary distinctions, he would not admit a present, and still less a future, equality of conditions. The new Constitution nevertheless had to take this potential future into consideration. There were still not agrarian laws in America, but a levelling spirit was beginning to make itself felt, notes Madison (who probably knew of the agrarian law the Pennsylvania constitution had considered and rejected). Population growth will transform work conditions while universal suffrage will transfer power toward the oppressed classes who will demand an equal distribution of resources. How can oppression of a propertied minority by the majority be avoided without abandoning republican principles? Among other things, by the creation of a wise and virtuous second house, whose nine-year term of office would guarantee its independence and whose age-based conditions for eligibility would assure both wisdom and experience. Madison's counter-sociology here brings out an originality of American social conditions which Pinckney had misunderstood. Not only does there exist no Crown and no nobility; there no longer are any homogeneous and organically connected social groups (or pre-modern corporations) but rather just individuals with their own interests and activities whose social condition has evolved and will evolve further. A dynamic society demands a Constitution adequate to its inherent mutability. The *res publica* of such a society can be neither fixed nor presupposed. The prospect of a dynamic future that challenges the organic State which is at the basis of classical thought is founded on individualist premises. These premises replace the sociological politics of the mixed constitution with a liberal political sociology whose implications remained to be drawn.

The path toward a practical compromise was still long, although, on 29 June, Dr Johnson took up again the idea, already proposed by Sherman, of trying to guarantee to the States at least a negative liberty by organizing representation of one house of the legislative branch along the lines of equality between the States with the other organized proportionally. Ellsworth supported the same idea without claiming to justify it in theory. This compromise was violently rejected the next day by King, who was himself attacked by Dayton for his rhetorical excesses which were said to have substituted statement for proof and intimidation for argumentation. This kind of transgression had been rather rare in these debates (which were held, it will be recalled, behind closed doors precisely in order to avoid such excesses). Bedford returned to the defence of the small States, from the standpoint of *Realpolitik*, accusing the large States of a conspiracy – although Hamilton had already shown why this was not possible for sociological reasons. Bedford was in any case convinced that the large States had too great an interest in the continuation of the union to risk its dissolution. The small States therefore held a position of relative strength. The debates had again reached an impasse. It was proposed that a committee be set up to work out a compromise.[11]

## THE COMPROMISE AND THE PUBLIC DEBATE

The compromise proposed by this committee on 5 July attempted to take into account the fears of both sides, granting equal representation for the States in the upper house while basing representation in the lower house proportionally on population. This concession on equality for small States in the Senate was compensated by the fact that the popular house was to have the right to initiate all bills for raising revenues (which the upper house had the right to accept or to reject but not to amend). This proposal was not easily accepted; the threat of secession, images of civil war or unity conquered by the sword were brandished by some while others pleaded for the interest of humankind in preserving a unique republican experience that could still be saved by compromise. A new committee suggested a reapportionment of representatives based on changes of wealth and population in the States. This raised the question of the representation of slaves, who had been considered both as property and as part of the population. From grand compromises on principle, the delegates proceeded to compromises based upon self-interest. Local interests took the upper hand, for example, when King insisted that New Hampshire deserved three representatives rather than two. Regional interests also re-entered into the discussion. The eventual role to be played by the West was hotly debated. Gerry admitted his fear of seeing the West one day dominate the Atlantic States and proposed that a limitation be placed on the number of new States that could be admitted into the Union. The principle of a regular census of the population was accepted along with a compromise on the representation of slaves, who would be considered as three fifths of a person in electoral statistics. But nothing was yet resolved on the basic issues.

The principal compromise was again put into question during the debate over taxes. Gouverneur Morris criticized the conflicts of interest that this threatened to revive. Either the conflict is real, he said, and the only thing to do is to agree to separate amicably; or else not all interests can claim equal protection. But in the latter case, how was one to distinguish between them? A society without estates or orders is a homogeneous society in which all interests are qualitatively equal. A proposal by Randolph attempted a new compromise by defining the instances in which equal representation should be granted to all the States. This idea already figured in his original plan, which provided for representation by population or fiscal contribution 'as the one or the other rule may seem best in different cases'. But once again, how can one define these situations? The debates were again at an impasse as tempers rose; the atmosphere became rather pessimistic. As if they wanted to gamble everything on an attempt to break this impasse, Paterson and Randolph reached an agreement on a proposal that the rule imposing secrecy be lifted and that all the delegates return to their constituents rather than continue a frustrating and sterile debate. Randolph asked for adjournment in an ambiguous statement that might have been interpreted as the declaration of a rupture. Pinckney saw in this the end of all hope; but Paterson and other delegates from the small States proved intransigent. They ended up winning their case. The compromise was agreed to on 17 July. Provisions granting the States representation in the Senate as well as jurisdiction over domestic policy matters were adopted. The idea, dear to Madison and the nationalists, of granting Congress veto power over State laws was abandoned. Sure enough, the large States had too great an interest in preserving the union. The delegates could now proceed to the details – which were no simple matter.

The debate over how to nominate the executive and how this office should function depended on a conception of the principle of its representative nature. Wilson noted that the delegates were unanimously against the principle of the legislature designating the executive, unless the executive were not subject to re-election. Direct election was a better solution, since the executive was to serve as a counterbalance to the legislature – which assumed that he could be re-elected and that there be an independent basis to his power. Paterson proposed that this officer be nominated by electors chosen for this purpose by the States. Once again a compromise between popular and state sovereignty had to be found. Madison insisted that the separation of powers implied also their mutual independence. The method for nominating the executive should serve to set him apart from all legislative pressure. Popular election would fit this criterion, but the conditions for the exercise of suffrage in a large country still posed problems. Madison therefore accepted the method of choosing electors as the best possible solution. But how to choose them? The debate of 20 July did not answer this question. So as not to remain in this impasse, and since the old fear of executive power was still alive, the delegates turned to the problem of impeachment, still from the standpoint of safeguarding the independence of the executive as required by the doctrine of the separation of powers. The Convention had agreed the day before on a six-year term, a length of time considered necessary to assure steadfastness in the execution of his duties, which were assumed to be sometimes unpopular. Abuses of this independence now had to be guarded against while also preserving it. The solution finally found, which divides the roles between the two houses and the judiciary, is an elegant illustration of the American science of checks and balances, but we no longer need to follow here the details of how it was worked out.[12] The great pragmatic principle on which unity was to be built had finally been attained: the President would be elected to a four-year term; he would be at the same time dependent upon both houses, in case of impeachment and for the confirmation of other executive officers that he would nominate; and he would be independent of them because he would be selected by electors chosen in the States, possibly even by a popular vote.

Although the debates, which lasted until 8 September, no longer posed a challenge to the compromise that had been worked out, they did reveal that this compromise was based upon practical necessities and not on a theory or even on a 'science' applied to a resistant reality. The alleged science of checks and balances lent itself to arguments based on the self-interests of all sides. Finally, the compromise draft that brought about unity was recast for stylistic purposes by a committee led by Gouverneur Morris. The proposed Constitution was then sent to the Congress of the Confederation with the request that it be submitted to conventions specially called for this purpose by the States so that the people could express themselves on the issue of its ratification. Before signing, Randolph took the floor once again on 15 September to express his dissatisfaction. He asked the Convention to add to the document a call for amendments, which would be discussed at a second Convention. Mason supported him, insisting on the role to be played by the people, who until now had been excluded by the secrecy of the deliberations. Gerry added a list of eight detailed criticisms and three objections in principle that prevented him from approving the work of the Convention. Randolph's proposal was rejected unanimously and the Constitution was adopted. A statement from the venerable Franklin recommended that everyone sign the document in order to preserve unity in the eyes of public opinion and because the new Constitution assuredly was better than the one presently in force. The formula Franklin proposed for signing the document indicates that the delegates were expecting resistance to their plan: 'Done in Convention by the unanimous consent of the States present the 17th of September . . . In Witness whereof we have hereunto subscribed our names'. The consent of the *States* present did not guarantee ratification by conventions in these States. Moreover, Gerry, Randolph and Mason refused to sign.

The debate could now continue on the public stage. The criticisms addressed to the Congress of the Confederation by Richard Henry Lee of Virginia did not prevent the text from being sent to the States, but neither did the Congress attach to it a statement of its express approval. The most determined opposition came from Virginia, led by Lee, Patrick Henry and Randolph, and from New York, where local politics fed the antagonism between Governor Clinton's faction and that of Schuyler (whose delegate in Philadelphia was Hamilton, whereas Clinton's representatives, Lansing and Yates, had departed before the debate was closed). Generally speaking, this opposition was rather heterogeneous in character, and the positions adopted were often conditioned by the influences of local politics. Strong opposition was found in the western parts of Massachusetts and Pennsylvania whose self-sufficient communities felt threatened.[13] In general, local politicians could find an interest in exploiting the populist vein of resentment against other claimants to local power. In New York, for example, Clinton had made himself famous by his populist proposal to tax people proportionally to their real wealth. Finally, there were, of course, many sincere opponents who could invoke the old and dear principles for which they had declared independence and made war. But others supported the new institutions precisely because they feared that the liberty they had won was being stolen by the enemy within or was being wasted away by internal struggles. To these advocates of the Constitution were added many urban artisans who had suffered from the recession that followed the war and from the rise in English imports that were being sold at low prices as a way of recapturing the old markets. These artisans could argue that national taxes would affect only the rich; that unity would protect American commerce; and even that the young nation, full of vigour, would place military orders that would create new jobs.[14] The advocates of the Constitution, therefore, were not only speculators and members of the propertied classes, as the 'progressive' historians' thesis later maintained.

At the level of principles, the objections were varied. Many of the ideas and arguments were well known. Some saw in the establishment of a national government the beginnings of the kind of corruption they had combatted in the Court at London. Others criticized the power of the executive, some proposing to add to it a council that would guarantee against possible abuses. The elimination of annual elections were often denounced, as this practice had been at the heart of Old Whig politics. Opponents often used variations on the three arguments of principle raised by Gerry at the close of the Convention. They denounced the implications of the clause granting the national legislature the power to make all laws it considered 'necessary and proper' for the maintenance of the union. Congress's unlimited power to raise armies and to levy taxes was also rejected, notably because of the experience that had not so long ago led to the establishment of Walpole's 'corrupt' oligarchy. Further, some clauses seemed in certain cases to allow for trial without jury, thereby appearing to confirm the oligarchic aims already being ascribed to the nationalists. Finally, on top of everything else, the opponents of this Constitution constantly harked back to their conviction that the Convention had exceeded its mandate; the thesis of a political *coup d'état* was in no way the invention of historians of our century. This distrust of the political, inherited from the struggle against England, was widely shared. The nationalists who had cleverly renamed themselves 'Federalists', had first to combat this distrust. Indeed, it is with regard to this general rejection of the political that the most prevalent criticism may be understood: namely, the absence of a Bill of Rights, which would have protected people from political interferences in private life.[15]

The first convention held in a large State was that of Massachusetts, where Gerry led the opposition. The critiques were many and varied. Biennial elections for the House were condemned along with the acceptance of slavery and the lack of any provision guaranteeing that all public officials would be Christians. Luxury, corruption and the greedy pursuit of power were denounced, as were pride and ambition, which were thought to harm the sentiments of frugality, republicanism and patriotism. The *Boston Gazette* accused the advocates of the Constitution of accepting bribes – paid, moreover, with 'foreign' money – that is to say, from the other States. Along the same lines, fears of the establishment of a standing army during peacetime were expressed, for, it was said, this would bring into the State foreigners (again, those from the other federated States) to collect taxes, exactly as the old English masters had sent their tax officials accompanied by troops. Lawyers, men of letters and the rich were attacked as the true beneficiaries of this new system. The defence of local liberty went hand in hand with a sort of ascetic puritanism, which seemed to doubt the steadfastness of its own virtue. Thus, to cite only one example, a small farmer, Amos Singletary, rose to declare: 'These lawyers, and men of learning, and moneyed men, that talk so finely, and gloss over matters so smoothly, to make us poor illiterate people swallow down the pill, expect to get into Congress themselves; they expect to be the managers of this Constitution, and to get all the power and all the money into their own hands, and then they will swallow up all us little folks, like the great *Leviathan*, Mr. President; yes, just as the whale swallowed up *Jonah*. This is what I am afraid of'. But another small farmer was quick to respond to him. After having mentioned Shays' Rebellion, Jonathan Smith stated that 'Had any person, that was able to protect us, come and set up his standard, we should all have flocked to it, even if it had been a monarch; and that monarch might have proved a tyrant; – so that you see that anarchy leads to tyranny, and better have one tyrant than so many at once'. This perfectly classical response to the pre-modern criticisms expressed by Singletary was accompanied by the reproach that Singletary was wallowing in his own resentment. Smith and his fellow supporters were right, but the balance was tipped ultimately to the side of the advocates of the Constitution only when their adversaries announced, just before the vote, that in case they were beaten, they would continue henceforth their battle within the framework of the new institutions. Finally, after a long and detailed reading of the entire document, the Massachusetts Convention adopted it by 187 to 168 – a margin of 19 votes out of a total of 335; a change of ten votes would therefore have defeated the ratification effort.

The polemics were even more ferocious in Virginia, where the flamboyant hero of the Revolution and the governor of the State, Patrick Henry, fought against the calm and logical Madison. First, Henry denounced the opening statement, 'We the People of the United States, in Order to form a more perfect Union . . . do ordain and establish this Constitution for the United States of America'. According to Henry, this preamble, legally speaking, should have declared: 'We the States of the United States . . .'. The authors of the Constitution were therefore accused of having gone beyond their mandate. No, responded Randolph, who had changed sides after the Massachusetts experience; the Articles of Confederation could not really have been repaired. Randolph explained that he now supported the new Constitution and that he would propose amendments within the framework of the procedure prescribed therein. This defection demoralized the opponents of the Constitution. Mason, who maintained his opposition, evoked the danger that the national will would destroy the State governments, just as the old principle of *imperium in imperio* predicted. History seemed to him to indicate that only a monarchy can govern a large territory; popular governments are made for small communities. But, responded Pendleton, the national will established by the Constitution is not limitless, as you well know; and one of these limits resides precisely in the right of the States to legislate within their own domain. Nevertheless, the most important criticism concerned the lack of a Bill of Rights.[16] But rather than insisting on this point, which undoubtedly would have attracted the support of other delegates, Henry and his fellow opponents launched a line by line attack upon the Constitution in a marathon session that seems to have ended up harming their cause, notably among those who were convinced of the need for a serious reform of the Confederation but who were frightened by the nationalism underlying the proposed document. In his final speech, like Massachusetts opponents of the Constitution, Henry rejected in advance any recourse to violence (which had been mentioned during the debates) and promised to struggle peacefully within the framework of the new institutions for the defence of liberty. A proposal that would have made ratification subject to the annexation of a Bill of Rights was rejected by 88 to 80. The motion to ratify was then adopted 89 to 79; a change of six votes would have tipped the balance against the new Constitution.

With Virginia's ratification, and that of Massachussetts, there remained only the crucial vote of New York. The nine-State quota necessary for formal ratification had been reached, but New York was a geographically crucial State for the country's practical political unity. The course of its debates were decisively influenced by the publication in several newspapers of a series of articles written under the name of 'Publius' by Hamilton, Madison and Jay and collected under the title of *The Federalist*. This document constitutes the most mature expression of the thought and of the actual situation that gave birth to the American Constitution. The history of interpretations it has given rise to and the role they played in helping a Constitution written two hundred years ago to endure so long would by themselves merit a separate study. Our goal will be different. The compromise that allowed for the creation of the Constitution had been justified above all on pragmatic grounds. The political theory of the time was invoked only after the fact in order to legitimate compromises already decided upon. And yet, as both Pinckney and Madison had insisted for their own reasons, America was not Europe. What would be the result of applying European political theory to a novel situation? What is the new political practice that results from it? Does it answer the questions left up in the air by the contradictions resulting from the opposition between republican thought and the political concepts of American Old Whigs? The 85 essays included in *The Federalist*, written at a rate of two or three a week during the period preceding the New York Convention, follow the debate and try to respond to the questions, doubts and objections raised by Publius's contemporaries. *The Federalist* is therefore not a book of political philosophy but rather the expression of a new politics still feeling its way. Like the Revolution itself, this book is to be interpreted in its own practice.[17]

# 11 History Reflected: How to Represent Popular Sovereignty?

We have seen that the Constitution was the product of a series of practical compromises and that the concrete content of the application of the 'science' of the separation of powers and the system of checks and balances was in fact the result of a debate among opposing interests. The Constitution is a short and often a quite ambiguous document. Whereas the Articles of Confederation explained in detail the limits and obligations of the central authority, the Constitution allows a broader interpretation of its role. For example, the long list of the powers of Congress in Article 1, Section 8, concludes by granting it the right 'To make all Laws which shall be necessary and proper to carrying into Execution the foregoing Powers, and all other Powers vested by this Constitution in the Government of the United States, or in any Department or Officer thereof'. The first part of this clause is already rather generous; the second part can become perfectly elastic. The history of the Constitution and therefore, in a certain manner, of the Republic can be written from the standpoint of the constitutional battle between the States and the national government. But such a history explains nothing: if the Constitution is elastic, the dynamic through which its potential is realized must still be comprehended. If we are justified in treating *The Federalist* as the theoretical reflection of the new politics that emerged from the Revolution, this is because of its function as a political pamphlet involved intimately with the events that produced the Constitution, events which continue to influence the sense of the politics for which it is the framework.

The first two paragraphs of the first number of *The Federalist* define the apparently opposite poles that structured the American Revolution since its beginning.[1] There is first of all the rationalist if not utopian goal of trying to construct a scientific politics. It is not by accident that the authors of *The Federalist* adopted the pseudonym 'Publius' rather than Brutus, Cato, Caesar or any of the other pseudonyms used frequently by the pamphleteers of the era. The Publius depicted by Plutarch is not the defender of a threatened republic, as the Old Whig style of thought would have had it, but one of its founders, comparable to Solon in

Athens. Thus, the first paragraph insists that 'It has been frequently remarked that it seems to have been reserved to the people of this country, by their conduct and example, to decide the important question, whether societies of men are really capable or not of establishing good government from reflection and choice, or whether they are forever destined to depend for their political constitutions on accident and force'. Publius emphasizes the responsibility Americans now have on their shoulders: 'A wrong election of the part we shall act may, in this view, deserve to be considered as the general misfortune of mankind'. But the author of these words, Hamilton, might recall the five-hour speech he had delivered to the Convention on 18 June, when he insisted that the history of republican experiences justifies the advocacy of a strong government based on an aristocracy and combined with a monarch named for life! He cannot pretend to believe that a new application of the old political science would allow the country to avoid these difficulties, which seem to be inherent in the social existence of individual men. If he claims that the 'good choice' is now within the grasp of the American people, he must be inspired by another conception of the political.

The second paragraph of the first number is more disillusioned, no doubt as a reflection on the political experience of the Confederation. This 'good choice' is 'a thing more ardently to be wished than seriously to be expected'. Indeed, 'the plan offered to our deliberation affects too many particular interests, innovates upon too many local institutions, not to involve in its discussion a variety of objects foreign to its merits, and of views, passions and prejudices little favourable to the discovery of truth'. Still more concretely, the next paragraph adds that among the obstacles the new Constitution will have to face is 'the obvious interest of a certain class of men in every State to resist all changes which may hazard a diminution of the power, emolument, and consequence of the offices they hold under the State establishments; and the perverted ambition of another class of men, who will . . . hope to aggrandise themselves by the confusions of their country . . .' More than a pre-emptive counter-attack, these arguments express the new sociological orientation that had begun to appear, for example, in Madison's essay on 'The Vices of the Political System of the United States', and at the Convention.

Publius knows that he cannot disregard the actual social situation. In the following seven essays of *The Federalist*, he is satisfied to praise the advantages of a national political union over the precarious and uncertain ties of the Confederation. Then, in Number 9, he resumes the task of social analysis from the standpoint of classical political thought: 'It is impossible to read the history of the petty republics of Greece and Italy without feeling the sensations of horror and disgust at the distractions with which they were continually agitated, and at the rapid succession of revolutions by which they were kept in a state of perpetual vibration between the extremes of tyranny and anarchy'. Publius emphasizes further 'the tempestuous waves of sedition' and 'party rage' as the vices of these republican governments. The lesson had not been forgotten, as Publius well knows. He had promised to examine six topics – the advantages of the union, the shortcomings of the Confederation, the need for an energetic government, the conformity of the new constitution to republican principles, and its analogy to the State constitutions, as well as the contribution it makes to the preservation of liberty. This initial plan was modified as practical needs arose and the objections of critics surfaced. *The Federalist* is decidedly not abstract theory.

The aristocrats, monarchists and 'advocates of despotism' are not the only ones to use the pretext of these sad lessons of history as a ground for rejecting the idea of a republican government founded on 'the very principles of civil liberty'. This is also the argument of the opponents of the new Constitution who fear that a national government will weaken their local power. Publius notes, however, that 'the science of politics, . . . like most other sciences, has received great improvement. The efficacy of various principles is now well understood, which were either not known at all, or imperfectly known to the ancients. The regular distribution of power into distinct departments; the introduction of legislative balances and checks; the institution of courts composed of judges holding their offices during good behaviour, the representation of the people in the legislature by deputies of their own election . . . are means, and powerful means, by which the excellencies of republican government may be retained and its imperfections lessened and avoided'. All the protective methods mentioned in this ninth number of *The Federalist* were applied in the elaboration of the Constitution. Publius also points out another method, this time sociological rather than institutional, for guarding against the internal ravages of a republic. This protection is taken up again in Number 10.[2] Before turning to it, we should note first that the Republic, which Publius claims is both viable and desirable, is founded on what he calls 'civil liberty' or popular sovereignty. This foundation plays a role, at once positive and negative, of motive force and limit point. The institutional analysis of this role will allow us to understand both Publius' optimism and the new politics underlying his optimism.

The techniques that allow modern political science to order institutions in such a way as to preserve civil liberty are not without their dangers. The balance established among the institutions thus organized can be so delicate that they threaten to interfere with one another, thereby paralyzing the entire system; or, if they are too well calibrated, they may collapse like a house of cards at the slightest breeze. At the other extreme, the divisions that are supposed to guarantee the separation of power among the branches or between the government and civil society can prove to be too great, provoking a *de facto* split that reduces both sides to impotence. These two cases, to which Publius refers in Number 47 (which introduces a detailed discussion of institutions that begins in Number 51), are avoided by the Constitution, thanks to the role it grants to popular sovereignty. Popular sovereignty serves, first of all, as a motor that prevents the machinery from jamming up; it acts at the same time as a sort of glue, assuring that the separation of powers does not culminate in their becoming wholly autonomous from each other. This positive role attributed to popular sovereignty may be seen in the functioning of the bicameral legislature which, it seemed to the participants at Philadelphia, could only be justified on pragmatic grounds in the compromise that granted the States equal representation in the Senate and representation proportional to population in the House. This pragmatic justification was, in a certain sense, more satisfying than the arguments in favour of bicameralism advanced by John Adams and implemented, for example, in Massachusetts or in Virginia. But the analysis of *The Federalist* opens new ground.

The fact that the American Republic is founded on popular sovereignty implies that its government is necessarily *limited*. This idea of a limitation of governmental authority had been present since the inception of the conflict with England, for example when Otis invoked a sort of natural law that would restrain the power exercised by Parliament. It reappeared in the rejection, by the citizens of Massachusetts, of a constitution that did not originate from a convention specially elected for this purpose. It had been actualized in another form in the institution of a council of censors in Pennsylvania, which functioned as a sort of popular senate. We now encounter it again in *The Federalist*. Otis' concerns, for example, reappear in the explanation, at first sight surprising, offered in Number 84. Publius argues that the Constitutions's affirmation of popular sovereignty obviates the need for a Bill of Rights since there is now no separate and distinct power against which the people have to be protected. This suggests that the natural rights which Otis ultimately had to confer upon the self-correcting parliamentary process are now connected to the political dynamic of the

Republic.[3] Similarly, the concerns of the citizens of Massachusetts appear in Numbers 38 and 39 which stress the idea that it is up to the citizens, assembled in a convention, rather than the States to ratify the Constitution. The same preoccupation is expressed in the argument concerning the Constitution's amendment process, which can be initiated either by the Congress or by the States, but must finally obtain the support of both. Finally, and perhaps most importantly, the role played by the Pennsylvania Censors is assured now by the judiciary, the guardian of the Constitution and, through its judgements, the interpreter of a popular sovereignty whose concrete content is open to constant change. These multiple roles assumed by popular sovereignty which culminate here in a judiciary that has become truly an autonomous institution of government, suggest the presence of a new way of thinking about the political framework within which politics occurs. The creation of a constitutional judiciary transforms this branch into a genuine political counterbalance to the other branches of government. This innovation was made practically necessary by the multiplicity of laws passed by the State legislatures, which challenged the relation between the generality of law and its application to particular cases. There remained, however, the problem of finding a political form for this innovation. Publius broaches this subject within the context of his analysis of the judiciary. The judiciary does not represent a specific political *virtue*, as it might in the classical view of politics; rather, it protects popular sovereignty against political laws, the universal application of which risks violating the particularism inherent in social interests.

Historians and lawyers are still debating over the 'intentions' of the Founding Fathers on the subject of 'judicial review'. For some, this idea of granting such vast power to the judiciary was far from the will of the Convention – which, after all, had rejected a proposal to grant the national government veto power over state laws despite the tenacious defence of this proposal offered by Madison and his supporters. Madison finally had to concede this point, and it is doubtful that his opponents would have allowed him later to insert this power elsewhere in the Constitution. The doctrine of judicial review therefore appears to have become rooted in constitutional practice only afterwards, under the pressure of political circumstances the Founders had not foreseen. Other contingencies could then be said to make it necessary to limit this power that had become, according to some, 'exorbitant'. As President Andrew Jackson might have asked in the 1830s, how many divisions does the Supreme Court have? But if the Constitution is indeed the result of a compromise, and if the brevity of its wording lends itselt to ambiguities, one cannot rule out the possibility that the authors had written a document open to the future, and that the doctrine of judicial review is implied in that orientation. From this standpoint, *The Federalist* would be part of a political evolution foreseen by the Founding Fathers.[4] Historical interpretation, however, is not crucial here; we need to see rather what is at stake on the theoretical plane.

In Number 78, Publius explains how popular sovereignty limits the action of government. As is often the case in the *The Federalist*, he begins with a criticism of the Constitution in order to refute it. 'Some perplexity respecting the rights of the courts to pronounce legislative acts void, because contrary to the Constitution, has arisen from an imagination that the doctrine would imply a superiority of the judiciary to the legislative power'. This would indeed be true if the Constitution had limited itself to juxtaposing three autonomous branches of government without establishing positive ties between them. But, replies Publius, 'There is no position which depends on clearer principles than that every act of delegated authority, contrary to the tenor of the commission under which it is exercised, is void'. If this position is not accepted, he concludes, 'the representatives of the people are superior to the people themselves', which is evidently absurd in a republic. Publius might well have asked about the provenance of his opponents' criticism, which forgets the lesson learned during the conflict with England: that the legislative assembly cannot act as constitutional judge of its own authority. The people do not give to their representatives the right to substitute their own will for that of the people. We should not, however, deduce from this refutation the idea of binding instructions as the means to preserve popular sovereignty. 'It is far more rational to suppose that the courts were designed to be an intermediate body between the people and the legislature in order . . . to keep the latter within the limits assigned to their authority'. This implies that the Constitution, as the fundamental law, provides the starting point from which judges are to evaluate the positive laws passed by the legislative assembly. In case there is a contradiction, it is the Constitution that prevails, for it represents the will of the people, manifested within the framework of the conventions designated for this general and political end and therefore distinct from the particular and interested manifestation of this will that expresses itself when it elects representatives to the legislature.

This doctrine of constitutional supremacy, and therefore of the pre-eminence of the judiciary, which is the interpreter of the Constitution, appears at first sight perfectly coherent. The positive laws voted by the legislature and the administrative actions undertaken by the executive are therefore subject to judicial review. But under these circumstances, the Constitution itself runs the danger of being transformed into positive law and being put on an equal footing with other laws; for, we must not forget, this document, the fruit of compromise, remains open to new questions and to the advent of the new. It is often said that the Constitution itself is modified by judicial rulings, but the situation is more complex. Indeed, the Constitution and popular sovereignty, of which the former is the expression, must not be confused. The Constitution and the judiciary which serves as its guardian both depend on popular sovereignty; the sovereign people can make amendments to the Constitution or demand the convocation of a new constitutional convention. The judiciary and the Constitution *represent*, therefore, this popular will of which they are the always-revisable expression and which in a certain sense is *everywhere and nowhere*. The sovereign will of the people is what makes institutions function and interact; but none of these institutions can claim to be its complete and total incarnation. This difference explains, once again, the dynamic of the system, and the reason that it is open constantly to the new.

The interpretation of judicial review in terms of the concept of popular sovereignty or popular will as laid out in Number 78 of *The Federalist* may be better explained and can be confirmed if we apply it to the analysis of the controversial role played by the Senate in a bicameral legislature. Our interpretation in Number 78 did not explain fully the distinction between the sovereign will of the people that establishes a constitution and the expression of this will in the election of its representatives or of its executive. As we know, the institutional difference between these two expressions of the popular will is due to the fact that the Constitution was the work of a Convention and that the process of amending it requires strong majorities (2/3 and 3/4) from the national and State representative authorities, whereas election depends only on a bare majority. What is the implication of the contrast between the solemnity and difficulty of making constitutional decisions, and those regular expressions of the will of the sovereign people that occur in public life? What is the difference between the representativeness of the President and that of a member of the House? Or again, between that of a national Senator and that of a State representative? Since it is the same citizens that vote in each of these cases, how can one attribute different powers to them in different cases?[5] The dilemma is all the more difficult since the Americans had come to recognize that their society was homogeneous and lacking the corporative orders that might have provided a social basis for political distinctions. The question is not new: John Adams had tried to filter this popular expression in a way that would recruit ever more qualified representatives to fill important posts; we have seen the difficulties Virginia encountered in attempting to define the conditions for eligibility to the upper house; and we have explained why Pennsylvania refused to envisage any distinctions among its representatives, and, in the last analysis, between the representatives and the people. But the Senate proposed by the new Constitution is the expression of a practical compromise between the interests of the States and those of the nation. Publius concedes this fact; yet his explanation draws from it implications that go further on the theoretical level.

We have seen that all the delegates to the Convention (except for Franklin) were, from the beginning, advocates of the form of bicameralism proposed in the Virginia Plan. Their argument was simple, and conservative in the classical sense of the term. Publius sets forth the logic of this argument in Number 63. He speaks of the historic role of the Senate in republics as 'an anchor against popular fluctuations' and he insists on the parallels with the present American situation, characterized as it was by 'a numerous assembly frequently elected by the people'. Finally, he adds, in the tone typical of *The Federalist*: 'To a people as little blinded by prejudice or corrupted by flattery as those whom I address, I shall not scruple to add that such an institution may be sometimes necessary as a defence to the people against their own temporary errors and delusions. As the cool and deliberate sense of the community ought, in all governments, and actually will, in free governments, ultimately prevail over the views of its rulers; so there are particular moments in public affairs when the people, stimulated by some irregular passion, or some illicit advantage, or misled by the artful misrepresentations of interested men, may call for measures which they themselves will afterwards be the most ready to lament and condemn'. This experience ought to have taught Americans, 'in these critical moments, how salutary will be the interference of some temperate and respectable body of citizens, in order to check the misguided career and to suspend the blow mediated by the people against themselves, until reason, justice and truth can regain authority over the public mind'. Even while granting the practical necessity of this salutary intervention, Publius still has not explained where this 'temperate and respectable body of citizens' will come from nor how the people, in the grips of this 'irregular passion' and agitated by their desire to obtain for themselves 'some illicit advantage', will be able to recognize and choose these superior citizens as their representatives.

The existence of a Senate challenges the direct expression of the sovereign people and their capacity for self-government. To explain this, Publius appeals to what he calls a *modern* definition of a republic. The distinction between this modern form and that of the ancient republic rests on the type of representation employed. Publius admits that the Ancients were familiar with the principle of representation. He shows how the Athenians before Solon elected archons; he speaks of the Carthaginian Senate which was also an elective office; he describes how the ephors of Sparta and the tribunes at Rome were also popularly elected. But, he continues, 'From these facts, to which many others might be added, it is clear that the principle of representation was neither unknown to the ancients nor wholly overlooked in their political constitutions. The true distinction between these and the American governments lies *in the total exclusion of the people in their collective capacity*, from any share in the *latter* and not in the *total exclusion of the representatives of the people* from the administration of the former' (emphasis in the original). This interpretation, surprising as it is at first sight, may be explained by recalling what Americans had learned during the debate with England. In the English system, the people were supposed to be embodied in the House of Commons, just as the aristocracy was to find its incarnation in the Lords. The entire polity was fully and actually represented by 'the King-in-Parliament'. What Publius rejects here, in the American case, is the notion of representation as the *real* incarnation of social interests or alleged political virtues. Just as the idea of binding instructions for delegates had proved to be not only impractical but a theoretical contradiction due to the fact that the delegate thus bound was only an ambassador from a foreign power within a republic (which for this very reason no longer incarnated a *res publica*), so there is a rejection here of the *immediate* transfer of social or impassioned interests into the political sphere, which would otherwise be reduced to an antagonistic association incapable of giving itself a unified political form.

Publius' explanation for the rejection of an immediate representation of the social into the political sphere turns the pre-modern theory of the political on its head. It is usually asserted that excluding social interests was typical of classical republican politics. Publius affirms the contrary when he insists on the new form of representation worked out by modern political science. To understand this innovation in the relationship between the political authorities and the social base, we must return to the difference between American society and the European societies which served as the starting point for elaborating classical theory. One can say that the England presented as the model of the theory of the mixed constitution was in itself already a Constitution, whereas the United States sought to endow itself with one. But what is this entity – the United States – that is in search of a Constitution? It is the people who won its sovereignty in the struggle against the English. *The Federalist* insists now that this social unity needs a political form capable of protecting it against enemies both foreign and domestic. As in the case of the judiciary, what is to be represented – popular sovereignty – is at one and the same time *everywhere and nowhere*. This affirmation seems to lend itself to the accusation by the 'reality principle' of the progressives that this is a political mystification masking the reality of social power. But the situation is more complex. We have seen that, from the very first number of *The Federalist*, Publius does not in the least deny the role of economic and social interests in the political system. He returns to this role in the famous Number 10. We have now come full circle; the institutional interpretation leads back to its theoretical grounds.

The first lines of Number 10 of *The Federalist* express frankly its apparently conservative goal. 'Among the numerous advantages promised by a well-constructed union, none deserves to be more accurately developed than its tendency to break and control the violence of faction'. The existence of factions is an evil inherent in popular governments in a society founded on interest rather than virtue. The Confederation was undermined by factions which rendered the government unstable and that subordinated the public good to party conflicts. The result was that 'measures [were] too often decided, not according to the rules of justice and the rights of the minor party, but by the superior force of an interested and overbearing majority'. This reference to the tyranny of the majority is familiar; we know also that the minority to be protected had social and self-interested origins. How can one represent this sociological fact on a political level when the notion of a republic that expresses the common good seems to exclude by definition the existence of a political minority? Publius' definition of a faction is not precise about its nature and its roots. 'By a faction I understand a number of citizens, whether amounting to a majority or a minority of the whole, who are united and actuated by some common impulse of passion, or of interest, adverse to the rights of other citizens, or to the permanent and aggregate interests of the community'. The last part of this definition suggests that a faction can be qualified as 'social' when it infringes on the rights of other individuals and as 'political' when it challenges the interests of the community as such. Publius does not go into greater detail; he makes nothing of the first clause, which defines faction first as a majority! Rather, he proceeds to the remedies that may be adopted.

The political specificity of Publius' analysis is apparent when he rejects a first sort of possible solution. When faced with a danger, one can either act on its causes or limit their effects. To eliminate the cause of factions would involve the destruction of the kind of liberty that is essential to the republic's existence. Publius rejects this option, just as he rejects another remedy, that of alloting to each citizen the same passions and the same interests – which is neither possible nor desirable. His political analysis is thus not idealistic; the goal is not to impose a form of behaviour on society. Rather, Publius seeks to predict and to explain what takes place beneath the properly political. Just like popular sovereignty, which cannot be really incarnated in political institutions, liberty is a right whose ability to express itself in political institutions must be limited in order precisely to safeguard it. This paradox, which once again seems to grant in theory what is denied in reality, must be explained.

The liberty which is the foundation of the Republic at the same time that the Republic is charged with providing it with a framework and protecting it nevertheless must be given a concrete form. When Publius explains that 'the diversity in the faculties of men' is at the origin of 'the rights of property' and when he affirms a short while later that 'the most common source of factions has been the various and unequal distribution of property. Those who hold and those who are without property have ever formed distinct interests in society', it appears that the Constitution must be interpreted as a way of legitimating the social domination of the propertied classes. But this initial analysis of the divergence of interests is complemented by the political principle that 'the protection of these faculties is the first object of government'. And the apparent determination by the economic is nuanced by the statement that 'so strong is the propensity of mankind to fall into mutual animosities that where no substantial occasion presents itself the most frivolous and fanciful distinctions have been sufficient to kindle their unfriendly passions and excite their most violent conflicts'. Factions are not simply economic. They are social; they threaten other social interests, and thereby endanger the only unity that encompasses them and whose role is to preserve them, namely, the political. Publius' analysis therefore is sociological only as a prelude for better specifying the political dimension.

If factions neither should nor can be eliminated, their effects must therefore be controlled. Two means are open to consideration. One can prevent the formation of a majority sharing common passions and interests; or one can prevent the realization of their plans, should such plans arise. The first solution is apparently political. Publius explains that pure democracy is not desirable because of the danger that a majority will be seized by a common passion at the expense of a minority – or of an obstinate or rebellious individual. As opposed to direct democracy, Publius argues that the representation-based republican form of government offers two advantages. First, as regards the choice of leaders, representation serves 'to refine and enlarge the public views by passing them through the medium of a chosen body of citizens whose wisdom may best discern the true interest of their country . . . The public voice, pronounced by the representatives of the people, will be more consonant to the public good than if pronounced by the people themselves, convened for the purpose'. We have already encountered this solution in the Massachusetts of John Adams; popular sovereignty is filtered, refined, and transformed by its presence in the republican public sphere in order to take on a form capable of being recognized at the properly political level. The particular, passionate and irrational character of private interests will then give way to a general, rational and non-passionate public expression. Danger is avoided in as much as sociological reality, just like popular sovereignty, is preserved without becoming identified with the ruling power itself.

Publius is not so naive as to believe that a political solution based on the elimination of the social from the political sphere[6] would really and effectively put an end to social interests. His analysis of the origin of factions shows, on the contrary, that he in no way wishes to suppress them. But he recognizes the possibility of the triumph of a demagogue who would mobilize the people to vote for him before betraying their true interests. Here he introduces a second solution, which we have already encountered in Madison's essay on 'The Vices of the Political System of the United States' and in Number 9 of *The Federalist*. Contrary to what had been foreseen by Montesquieu (whose republic is not representative in the modern sense), it is the very extent of the American Republic that will preserve it from the danger of factions.[7] The process of filtration which assures that the Republic will have representative institutions is reinforced by this geographical fact. As was the case with the justification for the distinction between the two houses of the Virginia legislature, the vast size of the territory that makes up the Republic implies that there will be more electors for selecting each representative and that it will therefore be less easy for these electors to be deceived. Similarly, those standing for election will have to be worthier individuals in order to win the attention of a greater number of their fellow citizens. The size of the territory also plays a role on the social level. It creates a multiplicity of diverse interests, with the result that, as in the case of religious sects, each ends up recognizing a common interest – namely, the need to protect minority rights.

The analysis of factions in the Number 10 is often improperly reduced to a sociology of interests, the free play of which would counterbalance the drawbacks of factions. It follows that the analysis neglects the role assumed by the political in the constitutional structure. But looking a bit more closely, we see that it is rather the indissoluble tie between these two domains that is being demonstrated. It is true that a danger may arise from social interests dominating the political authorities, but the suppression (or the standardization) of these interests is no less dangerous. Factions are therefore both necessary and dangerous, and the political must be able to protect itself without in its turn threatening social liberty. The doctrine of a republic based upon interest and covering a large territory therefore does not replace political theory. Indeed, this is what was already brought out in the discussion of the Senate in Number 63, where Publius returns to the earlier argument: 'It may be suggested that a people spread over an extensive region cannot, like the crowded inhabitants of a small district, be subject to the infection of violent passions or to the danger of combining in pursuit of unjust measures. I am far from denying that this is a distinction of peculiar importance. I have, on the contrary, endeavoured in a former paper [he is referring to Number 10] to show that it is one of the principal recommendations of a confederated republic'. But, he continues, 'at the same time, this advantage ought not to be considered as superseding the use of auxiliary precautions'. These 'auxiliary precautions' are incorporated in the structure of the political institutions whose general plan is outlined in Number 51, in which the sociological doctrine of a extended republic also reappears once again: 'Whilst all authority in it will be derived from and dependent upon society, the society itself will be broken into so many parts, interests and classes of citizens, that the rights of individuals, or of the minority, will be in little danger from interested combinations of the majority. In a free government the security of civil rights must be the same as that for religious rights. It consists in the one case in the multiplicity of interests, and in the other in the multiplicity of sects . . . and this may be presumed to depend on the extent of the country and number of people comprehended under the same government'. Sociology thus remains present in the properly political analysis, which it in no way eliminates, any more than the political analysis neglects social facts. But the relation between the social and the political has yet to be determined.

The principle of a popular sovereignty that is present everywhere and nowhere in republican institutions is explained in the four essays (Numbers 47 to 50) that introduce the theory of government properly speaking. Publius answers the objection that the Constitution violates Montesquieu's idea of the separation of powers. As we have already seen, a too rigid separation could lead to a breakup; at the other extreme, over-integration could provoke institutional paralysis. What is important to guard against is not so much infringement of the territory of one branch by another but the domination of one over another. The principle of separation had to be reformulated along the lines of the lesson learned from the debate with England: one cannot be at the same time both judge and a party in the same affair. In light of this maxim, it can be understood why Number 48 finds some justification for the fears of critics who worry about the misdeeds inherent in the invasive nature of power; they are quite right, says Publius, to distrust barriers constructed simply of words written on parchment. But these critics are mistaken when they concentrate on the executive authority established by the Constitution. That would be justified in a monarchy.[8] 'But in a representative republic where the executive magistracy is carefully limited, both in the extent and the duration of its power; and where the legislative power is exercised by an assembly, which is inspired by a supposed influence over the people with an intrepid confidence in its own strength; which is sufficiently numerous to feel all the passions which actuate a multitude, yet not so numerous as to be incapable of pursuing the objects of its passions by means which reason prescribes; it is against the enterprising ambition of this [legislative] department that the people ought to indulge all their jealousy and exhaust all their precautions'. A first illustration of this familiar argument is provided by the experience of Pennsylvania and its censors; another is presented on the basis of Jefferson's *Notes on the State of Virginia*, whose point may be summarized in essence by the idea that 'one-hundred-and-seventy-three tyrants [namely, the State's representatives] are as oppressive as a single one', and that the Americans had not fought to replace a hereditary tyrant with an elective one.

The rejection of legislative despotism takes on an explicitly anti-popular form in Numbers 49 and 50, an attitude which raises even more acutely the question of how to represent popular sovereignty. Jefferson had proposed the solution of a popular convention called at the request of two of the three branches of government – which he expected usually to be the judiciary and the executive. Publius notes first that to have recourse to the people in this way would deprive the government of the veneration that comes with tradition, without which even the wisest of governments cannot function. He adds that, since every government is founded upon opinion and since people become more stubborn when they believe their opinions have mass support, the calling of a convention would risk bringing about explosions of popular passion. For, he says in Number 50: 'When men exercise their reason coolly and freely on a variety of distinct questions, they inevitably fall into different opinions on some of them. When they are governed by a common passion, their opinions, if they are so to be called, will be the same'. This is why, concludes Number 49, 'it is the reason, alone, of the people, that ought to control and regulate the government. The passions ought to be controlled and regulated by the government'. But we saw in Number 10 that this idea of standardizing and controlling factions goes against the essence of liberty and therefore of the Republic. We must be careful here: what lends itself to standardization in this argument are the passions, not reason. The effects of a large-scale republic work in conjunction with those of a politics founded upon a diversity of factions since the latter were seen to be in fact *rational* results of human liberty. Sociological analysis, which seemed to give the irrational a legitimate place in the political sphere, changes its meaning; the interest that it legitimates is not the opposite of the political, as was the case in classical politics.

*The Federalist*'s critique of the various attempts *really* to incorporate popular sovereignty into political institutions cannot be reduced to the idea of a government of interests or to a form of protection for minority interests. We have seen that Publius is quite conscious of the difference between the social and the political. To give another example, at the beginning of Number 51, he states that 'the defect must be supplied, by so contriving the interior structure of the government as that its several constituent parts may, by their mutual relations, be the means of keeping each other in their proper places'. For the parts to be able to relate to each other in this way, they must be homogeneous with one another so that there can be no qualitative distinctions that would serve as the basis for a claim to superiority of one over another. Publius does not explain how this homogenization will take place (or how it has taken place); and we know that in the mixed or classical constitution, each of the branches is in fact essentially different in social content and not simply in function. Once this homogenization is carried out, Publius continues his argument, each department must be endowed with a will of its own, which means concretely that it does not depend on the other departments for the appointment of its officers. This apparently innocuous remark repeats the theoretical argument we have found elsewhere. It implies that all of the officers, in all the departments, issue directly from the people, no matter who nominates them, and that their authority is therefore ultimately drawn from, and founded upon, the people themselves. This extension of the 'modern' theory of representation to government officers might be surprising at first sight. Its implications permit a refinement of the American theory of representation.

Publius reintroduces the concept of interest, which he had first sought to remove from the political sphere, following apparently the classical model. In order to ensure the independence of the branches of government, 'the great security . . . consists in giving to those who administer each department the necessary constitutional means and personal motives to resist encroachments of the others'. The concept of a government officer is transformed here – as is the concept of interest. 'Ambition must be made to counteract ambition. The interest of the man must be connected with the constitutional rights of the place'. Publius knows quite well that his argument runs the risk of shocking people. 'It may be a reflection on human nature', he says, 'that such devices should be necessary to control the abuses of government. But what is government itself but the greatest of all reflections on human nature? If men were angels, no government would be necessary. If angels were to govern men, neither external nor internal controls on government would be necessary. In framing a government which is to be administered by men over men, the great difficulty lies in this: You must first enable the government to control the governed; and in the next place to oblige it to control itself'. This last obligation is fulfilled, Publius concludes, by the Constitution's mechanical arrangement of institutional checks and balances. The most important of these is the bicameral structure of the legislature, which limits the tendency of the legislative branch, in a republican government, to increase inordinately its power at the expense of the other branches. The existence of an upper house, reinforced by its federal character and make-up, is therefore justified by the mechanics which seeks to establish an equilibrium among the various interests. We are as far from classical justifications here as we are from the principles of a mixed constitution invoked by the authors of the first State constitutions.

Should we conclude that *The Federalist* furnishes a theoretical justification for the transformation of politics into sociology? This would, first of all, mistake the goal of these 85 essays, which were an attempt to rally support for the cause of the Constitution. It would also assume that the public to which Publius was addressing himself was simply that minority of propertied men who thought they were threatened by the creation of a national republican government. It is quite likely that this minority knew how to read between the lines; and it would not be wrong to see in the discourse of Publius the expression of the fears of those with property. But one must not forget that the established order itself was in crisis. If Publius is said to formulate what could be called anachronistically a 'class theory', one cannot, in any event, accuse him of masking his plans or of deluding those whom he sought to dominate. But the anachronism of this hypothesis suggests its inaccuracy. As we have just seen, Publius insists that 'you must first enable the government to control the governed; and in the next place oblige it to control itself'. That second task, which is the responsibility of the governmental structure, could eventually become the object of a political, or even an institutional or mechanical criticism. But it is more important to answer the first question: how to 'enable the government to control the governed'? This question had been posed to the Philadelphia Convention at the time of the introduction of the Paterson Plan, when Randolph insisted that the merit of his own proposals was that they avoided the need to apply coercion by instituting direct governmental authority over the citizen without depending on the mediation of the States. What is at stake here is the transformation of the power of coercion into rational and legitimate authority.

The key to the American constitutional system is found in the relationship that it establishes between the two concepts of popular sovereignty and representation. These were, of course, issues around which the entire revolutionary experience had turned. The relationship established by *The Federalist*'s reflection on that experience is paradoxical, to say the least. On the one hand, sovereignty is present everywhere and nowhere in institutions which, according to Publius, expressly exclude the *real* form of participation that had undermined the classical democracies and still threatens the representative Republic. On the other hand, the three branches of government as well as the government officers who set them in motion are said to be representative. If this is not a verbal mystification, what can it mean? What is the signification here of this concept of representativeness?

For the government to control the governed, it must be distinct from them; this is what *The Federalist* demonstrates in its analysis of the relationship between the social and the political, for example in the arguments developed in Number 10. Once this distinction is established, each domain can be analyzed according to its own institutional logic. And yet, they must not be separated too absolutely. This is why Number 51 reintegrates them in a unity that encompasses them both. Only then is the analysis of the institutions that make up the government possible (in Numbers 52 to 83). These institutions are called representative in as much as there exists now a homogeneous relationship between the represented and the representative. This homogeneity, which Publius had asserted but not explained, is explained in Number 51 which describes a 'policy of supplying, by opposite and rival interests, the defect of better motives, [which] might be traced through the whole system of human affairs, private as well as public'. This is the key to Publius' analysis; the same antagonistic logic rules private life and public life. But this logic is not irrational; once again, the social is not the negation of the political, as classical theory would have it. Social interest is not based on passion as opposed to reason. The fears of the Old Whigs – that interest leads to 'corruption' that benefits power at the expense of liberty – prove to be without foundation, but at the same time the hopes of the classical republicans – that virtue will triumph over private interest – are disappointed. Interest becomes at one and the same time the principle of government and its product – exactly like the virtue that was crucial in John Adams' widely copied *Thoughts on Government* which dominated constitutional theory during the confederal period. Popular sovereignty therefore continues in the role it played since the Declaration of Independence: that of a *symbolic legitimation*.

The refusal to embody popular sovereignty in one or another of the new institutions – or in the Constitution itself – explains the constant attempts of the Americans to dissociate the social from the political and to keep the latter free from the influence of the former. This was their objective during the struggle against England. At the outset, it was expressed through a purely political theory based on the ambiguity of relations between public and private liberty. But the experience of the Confederation taught Americans political sociology; it permitted them to redefine private liberty in terms of interests. The legitimation of the concept of minority interest in this context is undoubtedly due in part to the experience of religious sects and to the absence of an aristocracy that, as in Europe of the 19th century, would have proposed this concept, and thereby have delegitimated it just as quickly. But of greater importance for understanding the role given to social interest is the transformation of previous political theories into the political theory in which the experience of the American Revolution finally culminated. In Old Whig theory, society sought to protect itself from the political. Henceforth, the roles are reversed; it is the political that aims at maintaining itself, while the social appears as its premise, but also as a threat to it. This is the final irony: starting from a political theory that sought to protect a threatened liberty, the Americans now must search for forms that will allow liberty to be incarnated in a legitimate political authority. One could rewrite the history of the Republic from this standpoint, that of the nibbling away of the properly political sphere by a society whose power is limited only by the conflicts of interest and the factions that *The Federalist* sought to take into account and to explain.

# 12 History Rethought: To Understand Oneself as Revolutionary

The historical reading of this last phase of the Revolution is, in a certain sense, nothing but the lived experience of a republic at the point of reaching its bicentenary. Two centuries' experience is itself the critical reflection of the new political theory which took shape in the Constitution of 1787. This experience has sometimes carried with it severe critiques of the Founders, such as the Civil War which, begun in 1861, justified Hamilton's view that the true opposition was not between small and large States but between various regional interests.[1] Compared to such criticisms, the 17th Amendment's creation of a Senate directly elected by the citizens of each State (and no longer designated by the State legislatures along the lines of the federative principle that made possible the fundamental compromise at the Convention) appears simply as the application of American political science under new social conditions. Between these two sorts of criticism of the work of the Revolution lies a third type of reflection which asserts that the success of the American experience depends little on the constitutional practice of the Founding Fathers but rather on the natural qualities and egalitarian social structure of this new country. This type of criticism points out, for example, that the Constitution did not foresee the creation of a two-party political system as a guarantee for the stability of the government. It remarks that the House was not as radical nor the Senate as prone to anti-popular opposition as was originally anticipated. It adds that the framers of the Constitution as well as the authors of *The Federalist* thought of American society as divided and conflict-ridden whereas American history offers rather the image of a tranquil scene in which consensus prevails over division. We recognize in this type of criticism the theses of Tocqueville, taken up again and enlarged – often without his genius – by the school of 'consensus' or 'American exceptionalism'.

But these kinds of criticism remain overly simple. The question underlying the critique is ill posed, as it is with another common view which looks at American history from the perspective of the judiciary's role in American political practice. It is not false to affirm that American

205

history can be interpreted from the standpoint of the decisions handed down by the Supreme Court. Textbooks do not hesitate to draw up a list of great cases, showing students how the popular will as embodied in the Constitution is not only able to adopt a detached attitude when confronted with momentary passions but also, and above all, is able to evolve on its own – for example, through such cases as *Dred Scott v. Sanford* (1856), which presages the Civil War, *Plessy v. Ferguson* (1896), which consecrates the 'separate but equal' doctrine of segregationism, and *Brown v. Board of Education* (1954), which puts an end to segregated schools and gives birth to the civil rights movement. But this reading of American history supposes the legitimacy of the doctrine of 'judicial review' which grants to the Court an undoubtedly unmerited position of pre-eminence in theory as well as in practice. One cannot recommend too highly to those who want to understand the American system a reading of its judicial history. But we must not go as far as a recent Frenchman who, freshly graduated from the Harvard Law School, proposes to his countrymen the idea of a judicial system that, by its very operation, would replace the political dimension; this idea corresponds only very partially to the experience of the American people, even in the era of deregulation initiated under the Carter Administration and pursued by Reagan.[2]

The historical question that has yet to be raised is that of the revolutionary nature of American theory and practice such as they emerged from the revolutionary era. We have broached this problem through an analysis of *The Federalist*, although its most recent interpreter (Furtwangler) states that it 'does not turn out to be very satisfying as an account of the United States government – currently, historically, or ideally'. Nor have we forgotten the meticulous critique offered by the political scientist Robert Dahl and the debate aroused by his insistence that the principle theses of *The Federalist* are non-operative because their apparent logic rests on concepts that have no precise referents.[3] We also know that *The Federalist* corresponds neither to the ideas of Madison (who insisted on a national veto power over state laws) nor to those of Hamilton (whose interpretation of the Constitution, once in power during the Washington presidency, went far beyond what he had expressed under the name of Publius). We have already noted how little influence this text had on the contemporary debates over ratification, and we can add here the observation made by the French *chargé d'affaires* in New York at the time, L.G. Otto, who judged that 'this work has no use for educated people, and it is too erudite and too long for the uneducated'.[4] Finally, we know the wishes of the aged Madison, who refused to publish his notes on the debates of the Convention because 'its publication should be delayed till the Constitution's hold be well settled by practice, & till a knowledge of the controversial part of the proceedings of its framers could be turned to no improper account. . . . As a guide in expounding and applying the provisions of the Constitution, the debates and incidental decisions of the Convention can have no authoritative character'.[5] Nevertheless, despite all this, we have based ourselves on the Convention's debates and on *The Federalist* for our reading. Why?

Publius admits in Number 39 of *The Federalist* that the Constitution is the product of compromises that are inevitable in an assembly comprised of diverse interests. The Ancients were conscious of these kinds of difficulties; that is why their Legislator, the giver of the Constitution, was always a single man. But the Americans could not have recourse to such an external intervention. To this first difficulty Number 37 adds others, which any society encounters when seeking to give itself precise and comprehensive laws that would guarantee both the stability and the dynamism necessary for the health of the social organism. The search for balance between self-preservation by means of stability and self-mobilization in order to confront the unexpected is only another formulation of the mechanics of applied political science. Publius does not claim to have totally succeeded. But, he says, 'The real wonder is that so many difficulties should have been surmounted, and surmounted with a unanimity almost as unprecedented as it must have been unexpected. It is impossible for any man of candour to reflect on this circumstance without partaking of the astonishment. It is impossible for the man of pious reflection not to perceive in it a finger of that Almighty hand which has been so frequently and signally extended to our relief in the critical stages of the revolution'. One may smile at or congratulate the author for this lovely, and so American, turn of speech. We shall pass over the intervention here of the Almighty; but let us share in Publius' wonder by interpreting *The Federalist* within the setting of an interrogation – that of the Revolution – in which his text is a participant.

Two debates dividing historians are worth brief mention in the context of our reflection on the revolutionary nature of the system born of the Revolution. On the one hand, the defenders of the 'civic humanist', republican theory have attempted to refute Gordon Wood's thesis that a politics based upon interest, masterfully expressed in Number 10 of *The Federalist*, marks the end of classical politics. J.G.A. Pocock's *The Machiavellian Moment* is an attempt to develop a sort of dialectic in which Florentine *virtù* is opposed to the peaceable institutions of commercial Venice. This dialectic is supposed to have emigrated to England before crossing the Atlantic. As in any dialectic, the situations that are overcome must remain present, although latent, in the current configuration of circumstances. Thus, for example, the *frontier* is said to have offered the Americans the opportunity to practice Florentine *virtù*; and the stable configuration of institutions systematized by the political science of interests is said to be still confronted with the classical challenge of founding a truly virtuous politics.[6] Certain episodes in American history, like the coming to power of Jefferson's party, or that of Andrew Jackson 30 years later, would then be interpreted along the lines of this dialectic in order to reveal not only the persistence of the old classical politics but also and above all the dynamic role that it can be said to have continued to play during the major transformations of the Republic.

This is not the place to settle these historical controversies which, after all, go beyond the period with which we are concerned. The perspective of the civic humanists is tempting; their depiction of a structure in which the political seat of power is not reduced to a simple epiphenomenon of a struggle between qualitatively indistinguishable material interests is comforting to old habits of thought. The action of *virtù*, which arouses and animates the political, suggests that situations exist in which the individual is not reduced to the abstraction of his status as property owner and in which social relations go beyond the contract concluded between isolated and atomized individuals. This dialectic has the advantage, moreover, of reconciling the republican outlook with that of the Old Whigs who, as defenders of liberty, wanted to restore the original purpose of republican institutions. The frontier no longer is opposed to civilization, as it had been during the period we have examined; it no longer is the locus of anti-federalist resistance, sometimes rebellious, as with Shays' Rebellion, sometimes sullen and withdrawn into itself and into its own resentment; and it represents still less a regional interest threatening the national unity, as it would during the years leading to the Civil War. But so many blessings incite doubt. We can leave the matter here for the historian to decide. For us, it suffices to note that civic humanism is attacking a straw man. What is important is not to contrast an a- or anti-political theory based on social interest to classical political thought. The problem faced by Americans was not to replace the political by the social, even if the latter constantly threatens the autonomy of the former.

A similar error, based on an underestimation of the thought of the American revolutionaries, offers an explanation for the difficulty upon which political scientists such as Robert Dahl insist. If the sociological analysis found in Number 10 of *The Federalist* is valid, they say, why was it necessary, as Number 51 urges, to redivide the government. This critique is not without contemporary overtones, as found, for example, in James MacGregor Burns's *The Deadlock of Democracy* (1963). It is suggested that the separation of powers and the reciprocal protections it affords have paralyzed the American government. Well known problems can be cited, such as the difficulties a President encounters in trying to win ratification for a treaty signed by him but not yet approved by the Senate, or the deadlock that can occur when either the Senate or the House is dominated by a party different from that of the President. If it is true that social interests balance each other out in this large-scale Republic, is not a parliamentary system based upon the ultimate responsibility of the executive to the legislature preferable to the instability, deadlock or the inconsistencies of the presently checked and counterbalanced system of institutions? The limited government that the Americans have been seeking since 1763 would then be the product of its egalitarian and pluralist social structure alone.

A critique of this contemporary political science, which will also close this discussion, can simply return to the conclusions drawn from our reading of *The Federalist* within the broader framework of the post-1763 revolutionary experience. That text, as well as the political practice of the new system (which obviously does not follow in all its details the recipes of *The Federalist*), are revolutionary first of all in their theoretical approach. This theory puts in question both the classical republican premises and those of the American Old Whigs. If the existence of a *res publica* is not affirmed *a priori*, it is because society is not conceived as an organism whose political institutions exist to preserve stability. The presence of a frontier on their immense continent forced the Americans to integrate the future into their present perspectives. There is, certainly, a common good; but this common good is not predetermined and its nature can very well change through time. To object that other republics too aimed at the future and at expansion is not a decisive criticism. The originality of the Americans, indeed, is that their vision is founded upon a view of *federalism* in which new territories were welcomed on an equal and republican footing with the old ones. This innovative egalitarianism stems from the other innovation in American political thought. The combination of these two innovations explains the new federalism of the United States.

American political theory saw itself obliged to overthrow the Whig and the Old Whig theories that had in large part inspired the resistance

movement against England. The immense merit of Gordon Wood is to
have followed this evolution in its details. One of his conclusions sums
up well his insights: 'In America a constitution had become, as Madison
pointed out, a charter of power granted by liberty rather than, as in
Europe, a charter of liberty granted by power'.[7] The priorities were
inverted by the revolutionary experience, as our reading of *The
Federalist* suggested; it no longer was a matter of protecting oneself
against a pre-existing power but rather of building institutions that
would permit popular power to take shape. The difficulty, as we have
seen, stems from the fact that the expression of this popular power can
threaten the liberty that is its foundation. This is what explains the need
to add the checks and balances of Number 51 of *The Federalist* to the
sociological analysis of Number 10. It also explains why the label
'sociological' does not suffice to characterize the relationship established
between the social and the political. This last observation, finally, also
allows us to explain why the new American federalism did not become
shipwrecked on the reefs already charted by classical thought.

The analysis of the politics of factions in Number 10 demonstrated
above all the necessary existence of such factions in any free republic.
The idea that factions also represent a threat does not stem from this
theory but rather from the lessons of the classical experience. The
analysis in Number 10 emphasized, moreover, that the remedy to this
danger was in no case to be the elimination of the liberty of which
factions are the expression. At the same time, Publius rejected the
temptation to confront the problem of factions by attempting to create
common passions and interests, recognizing that this solution would be
harmful to the diversity which is constitutive of liberty. Once he laid out
this sociology of the large-scale Republic, Publius introduced a decisive
distinction between rational behaviour, which is expressive precisely of
this diversity, and behaviour governed by the passions in which the
masses share what is called a common opinion (or more recently, but
non-classically: public opinion). This distinction suggests that interest,
which is varied and which creates factions, is *rational*; it can therefore be
introduced into the political structures of the country without threatening them from within by introducing a principle alien to their essence.[8]
The result is a first stage of homogenization in which the relations
between society and the political can be defined in a manner that does
not deny the specificity of either the one or the other. There is no
essential conflict between the two spheres, which are not, however,
identical because it is the presence of the political that guarantees social
liberty against the self-destructive effects of factions.

To this first stage of homogenization corresponds a second one, situated within the political itself. Once all political institutions are thought of as representative, they are all equal on the qualitative plane. This equality – just like the mutual qualitative equality of interests – allows for the construction of a system in which the authorities do not encroach upon each other and can each *increase* their respective influence without threatening the autonomy of another, since all are based upon the representative relation. The task to be carried out by this arrangement is not only that of protecting a form of liberty whose ambiguous definition leaves open the question of whether it is private or public. This homogeneous structure also explains what makes the federalist system (even after the 17th Amendment) possible. The autonomous States conserve their autonomy exactly as free individuals continue to preserve their basic liberty. The States are represented on the national level just as are other interests. The difference between these States and other interests stems from the fact that the States are always at the same time political authorities ruled by the same modern republican logic that governs the nation. Although one might, conversely, be tempted to assert that factions 'represent' interests, that sort of representation is not a political form of representation. The difference between the two is that interests that organize themselves into factions seek *really* to embody themselves in these factions; this is why factions become passionate and, hence, irrational. The representation of the States and the representation of interests within the States avoid this difficulty because of the *symbolic* nature of republican sovereignty.

If the Americans overthrew and revolutionized inherited political thought, in what sense can their political practice be characterized as revolutionary? The answer to this question is of disarming simplicity. The doctrine, which some may call a mystification or a reification, of a popular sovereignty that is nowhere to be incarnated but everywhere present constitutes precisely the foundation of the new politics. It implies that power cannot become the monopoly of one interest or of a single branch of the government; and it also implies that each interest and each branch of government must apply themselves constantly to the task of appropriating power for themselves. If the term was not already in use to designate something else, one could talk about a 'permanent revolution'. It is better to speak, quite simply, about the impossibility of occupying or realizing once and for all a power that is *everywhere and nowhere*.[9]

This is, of course, too optimistic a conclusion, and the bicentenary history of the United States could easily be invoked in order to apply 'the "reality" technique' to this simplistic, if not mystifying hypothesis. The response – which would invoke other episodes in American history, for example the Progressive era – would require another book, another debate. Nevertheless, a pessimistic conclusion is called for here. Can one always trust in the rationality of interest? As John P. Diggins rightly observes, *The Federalist* did not appeal to the 'self-evident truths' of the Declaration of Independence or to any other norm; Publius describes and explains simply what is. The triumph of American politics is precisely its ability to free itself from the schemata and categories inherited from classical thought and to look straight ahead. Has the landscape that then looms ahead remained the same? The answer to that question would also require a book of it own.

# Afterword

**The Philosopher, the Historian, and the Revolution**

Historians correctly warn their political-scientist friends against the danger of a sheerly present-centred reading of the stakes of politics. Thus, for example, French politics must be understood as overdetermined by the attempt to complete or to conclude the movement inaugurated in 1789. German politics has to be understood similarly as overdetermined by the early legal codification by Friedrich, and by the failure to complete the 1848 Revolution. American political history, on the other hand, has forgotten, if not repressed, its revolutionary origin. Americans act as if their revolution had been somehow pre-ordained, the logical outcome of the principles of freedom developing freely on a virgin continent. However they interpret their origins, the Americans do not consider their roots as *political*; their country is assumed to have been 'born liberal'. This should give the political historian pause; what *was* it, really, that American Revolution? Its anti-political results seem to invalidate the usual distinction between the social character of the French and the self-limiting political thrust of the American Revolution. And yet that argument correctly underlines the properly political *origin* of the American Revolution. The historian has to turn to the philosopher; how could the history that followed the American Revolution deny its own origin? The philosopher has to reread the originary movement in order to discover its operative presence within the historical path it originates.

The path of the American Revolution can be divided into three distinct moments of which the participants were fully conscious. There was first of all the slow ripening which began at the end of the Seven Years' War, known in those English colonies as the 'French and Indian War'. The situation was simple: the French had been defeated; the colonies no longer needed the protective power of England, whereas the mother-country, now master of an empire, had to take measures to govern its new possessions while repaying the debt incurred by the war. It was quite logical to attempt to make the colonies pay; the war had brought them benefits, and now peace would bring new profits. At the same time, it was quite traditional to govern the Empire by mercantilist

213

politics. But the colonials were headstrong provincials; they wanted above all to be left alone. They resisted the new measures, basing their protests on what they called 'the rights of an Englishman'. Although they were also driven by economic interests which they could not admit (perhaps not even to themselves), the colonists were forced during the years that followed 1763 to make clear what they meant by the 'rights' of an Englishman. Their first political formulation of these rights was presented by the Declaration of Independence in 1776. But the principles that underlie that Declaration can only be understood if the theoretical sedimentations that accumulated during 13 years of debates and struggles are taken into account.

The Revolution could not stop simply with the conquest of sovereignty. Once independence was declared, it had to be realized concretely – which meant first of all that the War of Independence had to be won. Hearts and minds had been transformed by the long debate concerning their rights; now the experience of the war gave a new sense to the autonomy that the Declaration affirmed. The colonies were 13, and proud of their differences; the majority of them took their autonomy so seriously that they felt it necessary to include the Declaration of Independence in their State constitutions. But the War of Independence was the struggle of an entire nation. The national constitution – which was not ratified until shortly before the end of the War – instituted a confederation of autonomous States. Such a political form could not guarantee the collective future. Once the war had concluded, centrifugal tendencies came to the fore. The loose confederal form had to be rethought. The key concept was representation, a notion whose problematic application to the relations with the mother-country had given a foretaste of the difficulties it entailed. Now the concept had to be used to conceive the relations between the sovereign nation and the sovereign States *and* those between the free citizens and the political institutions which were supposed to incarnate or at least guarantee that freedom. The relation between the representation of political sovereignty and the representation of social freedom had to discover a new articulation.

The debate concerning representation brought together the lessons of the first and the second periods of the Revolution. The Constitution of 1787 can be read as their synthesis. That Constitution is often interpreted in terms of its liberal and capitalist results. Such a reading evades both practical and theoretical problems. For example, the Constitution makes no provision for the existence of political parties, much less for the two-party system which is supposed to explain the remarkable stability of American politics. The Constitution does not explicitly provide for the process of judicial review which permits the dis-ideologization of politics by the mediation of the judiciary. These two institutions emerged in the wake of what contemporaries called the 'Revolution of 1800' which brought the Jeffersonians to power. But the image of a republic divided into political parties, as well as the idea that laws voted by the representatives of the people could be overruled by a non-elected branch of government, would have shocked those Americans who had learned to fight for their rights and for their autonomy during the Revolution. Indeed, those who affirm that these inventions are compatible with the Constitution are often criticized by the 'progressive' historians who see the Constitution as a conservative *coup d'état*, a kind of American 'Thermidor'. But the politics that underlies the 'progressive' critique avoids the problems that led the historian to philosophy, and the philosopher to history. The 'progressives' insist on the need to return to the principles of the Revolution as incarnated in the Declaration of Independence. They thus suppose that the Revolution could be defined simply, immediately, and conceptually. This permits them to avoid the challenge of *reading* the Revolution. They can then confine themselves to 'demystifying' the deviations of two hundred years of political history.

**Principles for Reading**

Rather than interpret it in terms of its realization, the reality of the American Revolution needs to be read from the standpoint of its self-theorization. That theory was constantly reformulated during and by the revolutionary experience. Its structure was doubly reflexive. At a first level, it articulates the three periods through which the Revolution developed; these can be defined respectively as the *lived experience* (*le vécu*) of the struggle for sovereignty, the *conceptualized* form ( *le conçu*) of that autonomy, and the political *reflection* (le réfléchi) of these first two moments. The lived experience corresponds to immediate or pre-political existence; the conceptualized form expresses the social relations instituted by that lived experience; what is reflected as the unity of these two moments makes explicit their political implications. This articulation is then repeated within each of the three revolutionary periods. For example, the lived experience of the first period corresponds to the brute givens of colonization, including two crucial absences: the existence of an open frontier and the non-existence of social orders. The colonials conceptualized their particular experience only when the English intervened in what had been until then a self-regulating society. The reflection of that autonomous society occurred when the question of political independence was posed explicitly. But that reflection was not a kind of Hegelian or idealist consummation.[1]

This doubly reflexive structure explains how each period takes up anew and develops the theoretical conclusions of the preceding one. The moment of the political in which one period culminates institutes the lived experience of its successor. An example will clarify the institutional functioning of this logic ( *logique institutuante*). The Declaration of Independence did not conclude the revolutionary experience; that declared independence had to be given adequate institutional form. The members of the Continental Congress left Philadelphia to return home; more important than the national struggle was the attempt to invent constitutions adequate to the particular *society* of their home States. That the 13 sovereign States should create different institutions from one another does not contradict the political unity realized by the Declaration of Independence. The social diversity becomes a contradiction only when it is necessary to *reflect* the national sovereignty in a confederal Constitution. That Constitution has to incarnate unity while conserving diversity in the same way that the social experience of the struggle against England was reflected in the Declaration of Independence that unified a diversified country. But that *political* unification of social diversity could only be unstable, in the first as in the second case; the reflective status of the political had not yet been defined; the Revolution had to continue. The unstable political unity of the Confederation thus presents the *lived experience* of the third period.[2]

Before turning to the articulation of the third period, the paradox from which we began must be underlined: the American Revolution was through and through a political movement, and yet it was incapable of understanding itself politically. The progressive critics who want to return to its supposed political principles forget that a Civil War broke out in 1861, opposing those who based themselves on the principles of the Declaration, those who defended the autonomy of the confederated States, and those for whom the Union was the supreme value. This suggests the need for a different reading of the political foundations of American history. Our categories of lived experience, its conceptualized form, and its reflected moment are useful insofar as they avoid the temptation to analyze effects in order to seek their causes. These categories cannot be imposed from without on a completed history; they are in principle open, like the American democracy originated by the

Revolution. Their foundation lies in a theory lived first of all at the pre-political level, then conceived at the level of the social, and finally reflected in a Constitution which can only be understood within the context of a revolution of, and by, the political. This is the sense in which the American Revolution is exemplary.

**Reading American Theory Historically**

The theoretical lived experience of the colonials was a mélange whose first expression was the demand for the 'rights of an Englishman'. That concept had the advantage of being at once historically rooted while remaining open, if not vague. This 'right' was expounded in terms of concepts drawn from natural or contractual law, from Greek, Roman, or English history, and of course from the Bible. When the English interventions forced them to conceptualize this 'right', the colonists had recourse to what is called Whig thought. Whig theory begins from the premise that the existence of society depends on the presence of a Power whose essence is to seek always to expand at the cost of Liberty, which must constantly defend itself. This theory could be interpreted historically in an optimistic or a pessimistic vein. The optimistic view sees Liberty reconquering its rights after the Norman conquest, first with the *Magna Carta*, then with the Bill of Rights and the Glorious Revolution which gave birth to a stable society organized around the new, limited, and balanced Power called 'the King-in-Parliament'. The pessimists, on the other hand, argued that conquering Liberty is not inevitably bound to be successful; the excesses in both directions that followed the Revolution of 1640 could be cited to warn against naïve optimism. These pessimists, appealing as well to a stern Protestant authority, could become critics of the established order; as such, they acquired the name 'Old Whigs'.

When Old Whig theory is turned against the established Power, its biblical roots lead it to encounter classical political theory. If Power can expand, the reason must be that Liberty has been 'corrupted'; Liberty lacks the virtue necessary for good politics, which must be founded on the distinction between the common good and private interest. Thus, the Old Whigs acquired the name 'Commonwealthmen'. This version of Whig thought dominated in the colonial struggle once the Americans were forced to define what they meant by the 'rights of an Englishman'.[3] From this starting point, the colonial opposition could conceptualize its claims at the social level; resistance was justified by a critique of the 'corruption' of the prosperous English society and by the appeal to colonial virtue. That virtue was no abstraction; it was affirmed through tactics of popular resistance whose result was forms of social self-government. This movement, initiated by the merchants, quickly passed to the direction of popular committees called Sons of Liberty. The social struggle became political once the question of sovereignty was posed. This passage to the political took time; it originated in the Old Whig political theory, which had to be led to reflect on the contradiction between the primacy of Old Whig Freedom and the equally Old Whig affirmation of its republican institutional form in the Commonwealth. That contradiction was hidden by the Declaration of Independence; it was conceptualized only in the second period, and reflected finally in the third.

The first Continental Congress met in 1774. This Congress had no legitimate political status. It could only propose resistance, suggest compromises to a Parliament which refused to grant it any political status, and finally dissolve itself to return to the States. That is to say, the first Congress depended on social conditions (including the social and economic interests of the English merchants to whom their compromises were in fact addressed). A second Congress met in 1775. Its delegates considered themselves still to be ambassadors from their States. But this time, after some inconclusive debate, the Congress opted for independence (and although it made a last attempt at conciliation, this gesture was directed now to the King, because social pressure had not affected the attitude of Parliament as it had in the past). On the basis of what 'right' did the delegates found their political claims? The Declaration of Independence incorporates two arguments: the proclamation of certain 'self-evident truths' is followed by a historical recapitulation of the misdeeds accumulated since 1763. That second and longer part of the Declaration clearly draws the implications of Old Whig logic: it shows that England had been 'corrupted' and that American freedom must separate itself from the Old World in order to protect its self-evident rights. This suggests that these rights define political sovereignty. But the Declaration did not propose any political institutions capable of guaranteeing those rights against their eventual corruption or the degeneration toward that anarchy that had followed the Revolution of 1640. This makes clear the contradiction in Old Whig thought; its resolution depends on a political reflection of the status of the Congress which issued the Declaration, whose sovereignty was founded neither on self-evident rights or truths, nor on the particularity of social conditions.

The now free colonists adopted the Republic as the reflected form of their new institutions. This catch-all concept hid an issue that had been present during the first period and which could now emerge as the lived experience of independence in the second period. This crucial problem was defined as the question of *representation*. England had sought to legitimate its mercantile policies by means of the concept of 'virtual representation'. A good power is one that represents the common good of society; the 'King-in-Parliament' is supposed to guarantee that representation by the immediate co-presence of the three Estates of the Kingdom in the elaboration of law. This implied that the colonies had no more need to be represented than did the English citizens of Manchester. But self-government had defined the lived experience of the colonists; they had invented theoretical refinements – for example, the distinction between internal and external taxes – in order to justify their resistance. Now free, their republican representation had to take a form different from the English model. The representation of social orders could not be adopted in a country which had no orders; but the positive mode by which sovereignty, freedom, or self-evident rights could be represented was not clear. What, in fact, was to be represented? The constitutions adopted by the independent States sought a social form adequate to the lived political experience of the first phase as it was now reflected by the question of representation.

The contrast between the constitution of Pennsylvania and those of the other States illustrates the difficulty that confronted the newly independent Americans. The colonial political leaders of Pennsylvania had sought to slow the movement toward independence whereas these same leaders, in the other colonies, had taken the direction of the movement. The new men who created Pennsylvania's free constitution were aware of the fact that their society was based on a relative equality of conditions. They adopted a unicameral legislature accompanied by a weak executive and an elected and revocable judiciary. All laws had to be made public and debated before being adopted a year later by the legislature. A Council of Censors was to be popularly elected every seven years to function like a sort of classical Senate permitting the people directly to repeal unjust or unpopular laws. These democratic measures were to assure a direct and continuous representation of society. They contrasted with the attempts made by the other States which sought to filter representation in order to make sure that it had an explicitly political status.[4] Thus, all of them instituted bicameralism, some made either the executive or the judiciary more independent, and none created a Council of Censors. These latter constitutions express a consistent Whiggism. They conceptualize representation as a technique for protecting social Liberty by means of a system of checks and balances. But without the existence of social estates whose essential freedom is defined by their political function as social orders, bicameralism or the executive or judicial veto could not be justified. The question of representation was not resolved, in Pennsylvania or elsewhere.

The problem of representation became explicitly political when the creation of a national Constitution became necessary. The States had been particularist even though the presence of a common enemy in war had unified them externally. The Continental Congress had no real power; George Washington's army appealed vainly to it for help. The Confederal Constitution proposed in 1777 was not ratified until 1781, shortly before the decisive battle of Yorktown. A country which had insisted so strongly on its rights made war without any legitimate political authority. There was never a proposal, as during the French Revolution, to mobilize the nation through the appeal to '*la patrie en danger*'. Once independence had been won, the Confederal Congress remained without power. Its members were representatives of the States constrained by binding instructions from home; they were incapable of creating a national politics. This weakness posed the political question which became the lived experience of the third period. The impotence of the nation put into question at once the direct democracy of Pennsylvania and the traditional Whiggism of the other States. This third period thus reflects at one and the same time the pre-political lived experience of self-evident rights and their representative conceptualization in autonomous societies of the States. The Old Whig primacy of Liberty and the republican insistence on the realization of the Commonwealth had to be unified in a Constitution which makes explicit the political status assumed by the Declaration of Independence and put into practice by the Confederal Congress.

The new Constitution was called 'federal' in order to convince the States that it would not rob them of their social freedoms. The debate concerning its ratification makes explicit the theory underlying the process of the Revolution as a whole. The opponents of the Constitution who criticized especially the lack of a Declaration of Rights based their arguments on the Whig theory which sees the political as a threat to freedom. But the political cannot be conceptualized as the guarantor of pre-political freedoms any more than the reflection of politics is the mere representation of pre-existing social rights; those freedoms and those rights are born with the political whose concrete realization they instantiate. That is why the proponents of the new Constitution had no difficulty, after ratification, in directing the constitutional adoption of a

Bill of Rights, which consists in the first ten Amendments to the Constitution rather than being inscribed as the preamble or premise of that fundamental law. The Constitution reflects a different lived experience of freedom and another conceptualization of a society in which that freedom is manifested. The Constitution is concerned with a freedom and rights which are directed to a future in which they can take on new forms. In a society without estates or orders, Liberty takes the form of equal and shared *political* rights; the Constitution founds only *the right to have rights*. The theoretical status of this foundation will permit us to explain the birth of political parties and the justification of judicial review.

### Reading the Framers' Reading

The reading of American history in terms of the theory of its revolution can be developed further if we consider the reflection on that revolutionary experience produced by the authors of *The Federalist Papers*. That volume of essays, written during the debate on the ratification of the Constitution, sought to reassure those who saw the new Constitution as a threat to the freedom of the individual or to the social rights of the States. But the analysis has implications that remain actual. For example, Hamilton (in Number 9) and Madison (in Number 10) sought to reassure the classical Whigs who feared that an 'extended republic' must necessarily fail. The danger they feared was the emergence of 'factions' which would proliferate necessarily because of the sociological diversity of a large territory. The multiplication of these factions was taken to be the prelude to the anarchy which, classically, is the prelude to tyranny. *The Federalist* accepts the sociological diagnosis but rejects its political implications. Factions are to freedom what air is to fire. Rather than seek to suppress them in the name of a wholly unified society, the authors of *The Federalist* see in them the guarantor of freedom because, in an extended republic, they will each be the counterweight to the others. This argument was taken up again by the pragmatic pluralism of liberal sociology in the 1950s. It could be used, *a contrario*, by the progressive critics who sought to explain the apolitical nature of a society whose political parties are condemned to be only coalitions of interests reduced to their common denominator. But these contemporary sociological explications neglect the constitutional structure; they reduce it – as did the constitutions of the 13 States – to a simple technique invented by a political science which is in fact simply a one-dimensional sociology.

A second analysis in *The Federalist* has contemporary relevance which illustrates the difficulty. This time, the authors attempt to explain the system of checks and balances set up within the Constitution itself. If the three branches of government were only articulated to block each other reciprocally in order to permit *society* to function according to its own rules, government would be blocked, politics would be impotent, and the citizen would be left to the mercies of the law of the strongest. The contemporary Right criticizes the doctrine of checks and balances as the root of the impotence, the inconstancy of the government and its incapacity to decide in the national interest; the contemporary Left sees in this same structure a social pluralism crowning the weakness of the political level which thereby assures the domination of capital. *The Federalist* takes up the problem in Number 51. 'In framing a government which is to be administered by men over men, the great difficulty lies in this: you must first enable the government to control the governed; and in the next place oblige it to control itself.' The sociological analysis of factions within an extended republic is not sufficient in this explicitly political context. Thus, the same Number 51 adds that, 'whilst there being thus less danger to a minor from the will of a major party, there must be less pretext, also, to provide for the security of the former, by introducing into the government a will not dependent on the latter, or in other words, a will independent of the society itself'. But how can this argument against the separation of politics from society be brought into harmony with the defence of a bicameral legislature whose Senate has precisely the function of checking the impetuous will of the majority?

The crucial argument is found in *The Federalist's* explicitly *political* theory of representation. Number 63 explains that the Senate stands as the federal instance since the Senators are named by the States. The three branches of government are, of course, all republican, hence all representative. *What* they represent, each in its own way, is the sovereign people. But this representation is not conceptualized in terms of the binding instructions given by society to politics any more than it is reflected in terms of the idea of virtual representation. After showing that the Ancients already made use of the principle of representation, *The Federalist* underlines the fact that 'the true distinction between these and the American governments, lies *in the [Americans'] total exclusion of the people, in their collective capacity'*. This apparently paradoxical assertion, underlined by its author, seems to confirm the progressive's denunciation of a constitutional *coup d'état*. But a different reading shows it to be in fact the foundation of *political* democracy. The sovereign people is *everywhere and nowhere*: everywhere, freedom always will find its champion: nowhere, none of the institutions of government can claim to *be* the totality of the people, to speak the truth of the people, to incarnate the reality of that political 'will independent of the society itself' which was criticized in Number 51. It is in this sense that the American Federal Republic institutes a democracy.

This theory of representation can only be understood in terms of the lesson learned in the course of the Revolution. The question of sovereignty debated with England had been determined by the dilemma of the *imperium in imperio*; the relation between the parts and the general interest of the Empire had to be brought to explicitness. Whig theory did not lend itself to a federal solution; hence, the colonists fell back on the Old Whig primacy of Liberty. That justified independence, but its limits became apparent during the elaboration of the State constitutions. Shays' rebellion, which finally brought the issue to a head in 1787, was not a *jacquerie* but rather the ultimate recourse of society against the State. It posed again the question of political power.[5] The Continental Congress represented the nation without being able concretely to incarnate it. Society functioned, but without political foundation; left to itself, it ran the risk of foundering into anarchy before becoming tyranny. The Framers of the Constitution had to find a political foundation capable of protecting society against its own worst instincts. That foundation, incarnated by the Constitution, was nothing but the sovereignty which had been affirmed already in the Declaration of Independence and practised by the Continental Congress; but this time it was thematized explicitly as political. The sovereign people, everywhere and nowhere, exists in the mode of the *symbolic*; it is that instance which permits society to act upon itself. The political medium established by the Constitution is neither the economy nor individual interest; democratic politics concerns rights, whose first and foundational right is the right to have rights.

## The Institutions of Democracy

This reading of the theoretical foundation of the American Revolution permits an explanation of the birth of two phenomena which today determine American political life. A republican politics is founded classically on virtue, that ability of the citizen to (be able to) abstract from his private interests in order to devote himself to the common public good. The Puritans of New England as well as the Cavaliers of the South were not shy in invoking that virtue which they defended against the corruption of English society. They proved their virtue during the first period of the Revolution when their social self-organization taught them their ability to govern themselves as a sovereign people. Once independence had been won, the prosperity had returned, they began to doubt themselves. The existence of new fortunes won by sometimes doubtful or speculative practices contrasted with a stern poverty which broke out in revolt with Shays, or made democratic Pennsylvania nearly ungovernable. Although all of the State constitutions contained provisions for protecting, even for creating, virtue, neither the Constitution of 1787 nor *The Federalist* makes it primary. That absence explains the place that the political parties came to occupy. Their roots in a still pre-modern schema of political thought explain why there could be only two parties. Each of them must be able to claim to incarnate that virtue which no longer has a place in the modern democratic constitution; and they can only make such a claim by denouncing their competition as – in a contemporary if not modern phrase – the representatives of the Evil Empire.

The birth of political parties is often explained by the opposition between the protocapitalist commercial and fiscal policies of Hamilton and the agrarian democracy of which Jefferson dreamed. But this sociologizes relations which are in fact political (and it forgets that the much-praised farmer of Jefferson was a small agrarian capitalist). Both parties had supported the new national Constitution; the agreed-upon task now was to give it a content that could endure. It would be a retrospective reading to reduce their propositions to their social implications. The French Revolution brought their divergences to a head. Jefferson's supporters saw in it the successor to their own struggles and hopes; Hamilton's allies feared that its anarchical course would contaminate their own republican experience. The Hamiltonians made fun of the generous and naïve optimism which prevented the Jeffersonians from understanding the hard requirements of governing a sinful and easily corrupted humanity; they admired the stable institutions of England, which they hoped would come into being gradually at home. The Jeffersonians could only see these attitudes as 'aristocratic', as 'monarchist', or as the preaching of 'anti-republicans' who had no confidence in a public opinion which they sought to control rather than obey. After a first period during which opinion deferred, as it had always deferred, to its established leaders who thus had no reason to act as partisan politicians, the Hamiltonians had to seek to identify themselves with a 'national interest' said to exist above and beyond everyday politics. Their party could base its appeal on the denunciation of the

Jeffersonians as meddlesome factional politicians, anti-republican because they placed partisan interests above the national interest.

The two parties that emerged from the founding period changed their names during the course of American history; yet that history has always been the scene of a struggle between two parties each claiming to incarnate a politics based on republican virtue. Treated as a system, this bipartite structure is essentially modern and democratic despite its pre-modern foundation.[6] To accept the fact that society is fundamentally divided and yet still one is to go beyond the classical conception of a republic founded on the *reality* of a *res publica*. It would be a simplification to reduce the birth of political parties to a socio-economic analysis; *The Federalist* already suggested that approach in Numbers 9 and 10 before moving to a properly political account. Nor should one follow the functionalist political scientists who see in the party system simply the reply by the political system to challenges posed by its environment. It is true that parties fulfill functions, for example, by binding the executive and legislative branches or by mediating relations between the citizens and the government, the States and the nation, or by levelling regional differences in the process of agglomerating diverse interests. But to limit oneself to these approaches is to avoid the essential philosophical question: how did it come about that society could be conceived as at once unified and divided? How could democratic practice be instituted and opposition be recognized as legitimate? Political modernity cannot be reduced to the criteria of a pseudo-Weberian rationalization process.

The modern nature of the system of political parties can be explained when we recall the way in which the Constitution articulates the *symbolic* nature of the political. Political parties exist in the same modality as do the branches of the federal government; none can claim to incarnate, once and for all, either power or knowledge of the common good or that of the law. This symbolic existence of the sovereign power was the foundation of the peaceful transfer of powers during the 'Revolution of 1800'. This same symbolic nature of power explains how the Americans came to accept *judicial review* by a non-elected branch of government. That practice was born in the wake of the 'Revolution of 1800'. Only a society whose essence consists in being divided can understand that there will always be a confrontation between two rights which claim to represent the common good at the same time that each knows that in the long run the political system can only refute both of them. The birth of the party system and the practice of judicial review are thus bound together by the heritage of the Revolution. American judicial practice did not remain long within the path traced by the *political* logic of the Constitution; contemporary American law seems rather to lend itself to sociological analyses or those of political science. Nonetheless, if one seeks to understand the properly political history of the country, one cannot ignore constitutional law and its foundation: the future-oriented right to have rights.

At the conclusion of this reading of American political history in terms of its Revolution, we can return to our categories of lived experience, its conceptualization, and its reflection. According to that schema, the lived experience of American history is the Constitution. The three phases of the Revolution, and their specific articulations, constitute the contents of that lived experience – contents capable of being reactivated and rearticulated. The conceptualized form of that American political life is the party system. Its developments can be understood in terms of the sedimentations of the lived political experience in the society. But the politics of the parties is in turn dependent on the reflected instance, which is the process of judicial review. Its foundation is not the individual as portrayed by the Whig vision of the small owner – although that interpretation could dominate judicial practice during long periods like the one that culminated in civil war. The foundation of constitutional law is not society; constitutional law is the foundation of society – as one saw, for example, during the Civil Rights Movement when judicial decisions catalyzed political action. That contemporary illustration makes it clear that the reflected form of the political is not the conclusion or the goal of political action. One cannot stress sufficiently the fact that the constitutional decisions concerning civil rights were founded by *Amendments* to the Constitution – indeed, by amendments voted after the Civil War – added to the amendments that constitute the 'Bill of Rights'. This means that the great transformation of contemporary American life can itself be understood only in terms of that first and primary political right which is the right to have rights. American politics is constantly confronted, as it has been since the Declaration of Independence, by the *question* of those rights which are taken to be 'self-evident truths'. In the last resort, these rights are evident only in light of political practice, which itself is founded on that first and primary right to have rights.

We have to listen one last time to the political scientists who introduce a *caveat*. The appearance of what has been called the 'Imperial Presidency' seems to show that American political life has come to be defined by the Presidency. This deformation of the system of checks and balances is explained today by the near-disappearance of the political parties whose legitimacy was founded by reference to that pre-modern notion of virtue; the modern Presidency seeks to present itself as the incarnation of the national interest. Hamilton seems finally to win. The confirmation of this new direction today would be the fantastic abuses of foreign policy-making power in the 'Irangate' affair. But that label recalls that before this latest scandal, there was 'Watergate', and that the reflected form of the political cannot be neglected. But one should not be an idealist either. American political life since the end of the Second World War has passed through periods during which it was first the judiciary, then the executive, and then the legislative branch which claimed to be the incarnation of that sovereignty which the Constitution institutes as symbolic, *everywhere and nowhere*. Although a usurpation cannot be excluded *a priori*, and although the established order cannot be treated as sacred, one has to admit that the Constitution furnishes the bases that permit a modern democracy to reaffirm itself. Beyond as well as prior to a politics based on interest, the American Revolution, by instituting democracy, founded politics as a struggle for right and for rights.

# Notes

## INTRODUCTION TO THE ENGLISH EDITION

1. The French tend to talk of 'events' when they are at the end of their conceptual rope; whence, for example, the 'events' of May '68.
2. But not the translator! David Curtis highlighted this oddity in one of several long letters in which he suggested his own interpretation, and criticism, of this book. I have incorporated some of his ideas, and tried to reply indirectly to others, in this Introduction.
3. I should perhaps express here my surprise, as I combed through the historians' research, at the absence of discussion of Arendt's *On Revolution*. I don't know how to explain this absence, other than by the disciplinary constraints of the modern American university. Perhaps this, too, was a reason for my decision to write the book in French.

   Palmer's study, *The Age of the Democratic Revolution, A Political History of Europe and America, 1760–1800*, 2 vols., (Princeton: Princeton University Press, 1959, 1964) seems also to have enjoyed less circulation than it is due – in this case, apparently, because it was seen as an instrument in the Cold War. Such, at least, is the argument of Jacques Godechot, the French historian who formulated a similar thesis concerning an 'Atlantic Revolution' (which included the Latin American liberation struggles). Godechot explains the context succinctly in the Preface to the second edition of his *La Grande Nation* (Paris: Editions Aubier Montaigne, 1983) pp. 7–11.
4. Liberalism in this context refers to *economic* liberalism; republicanism captures the more Anglo-American concern with *political* liberties. It is not my intention to even sketch here a topology of French political life in the 1980s. The interested reader will find discussions of that subject – and some of my own attempts to contribute to it – in chapters of my two recent books, *Defining the Political* and *The Politics of Critique* (both published by Macmillan: London, and University of Minnesota Press: Minneapolis, 1988). With regard to the present Mitterrand-Rocard government, and it's 'Socialist' claims, cf. 'Politics and the Political: Learning from Paris and New York', in *French Politics and Society*, Vol. 6, October 1988, No. 4; French trans. in *La Lettre internationale*, Nr. 20, mars 1989.
5. I should underline 'almost' here. I will turn in a moment to the methodological justification of my categorial structure; the reader concerned with my interpretation of Hegel will find a detailed account in *From Marx to Kant* (Albany: State University of New York Press, 1985), which also suggests the strictly philosophical motivations behind this essay, which stands as part of a comparison, still in gestation, of the birth of the modern stage in France, Prussia and the United States.
6. Note that I call it a modern *phenomenon*. The political can also have traditional forms; and its study goes back to the origins of philosphy – and of democracy – in Greece. I speak here of a modern phenomenon because modernity poses, for the first time since the Greeks, the *question* of the

political. In its traditional forms, the political is the source of *answers*; neither its genesis nor its normative validity is put into question.

7. It is not surprising that the hermeneutic project arose at the same time as the modern revolutionary project. Indeed, its early practitioners were animated quite explicitly by a reactionary goal, but one whose consequences need not be so one-sided; the romantic reaction can be seen as a defence of the individual against the abstract universality of the Enlightenment. One recognizes here in abstract form the problems of democratic republicanism evoked above. A useful recent attempt to establish the nature and limits of a modern hermeneutics capable of dealing with the problem of revolution is found in Johann P. Arnason, *Praxis und Interpretation* (Frankfurt: Suhrkamp Verlag, 1988). Arnason discusses the emergence of the hermeneutic problem in the context of continental philosophy (Habermas, Castoriadis, Heidegger) its Anglo-American former opposite (Frege, Wittgenstein, Putnam). For an English summary, cf. my discussion 'The Hermeneutic Dimension of Critical Theory', in *Praxis International*, Spring, 1989.

8. This structural account is of course highly abstract. It has the methodological advantage of permitting an understanding of the potential for failure in a revolutionary project. If one or the other of the moments is made absolute, or is lacking, the originary question, the problem of the political, is lost. I have attempted to illustrate this process in the two volumes mentioned in note 3, and will concretize it in the proposed study of the birth of the modern state mentioned in note 4.

9. The *Afterword* added to this volume develops the approach suggested here but not carried out in the book itself.

10. Andrew C. McLaughlin, 'The Background of American Federalism', in *The American Political Science Review*, Vol. XII, 1918, pp. 215–40. Richard Buel, Jr. kindly called my attention to this article.

11. Another function of the chapters on 'History Rethought' is to take account of other theoretical positions which appear to contradict my own, or to introduce interpretative standpoints outside of my framework.

12. This point was suggested to me by David Curtis' well-taken criticisms of my arguments. I do not necessarily draw the same implications from it that he would see.

13. Among the socialists, I have in mind particularly those identified as the 'second left' (or criticized as the 'American Left' by dogmatists who know no US history). Among the historians, I have in mind particularly the pathbreaking work of François Furet, *Penser la Révolution française* (Paris: Gallimard, 1978). Both developments, as well as my own arguments, are indebted to the pioneering work of Cornelius Castoriadis and Claude Lefort. For details, see *The Marxian Legacy*, especially the Afterword to the second edition (London: Macmillan, and Minneapolis: University of Minnesota Press, 1988), and my essay referred to in note 4 above.

14. The concept of 'erasure' was once again suggested by David Curtis, who points to its usage in Derrida, among other contemporaries. Despite my rejection of this argument, I must admit that I found no satisfactory way to deal with the question of slavery, and its political legacy, in my attempt to deal with the origins of contemporary American politics.

15. Karl E. Klare, 'The Labor-Management Cooperation Debate: A Work-

place Democracy Perspective', *Harvard Civil Rights – Civil Liberties Law Review*, Vol. 23, Winter 1988, No. 1, pp. 39–83. It is not clear that Klare wants to attribute, as I would, a *symbolic* status to the goal of 'workplace democracy'. On the other hand, he does reject emphatically the idea that there exist solutions which would put an end to conflict by means of a harmonious solution that makes the workplace into a miniature image of what the Marxist revolutionaries imagined to be a post-revolutionary *society* in which there is no longer any place for the political.

16. I did make a good number of minor changes in the manuscript, correcting several errors which had been pointed out to me, and adding connective tissue when it appeared that an argument was not as clear as it should be. I want to thank Richard Buel, Jr. for his critical comments, which helped me to understand the nature and limits of what I have done in this essay.


## INTRODUCTION

1. The interpretation of the French Revolution obviously was a smokescreen concealing more deep-seated differences between the opposing political camps. Adams' Federalist party was considered anglophile, aristocratic and (without perceiving the apparent contradiction) mercantile and pro-industrial; Jefferson's Republicans were said to be francophile, agrarian and democratic. This is obviously to simplify things in the extreme and to neglect the questions of political theory that underlay the division. For example, already in 1787, when he was American Ambassador to France, Jefferson refused to undertake the translation of Adams' book, *Defence of the Constitution of Government of the United States of America*, whose theoretical point of view went against the ideas of his friends Condorcet and the *philosphes*, who criticized Adams' aristocratic rationale for a bicameral legislature. Cf. Joyce Appleby, 'The Jefferson-Adams Rupture and the First French Translation of John Adams' *Defense'*, *The American Historical Review*, Vol. LXXIII, April 1968, No. 4, pp. 1086–91.
2. This alleged right later served to justify the system of legal segregation that reigned in the South after the Civil War. Decentralization is not always good in itself! Small communities are not necessarily composed of virtuous republicans.
3. See the provocative study by David W. Noble, *The End of American History, Democracy, Capitalism, and the Metaphor of Two Worlds in Anglo-American Historical Writings, 1889–1980* (Minneapolis: University of Minnesota Press, 1985), which examines the ups and downs of republican thought from Turner to the first Beard, the critic of capitalism; to the second Beard, poet of American democracy against a now international capitalism; to Niebuhr, the Protestant and Progressive critic of capitalism; to Hofstadter, who contrasts American democracy with its capitalist form; up to Williams, who curses capitalism and Marxism in the name of an American democracy he has rediscovered in the populist movement.
4. Neither Bailyn nor Wood seems to have developed their writings from the 1960s any further. The debate that they stirred up has turned historio-

graphical. Only J.G.A. Pocock and some of his students have continued along this path. But the work of Pocock is becoming more and more philological in character and no longer promises the vast panoramas found in his earlier book, *The Machiavellian Moment.* I will return to these issues later. For the following, cf. Bernard Bailyn, 'The Central Themes of the American Revolution', in *Essays on the American Revolution,* Stephen G. Kurtz and James H. Hutson (eds) (New York: W.W. Norton, 1973).

5. I am schematising an argument that is developed at length in over 600 pages of text. Wood's thesis does not necessarily culminate in the death of politics, only in its radical transformation. He notes that, according to Whig political theory, the opposition between liberty and power is a zero-sum game: if one wins, the other loses. On the other hand, the *sociological* perspective is favourable to a growth in both power and liberty. Wood seems therefore to have rediscovered a key idea found in the work of Hannah Arendt. The difficulty is that the kind of liberty that progresses at the same time as power seems to rest upon a private form of freedom. Nevertheless, this latter form of liberty becomes active and dynamic, whereas the political liberty of the classical theory aims above all at preserving society in its organic form. Wood thus speaks of a form of political thought that is *romantic* because it is innovative and open.

6. This is the thesis of Louis Hartz, laid out in a comparativist format in *The Liberal Tradition in America* (New York: Harcourt, Brace & World, 1955).

7. One may have expected the name of Locke and the concept of liberalism to be cited here. His name and some of the elements of his thought did become household words during this era; but his political thought, itself rather confused, does not seem to have played a determining role in the analysis Americans made of their situation. If one is talking about the Locke whose theory of private property is supposed to found liberal society, to attribute to him the historical foundation of the Americans' revolutionary thought is either a banal truth or an error. On the other hand, Locke, as the theoretician of the political contract between society and government, might have played a role at the beginning of the Revolution, but in that case this theory would have contributed to the constitutional confusion that came with independence. Yet again, one finds traces of Locke the thinker of the pre-political social contract in the constitutional period. In short, there are many Lockes.

8. Pocock distinguishes a plethora of currents among the Whigs at the time. He analyzes, for example, the distinction between sceptical Whigs, vulgar Whigs and independent Whigs, modern Whigs and honest Whigs. Pocock's essay is found in his collection, *Virtue, Commerce and History* (Cambridge: Cambridge University Press, 1985).

9. Some Americans drew more radical conclusions, insisting on the idea that the republic presupposes social equality, the communal ownership of goods, and a breaking of foreign commercial ties. Jeremy Belknap, for example, concluded in a letter to Ebenezer Hazard, dated 3 March 1784: 'If "Equality is the soul of a republic" then we have no soul'. When individuals are rich and the State is poor, is this not evidence 'that the people of this country are not destined to be long governed in a democratic form?' (Quoted in Gordon Wood, *The Creation of the American Republic,* p. 425).

10. From Webster's article, 'Government', in the *American Magazine*, 1 (1787–88) p. 142; cited in ibid., p. 378.
11. Jürgen Habermas, 'Natural Law and Revolution', in *Theory and Practice*, trans. John Viertel (Boston: Beacon Press, 1973), pp. 82–120.
12. From Letter VI of Dickinson's *Letters from a Farmer in Pennsylvania*; reprinted in Merrill Jensen, ed., *Tracts of the American Revolution, 1763–76* (Indianapolis: Bobbs-Merrill, 1978), p. 145.
13. Letter II; reprinted in ibid., p. 135.
14. Thus the Bill of Rights is not a part of the Constitution itself but constitutes the first ten amendments to the Constitution, voted by the first Congress which set in motion its new institutions. That other amendments can be added reinforces the argument that the Constitution is a *symbolic* mediation. Rather than realize the abstract norms that would define pre-political man, the American Constitution seeks to define *political* rights, which rights can be enlarged eventually with the help of this plural society. The extension of rights is not only accomplished through the process of amending the Constitution. The manner in which Supreme Court interpretations contribute to this effort again confirms the symbolic character of the political authorities established by the Constitution. Such interpretations are a distinct form of jurisprudential action, a hermeneutic that would have to be studied in its own right. Indeed, the designation of the judiciary as one of the three independent branches of government is a novelty in political theory; in pre-modern constitutions, this power had been given either to the executive or the legislative branch or to both of them together. Pre-modern society considered itself, in effect, as an organism from which division was excluded, whereas modern society legitimates the division of society in such a way that two rights can confront each other without one or the other being declared illegitimate.
15. The existence of *factions* in pre-modern society was the sign of a division that political practice had to transcend toward the common good. Modern society is by essence divided; the preservation of this division, which is the sign and the guarantee of liberty, is the very definition of the republic and explains the legitimation of the new system of political parties in the United States. On the latter, cf. the Afterword printed here, which was first published in the *Revue Française de Science Politique*, Vol. 38, April 1988, No. 2.

# Part 1

## CHAPTER 1

1. See the fine study by Elise Marienstras, *Les Mythes fondateurs de la nation américaine* (Paris: Maspero, 1976), whose subtitle explains its purpose: *Essai sur le discours idéologique des Etats-Unis à l'époque de l'indépendance (1763–1800)* (Essay on the ideological discourse of the United States at the time of independence). Marienstras denounces the ravages of a national

ideology that became nationalistic because it was founded upon the psychical, physical and often violent exclusion of the humanity of the Other: the Native American, the black slave, the European.

2. A new political and commercial Whig aristocracy had begun to form. The 'Glorious', and peaceful, Revolution of 1688 became its consecration.

3. See Jacques Godechot, *La Grande Nation*, 2nd edn, completely revised (Paris: Aubier Montaigne, 1983) and Robert R. Palmer, *The Age of the Democratic Revolution*, 2 vols (Princeton: Princeton University Press, 1959, 1964). These two books have not had the audience they merit, undoubtedly because at the time of their publication, as Godechot notes, they seemed to participate in the polemics over the Cold War.

   The situation sketched here is more complex, according to the historian Joyce Appelby, who detects the birth of a new type of thought centred on the new phenomenon of the market during the first part of the 17th century. The Revolution of 1640 and its aftermath seem to have wiped out this practical orientation, but Appelby argues that it survived in the colonies and it came to constitute – a century later – one of the progressive roots of the revolutionary movement. According to Appelby, it follows that the American Revolution is not a reaction against progress as incarnated in the English Empire. On the contrary, if America passed quickly from a political revolution for independence to a liberal transformation of the economy, this was because it was founded upon the free market thought of the 17th century. See Joyce Oldham Appelby, *Economic Thought and Ideology in Seventeenth-Century England* (Princeton: Princeton University Press, 1976) and, for the ideological implications, Appelby's 'The Social Origins of American Revolutionary Ideology', *The Journal of American History*, 64:4 (March 1978) pp. 935–58.

4. Apropos of Locke, see the critical analyses of J.G.A. Pocock, 'The Myth of John Locke and the Obsession with Liberalism', in *John Locke*, ed. Pocock and Ashcraft (Los Angeles: William Andrews Clark Memorial Library, 1980); and John Dunn, *The Political Thought of John Locke: An Historical Account of the Argument of the Two Treatises of Government* (Cambridge: Cambridge University Press, 1969). On the ups and downs of Whig theory, see Pocock, 'The Varieties of Whiggism from Exclusion to Reform: A History of Ideology and Discourse', in Pocock, *Virtue, Commerce and History*, op. cit.

5. Carl Lotus Becker, in *The History of Political Parties in the Province of New York, 1760–76* (Madison: University of Wisconsin Press, 1968; first edn, 1909), points to the existence of semi-feudal manors also in New York; their owners had the right, for example, to be represented in the Assembly and to dispense justice on their domains. This power was falling into decline as the movement for independence progressed. Some of these large landholding families, like the Livingstons, survived the period of the Revolution but with their minds transformed, as illustrated, for example, by the fact that they financed Fulton's first steamboat in 1807. Nevertheless, Berthoff and Murrin, in 'Feudalism, Communalism and the Yeoman Freeholder' in *Essays on the American Revolution*, ed. Stephen G. Kurtz and James H. Hutson (Chapel Hill: University of North Carolina Press, 1973), try to prove that there was a final surge of feudal privileges – as supposedly also in France

– on the eve of the Revolution. The position and the power of the upper chambers were to be upgraded and life peerages were demanded at the same time that certain semi-feudal taxes were to be reimposed after having fallen into disuse.

6. One also finds a first declaration of democratic intentions in this colony, which was founded in 1641. 'The government which this body politic doth attend unto . . . is a democracy or popular government; . . . that is to say: It is in the power of the body of freemen, orderly assembled, or in the major part of them, to make or constitute just laws, by which they will be regulated, and to depute from among themselves such ministers as shall see them faithfully executed between man and man'.

   One finds also in *The Bloody Tenent*, which states that civil government is ordained by God to preserve social peace, the following lines: 'The sovereign, origin, and foundation of civil power lies in the people (whom they must needs mean by the civil power distinct from the government set up). And if so, that a people may erect and establish what form of government seem to them most meet for their civil conditions. It is evident that such governments as are by them erected and established have no more power, nor for any longer time, than the civil power or people consenting and agreeing shall betrust them with. This is clear not only in reason, but in the experience of all commonweals where the people are not deprived of their natural freedom by the power of tryants'.

7. In *this* area, Locke's thought had a strong influence. John Dunn, who has written the most complete essay on this subject, notes that Locke's pamphlet, the *Letter on Toleration*, as well as his writings on education and the *Essay Concerning Human Understanding*, had the greatest influence on the colonists. See John Dunn, 'The Politics of Locke in England and America in the Eighteenth Century', in *John Locke: Problems and Perspectives*, ed. John W. Yolton (Cambridge: Cambridge University Press, 1969).

8. Louis Hartz has spoken in this context of a 'hebraism' according to which the Americans' feeling that they were a chosen people explains why, in contrast to the French Revolution, they did not seek to carry their revolution beyond the boundaries of their country. Nevertheless, American foreign policy has oscillated between an isolationism similar to the hebraism described by Hartz and an interventionism that wants precisely to bring the Good News, if not its institutional form, to the entire world.

9. Some contemporary historians, as we will see, wonder whether Scottish philosophy did not have a greater influence on revolutionary thought than the concept of individualism drawn from Locke.

10. Political alliances by marriage and the cumulation of multiple positions were long established practices among this aristocracy. Nothing could be done to prevent the former, but the plurality of office-holding was abolished everywhere after independence.

11. Richard Koebner's study, *Empire* (Cambridge: Cambridge University Press, 1961), attempts to show that the English spoke of Empire only to designate England and Ireland. Starting in 1740, this concept acquired a certain importance as the Americans began to define their place in the world and their future. That the English had not grasped the meaning of this American attitude explains in part their inability to understand American demands later on, when integration into the Empire revealed itself to be a

form of subordination to England. The Americans felt betrayed; the patriotism of which they had given proof during the Seven Years' War evaporated quickly. This explains only in part, however, why these 13 colonies alone, and not Ireland, India, the Caribbean, not to mention Canada, challenged the Empire.

12. One current in the English opposition interpreted English policy toward the colonies as an attempt systematically to strip Parliament of its power and to return to the situation prevailing before the Glorious Revolution. The tenacious, even obstinate research of a Namier was necessary to demonstrate that this was in no way the goal of the government. But Namier and his school reduce politics solely to visible and positive acts of a determinate group. Whatever the real intentions of George III, and his ministers, it is the context that gives political meaning to his actions.

13. One should not, however, exaggerate, as does James H. Hutson, when he tries to prove that the American revolutionaries did not abolish slavery, as might have been expected, because they felt themselves to be treated as slaves by the British and because, in order to free themselves from the accusation of being cruel masters, they 'projected' this accusation onto the English and cleansed themselves by means of their victory in the War of Independence. Hutson adds to this analysis of colonial psychology the claim that the colonists were tormented by their desire to be independent of a protective mother and therefore lived their struggle for independence as a matricide of which they cleansed themselves by their pretensions to a virile form of virtue. The result of this psychological trauma is said to be that they became paranoiacs; and since paranoia is a defence against latent homosexuality, the American Revolution can be said, ultimately, to be the result of a generalized panic over their homosexual tendencies! ('The American Revolution: The Triumph of a Delusion', in *New Wine in Old Skins*, ed. Erich Angermann, [Stuttgart: Klett Verlag, 1976]).

14. The imminence of another Anglo-French war remained in everyone's mind during this period. The French Foreign Minister, Choiseul, was already preparing his revenge, foreseeing an eventual split within the English Empire. France's *de jure* recognition of the rebellious colonies in 1778, after the semi-official aid that was already being offered, was the logical culmination of his policy. The English were aware of the danger, but they were divided among conflicting demands. Thus, for example, when the colony of New York refused to lodge English troops in 1767, the minister, Lord Shelbourne, hesitated to intervene so as not to encourage a reaction from the French. Similarly, the colonies had to act in the context of the threat of a division among themselves which could then be used by one or the other of the two contending European powers. For the same reason, after independence, the confederated United States had to give themselves a more centralized Constitution in 1787.

## CHAPTER 2

1. The Albany Plan was responding to real needs, as was indicated by the flag and slogan it adopted: 'Join, or Die'. The colonies not only had to defend themselves but also had to provide eventually for some kind of mechanism

to enlarge their association as the process of colonization advanced toward the West. The assembly proposed in the Albany Plan would have granted representation to each colony according to the number of its inhabitants; and it would have been headed by a president-general named by the King. But when the abolition of the colonial legislatures was proposed as the corollary of this structure, Franklin himself responded in a pamphlet, *Letters to Governor William Shirley*, in December 1754. He pointed out that each colony was already in the habit of setting its own taxes and that there could be no question of changing this practice. This was in fact only a half-truth, for the president-general would have possessed a right to veto, and the traditional control the legislature exercised by means of the budget would no longer have been available, since this magistrate would be paid directly by the Crown. Thus, when it was seen that the Albany Plan would not be adopted, some politicians even proposed that it be imposed by England. A number of the ideas presented in 1754 were taken up later in the plan for the Articles of Confederation of the 13 independent States proposed by Franklin. But the powers granted to this president-general were not retained. The parochial attitude that doomed this national project remained embedded in the behaviour of the freed colonies. For example, John Adams spoke of the representatives from his State to the Congress of the Confederation as 'our embassy'; and as late as 1786 citizens of Maryland spoke of 'the nation' when referring to their State.

2. Although the affair took place in Massachusetts, these Writs of Assistance were applied in all the colonies and the protest against this kind of 'open hunting season' was unanimous. The importance of the protests against these Writs in crystallizing opposition in the colonies can be seen in the fact that the fourth of the first ten Amendments to the 1787 Constitution formally forbids this kind of police intervention. As O.M. Dickerson notes, it is surprising that an entire amendment should be devoted to this issue when freedom of the press, religion, and speech and the right to assembly and to petition for redress of grievances are dealt with in a single amendment (the first). On this affair, see O.M. Dickerson, 'Writs of Assistance as a Cause of the Revolution', in Richard B. Morris (ed.), *The Era of the American Revolution* (New York: Columbia University Press, 1939).

3. Blackstone's *Commentaries* were published only in 1765. His analysis codified Whig legal and political thought. Blackstone presents in particular an argument proving the omnipotence of Parliament which is based, among other things, upon the impossibility of a dual sovereignty in a single State (*imperium in imperio*). These two notions came to play a crucial role in the conflict with the colonies. For the moment, the important point is that Blackstone's argument is *modern*; he rejects corporatist doctrine handed down from a feudal system in which certain rights granted to constituted bodies are deemed absolute.

4. It is not the economic or fiscal wisdom of these measures but their political (and psychological) impact that is of importance. Nonetheless, a Marxist reading can see in them the outlines of an economic struggle between two nascent capitalist economies. Thus, Louis Hacker notes first of all that if only taxes were at stake, England would not have abandoned this fiscal policy so quickly in the face of American protests. For Hacker, the measures

aimed at strengthening the Empire – the introduction of stricter customs controls, proscriptions on the types of iron products the colonies could manufacture, the prohibition against issuing money in the colonies and finally, in 1773, the creation of an English monopoly on the sale of tea – can be understood if one starts with the requirements of English capital faced with the potential competition offered by the colonies. Cf. Louis M. Hacker 'The First American Revolution', in E. Wright (ed.), *Causes and Consequences of the American Revolution* (Chicago: Quadrangle, 1966). But other economists note that the colonies did well under the English system, which subsidized their exports within the Empire, protected their commercial trade against pirates as well as making safe their westward expansion, created a communications network and a postal service, made them the beneficiaries of a strong currency, and so on. These economic historians also point out that, after independence, the ex-colonies needed 30 years for their foreign trade to return to its pre-revolutionary level.

5. To speak of 'political opinion' in the colonies at the beginning of the 1760s is not self-evident, and may cause confusion. On the one hand, the situation in each colony would have to be analyzed. In Rhode Island or in New York, political groups organized around certain leaders who were seeking to secure for themselves seats in the legislature or judicial appointments as stepping stones to the upper house and as a way of furthering their commercial or speculative interests. In other colonies, such as Pennsylvania or Virginia, control continued to be exercised by well established persons with long-standing influence. On the other hand, there was no 'popular political opinion' at the beginning of resistance against English policy. Historians use Bagehot's concept of a 'deferential society' to describe political life during this era. As conflict with England intensified, a form of public opinion did develop, sometimes with the support of leaders whose interests coincided with such opinion, but often going well beyond the wishes of these leaders in both the content of its demands and the form of its actions. For illustrations, cf. P. Maier, op. cit.

6. This argument suggests that Otis' position is pre-modern in another sense. It is based on an identification of morality with politics, whereas the concentration of political functions in the State serves to separate these two domains. The unfolding of the American Revolution contributes to the clarification and modification of this distinction.

7. The distinction between internal and external taxes was later revived for his own purposes by Townshend. Seeking to avoid colonial protests against measures aimed at raising revenue, he asserted that his new regulations were aimed simply at managing trade within the Empire. The colonists then had to respond by challenging the very principle of taxes voted by Parliament, which boiled down to a *de facto* declaration of independence from it. But this took time. Edmund S. Morgan's 'Colonial Ideas of Parliamentary Power, 1764–66', *William and Mary Quarterly*, V:3 (July 1948), tries to free Americans of the accusation of hypocrisy. They are charged with having sought from the beginning to free themselves from Parliamentary control, but, not daring to avow this goal at the outset, they sought to hide behind half-measures like the distinction between internal and external taxes. But, according to Morgan, that distinction is absent from the colonial

arguments; the colonists distinguished only between legislation aimed at regulating the affairs of the Empire, which they accepted, and taxes that were simply a gift freely consented to by the colonial legislatures. But, what is striking in Morgan's argument is that the vocabulary (a 'freely consented gift') is, once again, pre-modern! The demand for independence would have to find another foundation.

It should be noted, too, that the distinction between internal and external taxes, or that between fiscal and legislative powers, is taken up again and applied in the Constitution of 1787. Its theoretical justification is found in numbers 33 and 34 of *The Federalist*.

8. This experience of direct democracy puts in question the frequent assertion that the colonists lived in a system of domestic democracy. Certainly the suffrage was rather general and society itself did not include any hereditary distinctions. But, as Merrill Jensen asks, is one really in a democracy when the same politicians are regularly re-elected because they control administrative posts (and honours), as was manifestly the case in Massachusetts? And since such control depended upon the distribution of sinecures, can one not say that the struggle against the English became confused with another struggle, this one domestic, over the issues of domination and of social autonomy? One is reminded of Becker's celebrated phrase: 'Home rule, or who shall rule at home?'

Jack Greene's response to the theses of Pauline Maier, to which I allude in the text, is worth mentioning here. Whereas Maier is surprised at the rapidity of people's conversion to republicanism, Greene asks, on the contrary, why they took so long, given that they had neither king nor established church nor landed aristocracy. But, one may respond, what is the connection between the institutional democracy practised in the legislature and a democracy based upon the participation of citizens? After all, the pre-modern conception of representation is that one chooses a natural élite whose virtue commits it to a life of public service. According to this conception, one does not run for political posts, and the idea of rotation in office makes no sense. The only purpose of election is to eliminate those who do not merit it, not to select those who do.

With regard to mobs, cf. Gordon Wood, 'A Note on Mobs in the American Revolution', *William and Mary Quarterly*, Vol. XXIII, October 1966, No. 4, pp. 635–42.

9. The classic explanation of this concept is to be found in Burke, the representative of Bristol who had not set foot there between 1776 and 1780. The representative is elected to represent the common good; he ought in no case to be tied by the local interests of his electors, although they have the right, at the end of his term, not to re-elect him. See, for example, Burke's *Works*, vol. 2, pp. 95–7. A half century later, during the debate over the 1832 Reform Bill, this Whig concept was replaced by that of active participation, inspired by an argument that may be stated as follows: if my representative votes the way I would have voted, why then prevent me from exercising my right to vote? See the parliamentary debate reported in J.R. Pole, *Political Representation in England and the Origins of the American Republic* (Berkeley: University of California Press, 1971).

10. I am summarizing here what was obviously the result of a great debate in

each of the colonies; and I am describing it as the result of a debate whereas it was often public pressure that obliged lawyers and judges to proceed in their legal duties without using those legally required stamps. This popular pressure was transformed little by little into an autonomous self-governing society. Comparisons with the French Revolution, of course, can be made here. More important in the American context is the existence of the Stamp Act Congress. Like the Continental Congress which began in 1774, it furnished a *symbolic legitimation* for these decisions taken at the grass-roots level. We will see the development of this logic at the end of Part I, when we consider the Declaration of Independence.

11. 'Speech on Conciliation', in Burke, *Works*, vol. 2, p. 125.
12. We have already alluded to one of Dickinson's arguments. The governor of Massachusetts, Bernard, saw in these *Letters* a potential American Bill of Rights. His vice-governor and soon successor, Thomas Hutchinson, felt it his duty to respond, but his essay – which Bernard Bailyn calls 'one of the most revealing documents in the literature of the Revolution' – was never published. Bailyn gives a summary of it in *The Ordeal of Thomas Hutchinson* (Cambridge: Harvard University Press, 1974) p. 99. This essay, 'A Dialogue between Europe and America', is now published in *Perspectives in American History*, 8 (1974). The use of Locke in the argument between the two protagonists should be noted, as well as the fact that Dickinson's position was implicitly accepted ten years later, in 1778, by the Carlisle Commission, when it undertook a final attempt at mediation, which the American alliance with France rendered hopeless.
13. Gibbon's masterly analysis of the *Decline and Fall of the Roman Empire* was published in 1776. It seized the contemporary imagination more strongly than Adam Smith's *Wealth of Nations* and Jeremy Bentham's first introduction of utilitarianism, which were published the same year. The only rival to the impact of Gibbon's thought was the Declaration of Independence, that other literary event of 1776.
14. In fact, this competition and division had already been at work for some time. Writing under the pseudonym of 'A Chester County Farmer', Joseph Galloway explained that the non-importation policy was only a device on the part of New England to destroy trade in the other colonies. A contemporary Marxist would obviously detect here a struggle between an indigenous and *comprador* bourgeoisie or between the 'centre' and the 'periphery'. Whether true or false, this economistic approach does not explain the revolutionary nature of the Revolution.
15. This acceptance of illegality is worth noting. It is part of a transition toward a new social attitude tending to delegitimate inherited political authority. This attitude perhaps derives from the tradition of the 'moral economy' that the oppressed have always invoked, in Europe as well as in America. In the American context, this behaviour marks a transformation of tradition under the pressure of new political conditions.
16. Pennsylvania's history constitutes a unique chapter in the annals of the Revolution. A proprietary colony, it was controlled *de facto* by the Quaker élite and their allies who guaranteed it the freest institutions in all the colonies. The proprietors' supporters – sometimes allied with the politically excluded citizens in the western part of the state, those belonging to minority

sects and religions, and the non-English populations – led the opposition before the Revolution. Those who in other colonies would have been opposed to the English measures struggled here to strip the proprietor of his Charter and place the colony under a royal government! The result of this inversion of roles was that power was slipping from the hands of both factions as independence approached. Those who attained real power *via* the Association were the committees of artisans in alliance with people belonging to the liberal professions, those previously excluded from power in the West and a portion of the petty merchant class.

The action of the Associations, which became *de facto* governments in most of the colonies, are described contextually by a historian of the French Revolution, Robert R. Palmer: 'Revolutionary government as a step toward constitutional government, committees of public safety, representatives on mission to carry revolution to the local authorities, paper money, false paper money, price controls, oaths, detention, confiscation, aversion to "moderatism", and Jacobins who wind up as sober guardians of the law – how much it all suggests what was to happen in France a few years later' (*The Age of the Democratic Revolution*, vol. 1, p. 199).

17. In this context, Pauline Maier notes the role doctors played in the conflict, explaining their participation in terms of the unrecognized status of their profession and of the prevailing medical ideology, which depended on Newtonian science and on a conception of nature as good in itself – a view identical to Paine's. See *The Old Revolutionaries* (New York: Vintage, 1982).

18. The advocates of independence obviously did not want to criticize someone who had brought grist to their mill. The responses of the loyalists were subject to the censorship of the Association, which did not hesitate to get rid of 'false and dangerous' ideas.

19. The loyalists were not – especially at this time – traitors or wealthy landowners whose interests determined their politics. First of all, their theoretical position was that of the Whigs who had carried out the Glorious Revolution. A conservative social ideology can be seen in their (quite Whig) theory of a mixed government, where the aristocratic order, with its specific virtue, is considered as a necessary counterweight to a democracy that tends to dominate over the other virtues. The fear of 'corruption' by the democratic base dominates the loyalists' analyses, whereas the advocates of independence were animated by fear of 'corruption' based upon the machinations of the Crown. One might follow some historians influenced by the social sciences and speak of a 'loyalist personality', respectful of authority, lacking in autonomy, little tolerant of disorder, and inspired by the present and the past because of its fear of the future. During the debates leading up to independence, they rejected the subtle distinctions concerning internal and external taxes, taxes for revenue and taxes for the regulation of commerce. They could not accept the idea of loyalty due solely to the King. Virtual representation seemed to them a completely fair view since, as they said, the idea of consent does not mean that one should refuse to obey laws legally voted upon just because one's own candidate has been beaten. And, on the practical level, they did not think it was impossible to reach a compromize with England, a country to which they were attached by both sympathy and habit. The most effective loyalist argument, because it was

truly anti-modern, sees Revolution as a break with the positive evolutionary development of liberty as well as the rise of greedy upstarts who are incapable of truly enjoying their wealth and who are dominated by the lower classes they must court in order to establish themselves in power. Finally, we must emphasize that many became loyalists for reasons extrinsic to the conflict with England, as in the case of the Regulators in North Carolina or the little people in the West who wanted to strike a blow again East Coast domination.

## CHAPTER 3

1. Galloway's pamphlet is important because this eminent representative of the old colonial élite finally addressed the public at large. In 'The Democratisation of Mind in the American Revolution' in *The Moral Foundations of the American Republic*, ed. Robert. J. Horwitz (Charlottesville: University of Virginia Press, 1979), Gordon Wood traces the changes in the style of politics from the colonial era to the birth of the political party system in the years after 1790. The salient feature, according to Wood, is the opening of the debate to an ever broader, but at the same time less and less literate, public. Thus, for example, Paine's *Common Sense* is distinguished from other pamphlets written at the time by its lack of erudite quotations from the classics, constitutional law, or other sources known exclusively to an élite. Similarly, Wood notes that a satirical style was employed less and less, for its effects can be felt only in a small circle where allusions could be understood without any need laboriously to point them out. Satire was replaced by invective, more and more demagogic in character, and the old élite was beaten on the rhetorical plane even before the argument began.

2. The members of the Lee clan of Virginia were already fiery advocates of independence. The two Adams, John and Samuel, represented Massachusetts. At the time, Samuel was the better known because he was the leader of the Boston radicals. (Later, John, his cousin, was disappointed when, upon arrival in Paris to represent the new nation, people expressed their disappointment that they were meeting 'the other Monsieur Adams'.) Samuel remained an active politician in Massachusetts while John went on to hold national office, including the presidency.

   While it is true that certain people were pulling the strings behind the scenes, we must understand the logic behind their choice. The leaders of Massachusetts knew that their colony had a bad reputation for acting rashly, being controlled by the rabble, and seeking to push others further than they themselves were willing to go. The alliance with the aristocratic gentlemen of Virginia was necessary to the success of a radical policy whose results the politicians of other establishments might have reason to fear. And the alliance itself had to be realized slowly, leaving to the events themselves the role of instructor. This sage policy, built upon compromises and precautions, was to be repeated in the movement leading to the adoption of a new Constitution in 1787.

3. They feared too that their absence might permit France, which was still

seeking vengeance against England, to support or even to bribe the delegates advocating independence as a way of weakening the Empire.

4. For Hannah Arendt, the phrase *'we hold* these truths to be self-evident' should not be interpreted as if the Declaration was stating absolute or pre-political truths. Just as the Declaration appeals to the 'opinions of mankind' in the first paragraph, so the statement of self-evident truths expresses merely the intersubjective and always revisable nature of the political sphere. It is difficult to support Arendt's interpretation historically, and 'radical' Americans, who often appeal to the Declaration against the Constitution as a way of justifying their social criticism, tend to treat these truths as absolute. Nonetheless, the fact that the affirmation of such truths is followed by a theory of government that emphasizes the need for the consent of the governed tends to confirm Arendt's interpretation.

5. One could also have written 'united States', as was suggested above. The ambiguity is that the Declaration is made by representatives of States that are 'assembled' or united in Congress. The unity in Congress seems to be the premise of the independence, or difference, of the very States whose sovereignty is affirmed by the act of Congress. (This is the title in Jefferson's copy; the Final Parchment version has simply 'The Unanimous Declaration of the Thirteen United States of America'.)

6. The optimism of '76 was far from universal, as the resonance of the loyalist counterattack shows. But, the loyalists failed to organize themselves, not because they were an élite separated from the masses but rather because they had no real 'cause' to promote. The advocates of independence had momentum on their side (with the aid of English stupidity). The Association's committees encountered problems in extending their jurisdiction beyond the local level and even in garnering the quorum required for taking decisions. Thus in the State of New York, many committees were not even represented in the radical institutions; the quorum was to be lowered several times and there was recourse to 'Committees of Public Safety' that had to operate when a quorum was not obtained. And the factors often cited by the optimists, such as demography, trade, expansion and immigration, became problems for the united nation, once its unity was confronted by issues other than the existence of a common enemy.

## CHAPTER 4

1. Concerning the direct influence of the American Revolution on the French, Forrest MacDonald tried to relate the geographical origins of the French troops who participated in the War of Independence to the areas where, beginning in 1789, conflicts were frequent and heavy. Claude Fohlen has effectively demonstrated the improbability of this thesis, given the problems of language, the way the troops were recruited, and the fact that those who were enrolled in the army at this time were the most deprived of Frenchmen. Their native regions were therefore likely to engage in revolutionary activity even if the American Revolution had not taken place. Fohlen's article also demystifies the image of a nobility enamoured of liberty after the fashion of

Lafayette, who is sometimes said to have been the spearhead of at least the first phase of the French Revolution: after all, future counter-revolutionary Count de Fersen also participated in the French military campaign in America. See Fohlen, 'The Impact of the American Revolution on France', in *The Impact of the American Revolution Abroad* (Washington DC: Library of Congress, 1976). Apropos of Lafayette, see Lloyd S. Kramer, 'America's Lafayette and Lafayette's America: A European in the American Revolution', *William and Mary Quarterly*, 1981.

2. The actors were conscious of the stakes. As was noted in the Introduction, the son of President Adams, and future president himself, John Quincy Adams, took responsibility for translating Friedrich Gentz's *A Comparison of the French and American Revolutions*, which appeared at the time of the 1800 election, when power passed from the party of his father to that of Jefferson.

   On the American reactions to the French revolution and the influence of the latter on the Americans' own self-understanding, see the excellent study by Richard Buel, Jr. *Securing the Revolution. Ideology in American Politics, 1789–1815* (Ithaca: Cornell University Press, 1972).

3. Another testimony to the spirit of the times is found in the archival work that began around this time. Peter Force published the first of the hundreds of volumes that make up *The American Archive*. Jared Sparks had already begun editing the *Diplomatic Correspondence of the American Revolution* in 1829, of which 12 volumes eventually appeared. Sparks also undertook the editing of Franklin's *Works* in ten volumes, beginning in 1836. His masterpiece was his *Life of Washington*, a bestseller that appeared in 1839, the year Sparks was invited to give the first academic course on the history of the American Revolution at Harvard University.

4. The best known representatives of this trend are George Louis Beer, Herbert L. Osgood, Lawrence H. Gipson, and Leonard W. Labaree. Gipson's analysis is laid out in the 14 volumes of his major work, *The British Empire before the American Revolution*, which was published between 1936 and 1969. For discussions of this historiography, cf. Richard B. Morris, *The American Revolution Reconsidered* (New York: Harper & Row, 1967), Esmond Wright, 'Historians and the Revolution', in *Causes and Consequences of the American Revolution* (Chicago: Quadrangle, 1966), and Jack P. Greene, 'The Reappraisal of the American Revolution in Recent Historical Literature', pamphlet 48 of the American Historical Association, 1967.

5. We will return to the consensus school and its critique, apropos of the analysis of the confederation era and its transformation by the Constitution of 1787. Daniel J. Boorstin, Richard Hofstadter and Louis Hartz have developed the most complete syntheses of this point of view. Criticisms of this school come from two directions: the republican synthesis, and a New Left historical viewpoint that sought, in the image of E.P. Thompson's *The Birth of the English Working Class*, to create a popular history, a history of the voiceless. For my part, I tend to think that an alliance of these two viewpoints could explain American exceptionalism!

6. John Dunn, the author of the most complete essay on this question, notes that already in 1698 the Irishman Molyneux based himself on Locke's

*Treatise* to denounce English policy in Ireland. The colonists perhaps knew of this text, but it is hard to see what possible solutions could be drawn from it concerning their own situation. Thus, after a study of university and personal libraries, book advertisements, pamphlets and newspapers of the era, Dunn states that 'the precise application of the book varied enormously, but the form remained identical. There existed a legal order, and the political moves of the English government or the governor of Massachusetts were in breach of this order. Endlessly the work of Locke was summoned to expound the tautology that illegality was not legal'. See John Dunn, 'The Politics of Locke in England and America in the Eighteenth Century', in *op. cit.*, p. 75. One might also note the anecdotal fact that Locke's patron, Shaftesbury, was a member of the company that founded the colony of Carolina, for which Locke proposed a Constitution that was hardly liberal in outlook! Moreover, Locke himself would have acquired a title of nobility had the company not gone bankrupt!

7.  Pocock seeks to show that socialism and classical political thought have been obsessed by the role supposedly played by a type of liberal social thought that denies the importance of the political. According to Pocock, the 'myth' is to be found precisely in the idea that this liberal thinking about society has played an important role. In his opinion, the choice of social liberalism is made unconsciously through a sort of mental slip whose movement Pocock seeks to trace in his various studies. Historians therefore cannot invoke Locke as the founding father without doing violence to reality. See 'The Myth of John Locke and the Obsession with Liberalism', in *John Locke*, op. cit.

    Pocock seems to revise his argument in a recent essay. He now sees a role for Locke's thought in the period preceding the Declaration of Independence, when there was recourse to the idea of a contractual relationship between the colonies and the mother-country. Pocock also sees a trace of Locke's influence in the argument that the dissolution of English authority does not imply the dissolution of society itself. See 'The Varieties of Whiggism from Exclusion to Reform: A History of Ideology and Discourse', in Pocock, *Virtue, Commerce and History*, op. cit. To grant Locke such a role does not weaken the pertinence of Pocock's major argument, which insists on the distinction between social liberalism and political thought.

8.  See 'Natural Law and Revolution', loc. cit.

9.  One might note in passing that the violent attack in Burke's *Reflections on the Revolution in France* does not refer to Locke, any more than does Gentz's comparative study of the two revolutions. There are theoretical reasons for this. Locke's social contract theory can explain quite well the relation between civil society and government, but it cannot explain how society as such is constituted for the simple reason that one cannot enter into a contract with oneself and one cannot presuppose the existence of a government with which society would, *then*, enter into a contract. If the Declaration of Independence was founded merely on a Lockian theory of natural law, we would be dealing only with a War of Independence and not with a Revolution.

10. As noted in the Introduction, I have not found serious reflections on the validity of Arendt's thesis among historians. This is surprising in so far as those of whom I will be speaking in a moment exhibit a certain philosophical sophistication, and their thesis is not alien to Hannah Arendt's.

11. A summary of other contributions to Bailyn's thesis and to the amplification of his work is provided by Robert E. Shalhope, 'Toward a Republican Synthesis: The Emergence of an Understanding of Republicanism in American Historiography', *William and Mary Quarterly*, XXIX:1 (January 1972) pp. 49–80. See also the less enthusiastic essay Shalhope published ten years later: 'Republicanism and Early American Historiography', *William and Mary Quarterly*, XXXIX (1982). Caroline Robbins' book was published by Harvard University Press in 1959.

12. The role of the 'dissenter' tradition in the churches must be added to Bailyn's thesis. The article by Richard Buel, Jr., 'Democracy and the American Revolution: A Frame of Reference' (*William and Mary Quarterly*, XXI:2, 1965), shows quite well the important contribution made by sermons preached and then published in pamphlet form during this period. I have not emphasized this religious dimension, assimilating it rather, as does Bailyn, to Old Whig theory, in so far as these thinkers were affected by the religious and political experience of the Puritans.

    Shalhope's second article notes that Bailyn's thesis neglects, among other things: regional differences, class relations, other ideologies – especially religious ones – and the rise of a politics of popular participation that challenged the old corporatist model.

13. This is why the Wilkes affair was so important for the development of the pro-independence mentality. See Pauline Maier's article, 'John Wilkes and American Disillusionment with Britain', *William and Mary Quarterly*, XX:3 (July 1963) p. 373–95.

14. This term is used by Bailyn in a 1973 essay, where he seeks to take stock of his own work, 'The Central Themes of the American Revolution', in *An Interpretation*, ed. Stephen G. Kurtz and James H. Hutson (New York: W.W. Norton, 1973). Bailyn bases his definition of ideology on Clifford Geertz's 'Ideology as a Cultural System', in *Ideology and Discontent*, ed. David Apter (Glencoe: Free Press, 1964). Ideology is said to be 'an elaborate map of social reality, part of a pattern that made life comprehensible'; later Bailyn speaks of 'maps of problematic social reality' which draw together 'values, attitudes, hopes, fears and opinions that lead to a perception of the world and action on it'. Ideology thus 'mobilises a general mood, "a set of disconnected, unrealised, private emotions" into a "public possession, a social fact", and shapes what is instinctive, giving it direction . . .' (p. 11). Bailyn grants that the colonists' ideology could not help them to understand the diversity of views that emerged with independence.

15. See the harsh attack on Wills offered by Ronald Hamowy in 'Jefferson and the Scottish Enlightenment: A Critique of Garry Wills' *Inventing America: Jefferson's Declaration of Independence*', in *William and Mary Quarterly*, 1979. Hamowy notes (p. 523), for example, that the earlier draft of the Declaration spoke of '"all men created equal *and independent*"', which contradicts the Scottish thesis of the social nature of man. The source for the

idea of the 'pursuit of happiness' seems rather to be Wilson's 1774 pamphlet, the *Considerations*.

Nonetheless, one should recall anecdotally that the expert on Scottish philosophy and president of Princeton University, Joseph Witherspoon, had among his students a future President, a vice-president, 21 senators, 29 members of the House of Representatives, 12 governors, 55 state legislators and 33 judges, including three who sat on the Supreme Court of the United States!

# Part II

## CHAPTER 5

1. In his *Defence of the Constitutions of Government of the United States*, Adams wrote that when 'the present states become . . . rich, powerful and luxurious, as well as numerous, their . . . good sense . . . [will] dictate to them what to do: They may [then] make transitions to a nearer resemblance to the British constitution' (cited by Douglas G. Adair, 'Experience must be our only guide: History, Democratic Theory, and the United States Constitution', in *The Reinterpretation of Early American History: Essays in Honor of John Edwin Pomfret*, ed. Ray A. Billington (San Marino, California: Huntington Library, 1966). Yet Adams' *Thoughts on Government* of 1775, to which we will turn in a moment, quite often inspired the authors of state constitutions. The *Thoughts* do not reveal the Anglophilia found in the *Defence*.

2. Although I am speaking here of Adams and Jefferson as archetypes, they were far from being the sole theoreticians of importance or renown. Each had played a role in the politics of his respective State – Adams as the main author of the Massachusetts constitution of 1780, Jefferson as governor of Virginia – but they both missed the great debates over changing the Confederation into a Federal Republic: The former was ambassador to England at the time, the latter was ambassador to France. What has been called here 'Jefferson's optimistic thought' was expressed most clearly in Tom Paine's pamphlet, *Common Sense*. It was against the influence exercised by this pamphlet that John Adams wrote his *Thoughts on Government*. Adams insisted upon the existence of conflict and divergent interests as well as the levelling spirit that had appeared with independence. An anecdote in Adams's *Autobiography* provides a significant glimpse into his state of mind. He meets a man,

A common horse jockey, . . . who was always in the law, and had been sued in many actions at almost every court. As soon as he saw me, he came up to me, and his first salutation to me was 'Oh! Mr. Adams, what great things have you and your colleagues done for us! We can never be grateful enough to you. There are no courts of justice now in the province, and I hope there never will another'. . . . Is this the object for which I have been contending? said I to myself. . . . Are these the sentiments of such people, and how many of them are there in the country? Half the nation for what I know; for half the nation are debtors, if not more, and these have been, in all countries, the sentiments of debtors. If the power of the country should get into such hands, and there is great danger that it will, to what purpose have we sacrificed our time, health, and everything else? Surely we must guard against this spirit and these principles, or we shall repent our conduct' (cited in Hannah Arendt, *On Revolution*, p. 300, n. 32).

3. It was a political civil war but also a social war, where political allegiance often was determined by the choice of one's immediate enemy, as we have seen in the case of the Regulators in North Carolina or of the Paxton Boys in Pennsylvania. In the case of the western part of New York State, which once was dominated by Sir John Johnson, the following figures show the results of five years of war: 700 buildings burned, 12 000 farms abandoned, hundreds of thousands of bushels of grain destroyed and nearly 400 widows and 2000 orphans made (see Edward Countryman, 'Consolidating Power in New York', *Journal of Interdisciplinary History*, VI:4 [Spring 1976] p. 654). It is often difficult to distinguish cases of patriotism motivated by socio–economic resentment from genuine revolutionary politics. And it is wrong to say that every non-rich loyalist was merely the victim of his own resentment; the choice of independence thus was no more obvious on the socio-economic plane than it was on the moral-political one. My discussion of the effects of the War of Independence is necessarily brief, given the goals of this study. For a detailed account of the strains and difficulties confronted in one small but central state, cf. Richard Buel, Jr., *Dear Liberty* (Middletown Conn.: Wesleyan University Press, 1980), which describes lucidly the 'dear' price paid in the battle for liberty!

4. We shall see these same concerns reappear during the Philadelphia Constitutional Convention of 1787, at which it was proposed that the 13 States form a strong federal unit in place of the loose confederation that then bound them together. The threat was realized later, when the Americans had to fight once again against the English, who took Washington, the new capital, in 1814.

5. The contrast to the later choices of the French Revolution should be clear. It is worth noting that the first French ambassador in the United States, Conrad Alexandre Gérard, saw the importance of this situation: 'The Congress won in moral authority what it lost in actual authority'. According to him it followed that there was no possibility of a dictator rising to power – but also that no first class individuals would want to become involved in the country's political affairs. Talent was invested elsewhere, especially in the States and in the army.

6. This description does not delve into the details of the economic basis for the creation of a real union by the Constitution of 1787. An analysis of that creation would have to examine, for example, the birth of the new juridical forms of commercial association adopted in various of the 13 States. The frustration merchants experienced due to the existence of different regulations in each of the States and the absence of a uniform commercial policy

are essential factors in the movement that put an end to the Confederation. Another aspect of the role played by economics is seen in the creation of banking institutions and the use of the (national and State) debts as a way of accumulating the capital required either for investment in new commercial or manufacturing enterprises or for land speculation in the West – this last option itself being another of the roots for the Constitution of 1787. But this financial programme became explicit only when Alexander Hamilton's policy was implemented during Washington's presidency in the early 1790s. Given that our goal is the analysis of political theory, it suffices here merely to mention these phenomena. A more cynical reading would insist on the importance of speculative interests in the march toward unification of the country. A more pessimistic one would underline the sheer incapacity of the State political institutions when faced with the burdens left by years of war.

7. Another demonstration of the idealistic and republican character of American political thought is provided by the debates over foreign policy. Felix Gilbert's *To the Farewell Address*, tries to demonstrate how the Congress, in rejecting European *realpolitik* and following the ideas of the Enlightenment (according to which free commerce between countries develops, enriches and renders virtuous all who participate), worked out a 'model treaty' for which its diplomats were supposed to win French acceptance. According to Gilbert, idealism was so strong that America preferred to run the risk of not receiving aid at all rather than to sacrifice its principles. Only slowly, he argues, did the Americans learn and begin to practise the art of diplomacy before refusing it again in the 'isolationism' of Washington's *Farewell Address*, which also rejected the ideal of teaching a new model of diplomacy to the Old World. Gilbert's elegant thesis, which is supported by a profound knowledge of the European world and of European thought, has been citicized empirically by James H. Hutson, in *The Quarterly Journal of the Library of Congress* 33:3 (July 1976).

8. This thesis was popularized by John Fiske in *The Critical Period of American History*, which appeared in 1888. The strongest criticism of the thesis was formulated by Merrill Jensen in *The Articles of Confederation* (1940, 1970). Behind the questions of historical analysis is found, of course, a political position with regard to the relative value of the principles of the Declaration of Independence and of those of the Constitution of 1787 which put an end to this 'critical' period. We shall return to this issue in Chapter 8.

9. Some States, like Massachusetts, resolved to pay back the debts incurred during the war. The taxes imposed for this purpose and the subsequent contraction of specie contributed to the recession that arose in 1786. This especially affected small farmers in the West, whose lands were often mortgaged and who were obliged, moreover, to pay their taxes in specie. The result was 'Shays' Rebellion', which was for many, as we shall see, the straw that broke the camel's back as far as the Confederation was concerned. Rhode Island, which followed the inverse – that is, inflationary – policy was equally unsuccessful as a model for solving state problems.

10. History could be interpreted, however, in another way, as indeed the authors of the Constitution of 1787 demonstrated. In his interesting article that was previously cited in note 1 of the present chapter, Adair begins with John Dickinson's 13 August 1787 remark at the Convention that

'Experience must be our only guide. Reason may mislead us'. He explains that the 'crisis' arose due to the fact that the classical experience was the sole model to which American political science could refer. According to him, this experience shows that democracy always leads to class struggle, and that the coexistence of small republics in ancient Greece gave rise to incessant wars before these republics inexorably fell into decline. It was therefore necessary to revise the overly democratic form of the States' governments and the too loose confederative structure that united them.

11. This return to the local level also masks or avoids the issue of the regional conflicts that had appeared in the Congress and to which no one knew how to respond. Thus, for example, France's insistent role of arbitrator was required in order to win acceptance for the Treaty of Versailles. New England insisted on its right to continue fishing in the waters that were available to it before independence; the South was ready to sacrifice these rights in exchange for a frontier border giving access to the Mississippi. France came down on the side of the South in this case, but an independent nation could not continually look to the French monarchy to settle its affairs.

## CHAPTER 6

1. The term has remained in today's American political vocabulary. One does not speak of the 'government' but of the 'administration'. This has no bearing, obviously, on the debates that have developed since the 1960s about the growth of presidential power – the famous 'imperial presidency' described by Arthur M. Schlesinger, Jr.
2. The difference between Montesquieu's theory and that of Delolme should be stressed. The latter did not insist upon the key role of the aristocracy in the mixed constitution, undoubtedly on account of his experience of Genevan politics. In this respect Delolme tends toward an Old Whig theory. At the same time, his theory of political institutions is founded upon their rootedness in the social structure. He therefore goes beyond the abstractness characteristic of the Old Whig orientation. But the existence of the aristocracy would have to be taken into account. It was to be represented in an upper chamber, but it was not justified as by Montesquieu, whose classical approach granted it a place on the basis of its specific virtue; in Delolme, the upper chamber is only a mechanism for preventing quick decisions taken under the influence of passion. One can see why the Americans identified more with the thought of Delolme than with that of Montesquieu: they had no artistocracy to be represented. On the other hand, as Gordon Wood notes, the concept of liberty found in Delolme is close to the one that American liberalism would develop. Liberty for Delolme is not political, and it is not exercised in the legislature or in the suffrage; according to Delolme, 'To concur by one's suffrage in enacting laws, is to enjoy a share, whatever it may be, of power', whereas liberty 'so far as it is possible for it to exist in a Society of Beings whose interests are almost perpetually opposed to each other, consists in this, that *every man, while he respects the persons of*

*others, and allows them quietly to enjoy the produce of their industry, be
certain himself likewise to enjoy the produce of his own industry, and that his
person be also secure'.* (Emphasis in the original; cited in Wood, op. cit.,
p. 609, n. 22). We shall return to this aspect below.

3. An expression of this popular spirit is retained in the preamble to the 1780
Massachusetts constitution, which declares that it is 'a social compact by
which the whole people covenants with each citizen, and each citizen with
the whole people, that all shall be governed by certain laws for the common
good'. This contract therefore assumes that the break with England brought
the State back to a Lockian state of nature, where social ties are preserved.
Others pushed this idea still further, with even more radical consequences.
Thus, in a public speech in Boston, Thomas Dawes declared: 'We often read
of the original contract, and of mankind, in the early ages, passing from a
state of nature to immediate civilization . . . the people of Massachusetts
have reduced to practice the wonderful theory'. (Cited in Wood, op. cit.,
p. 289).

4. Virtual representation and the idea that there *really* exists some*thing* shared
in common (a *res publica*) which the political machinery is supposed to make
visible to all go hand in hand. The English drew the logical conclusion when
in 1774 they eliminated the obligation that a representative reside in his
parliamentary division. American practice was moving rather in the
opposite direction, as J.R. Pole (op. cit.) shows. The difficulty with this
position, which is logical all the same, is entailed by the idea that this
common good really *exists*, that in a sense it predates political decisions,
which thus would be merely the prerequisite for its disclosure. One can
imagine another conception of the common good, according to which the
political process would be constitutive of this common good. But such a
common good does not belong to the organically unified and wholly
transparent society imagined by the classical theory of the mixed constitution.

5. This does not mean that the suffrage was universal. On the contrary, the
system greatly favoured the eastern part of the State, which obstinately
protected its position until the first reforms were made in 1830. Universal
suffrage (for white men) was granted only in the 1840s. At the beginning of
the Civil War, part of the State refused to secede and became the present
state of West Virginia. The history of the efforts undertaken to extend, and
also to restrain, the suffrage in Virginia is retraced in detail by J.R. Pole,
*Political Representation in England and the Origins of the American
Revolution*, op. cit.

6. One might reject the use of the label 'conservative' here, pointing out that
the majority can always transform its institutions so as not to privilege any
longer the abstract individual and the protection of private property. The
author could be accused of being anachronistic for asserting implicitly that
'socialism' was possible when its economic foundations did not exist. There
are two possible responses. One relies on the arguments of Louis Hartz's *The
Liberal Tradition in America*. The label 'conservative' designates merely a
political system that is unsuited to challenge its own premises and in which
novelty runs up against institutions that can adapt but cannot recognize
radical novelty as it emerges, for example, when the 13 seaboard States

became a continent and the nation asserted itself as an empire. The other response justifies the use of the label 'conservative', by the following comparison to the case of Pennsylvania.

If one wants to speak of 'conservative' in the usual meaning of the term, the constitution of Maryland was even more conservative. It provided for a system based upon property qualifications: one had to give proof of an income of £500 to be elected to the legislature; £1000 to become a sheriff, senator or congressional representative, and £5000 to become governor. Only citizens with an income of at least £500 could vote for senators. Thus, only 10.9 per cent of the citizens were eligible for the legislature, 7.4 per cent for the senate.

7. Pennsylvania's constitutional model was imitated under somewhat similar political conditions in Vermont, a territory whose borders had not been clearly drawn and which was coveted by speculators from New York and Massachusetts. A small group of inhabitants took advantage of their participation in the War of Independence and of the political confusions that ensued to set themselves free. As in Pennsylvania, the élite in the territory had been compromised and the population took advantage of this situation to endow themselves with a radical constitution. The territory's independence was enshrined in law in 1791 with its admisson into the Union as the fourteenth state – and the writing of a new constitution.

8. Once again, this proposal was formulated in explicitly political terms: 'That an enormous Proportion of Property vested in a few Individuals is dangerous to the Rights, and destructive of the Common Happiness of Mankind; and therefore every free State hath a Right by its Laws to discourage the Possession of such Property'. Against the interpretation I offer here, Eric Foner's book, from which I have drawn this quotation (p. 133), states that Pennsylvania's Bill of Rights was copied almost word for word from Virginia's Bill of Rights. Foner is, as always, too much the Marxist to recognize the role of the political as such in this State of Pennsylvania which he often analyzes quite pertinently in his study of *Tom Paine and Revolutionary America* (Oxford: Oxford University Press, 1976).

9. This was not the explicit argument of its authors, who invoked instead one of the aspects of Old Whig thought. This tendency appealed to an alleged Saxon tradition that was supposed to have disappeared with the Norman invasion. Its implications were developed in an anonymous pamphlet which appeared in Philadelphia in the spring of 1776, *The Genuine Principles of the Ancient Saxon, or English Constitution*, and which relied explicitly on Obadiah Hulme's *Historical Essay on the English Constitution*, published in 1771. According to the author, the Saxons lived in small communities in which each person participated in all decisions and in their execution. The end of this direct participation is supposed to have signalled the end of their mastery over their own destiny. It was therefore necessary to return to this ancient model, now that English institutions no longer existed.

10. It is not surprising that the committees of the Association were more active in this State than elsewhere during the war.

11. Opponents of the constitution saw in the duty to swear an oath of allegiance a manoeuvre designed to prevent them from being able to transform its institutions from the inside. The distinction between positive laws and the

basic Law had not yet been formulated. The debate in Pennsylvania was one of the factors that led to the eventual emergence of this distinction.

12. The French *philosophes* were surprised to learn that most of the newly independent North American States had instituted bicameral legislatures. The famous letter from Turgot to Richard Price (22 March 1778) served as the occasion for John Adams' *Defence of the Constitutions of Government of the United States*. Developed along these same lines was the criticism offered by Mirabeau, which was published in Philadelphia in 1786 under the title *Reflections on the Importance of the American Revolution . . . [of] Richard Price*. For his part, Condorcet observed that there was no place for a Senate in an egalitarian republic; since the nation was one, its legislature ought also to be singular. On this French reaction more generally, see Robert R. Palmer, *The Age of the Democratic Revolution*, op. cit.

13. Another difficulty already mentioned several times would be resolved shortly. This was the question of the disposition of the vast tracts of western land claimed by various States. Beyond the conflicts among these States with western frontiers, this issue aroused the jealousy of States with fixed boundaries, which had reason to fear that they would be put into the minority even if the practice of voting by politically equal States were retained. One of the merits of the Confederation is that it surmounted this difficulty, as we shall see.

14. During the Constitutional Convention of 1787 and in *The Federalist*, people were often reminded of the threat of a foreign country having recourse to the old tactic of *divide et imperium*. This argument in favour of a strong union was all the more pertinent as it was founded upon the experience of the colonies' struggle for their independence, as we have already seen.

15. As was mentioned earlier, in their correspondence, people at the time spoke of 'my country' when referring to their home State.

16. Jack Rakove demonstrates quite convincingly the non-theoretical character of the deliberations over the drafting of the Articles when he retraces their six successive versions, from Franklin's first draft in 1775, to the last, which modified the proposals offered by Dickinson in June 1776, before being re-examined in committee in May 1777. According to Rakove, the major task of the confederal Constitution was to legitimate the fact that the Congress had taken upon itself the initiative to declare independence and not to define the powers that had been granted to it. 'The deference that Congress commanded in the early years of the Revolution left it immune from close theoretical scrutiny. Removed from the daily exercise of coercive power, charged with framing general policies that all patriots felt obliged to support, venerated as "the collective wisdom" of the continent, Congress seemingly did not need to be subjected to the same constitutional restraints that other levels of government required', Jack N. Rakove, *The Beginnings of National Politics* (New York: Knopf, 1979) p. 151. This description corroborates the thesis of the symbolical character of the power exercised by the Continental Congress developed at the end of Chapter 3.

After a long analysis of the debates, Rakove concludes, apropos of the authors of the confederated Constitution that 'At a time when constitution-writers in the States were displaying an acute sensitivity to redesigning the architecture of government, transferring power from executive to legis-lature, the framers of the Articles never thought of confederation as an exercise in creating a conventional structure of government'. (p. 184). As for the attitude of the people, Rakove adds that 'Nothing of the general reception the Articles received suggests that Americans were deeply interested in discussing the nature of the union they were forming. No pamphlets were written about them, and when the Articles were printed in American newspapers they appeared only as another scrap of news, probably less important than reports of victory at Saratoga and almost certainly less controversial than a growing number of essays proposing remedies for inflation' (p. 185).

17. Beyond the conflicts between speculators, whose role in the movement toward independence we have already seen, we should note that this kind of problem would also arise due to the fact that some States had remunerated soldiers serving in their armies during the War of Independence with titles to western lands belonging to these States.

18. For those who see in the establishment of a metric system and a revolutionary calendar symbols of the radical nature of the French Revolution, it might be noted that Jefferson tried to apply Newtonian laws to develop a standard unit of measurement – he wanted to call it the 'ryttenhouse', after the American autodidactic scientist, David Rittenhouse – that would serve as the basis for a system exemplifying the originality of the New World. Rittenhouse convinced Jefferson of the scientific impossibility of this project which was to be based on an analysis of the movements of the pendulum. See Gary Wills' discussion in *Inventing America*, op. cit.

19. The issue of expressly delegated powers remained in the new Federal Constitution of 1787; one encounters it today in the phrase 'strict construction' and in the Tenth Amendment to the Constitution, which forms part of the Bill of Rights. As we shall see in *The Federalist*, Madison and Hamilton start from the premise that if the Constitution assigns to the government an obligation it must *ipso facto* also grant it the means to carry out this obligation.

20. If this theoretical analysis is valid, it confirms the argument of Merrill Jensen, for whom the Articles of Confederation were not only a viable form of government but also the faithful reflection of the ideas for which Americans had fought during the War of Independence. Its viability is precisely that of a liberal government – but this kind of government could not yet be conceived by the political theories of that era. What Jensen considers to be a kind of counter-revolution is in effect a reaction, in the strict sense of this term, by people who thought liberalism violated the basis of any just political institution. The Constitution of 1787 was not aimed at establishing, but rather at counteracting, the misdeeds of a liberal contractualism that was based upon an abstract conception of man. See the discussion of Jensen *et al.* in Chapter 8 below.

## CHAPTER 7

1. This refutes the argument that the advocates of independence were colonial politicians who joined the revolt only in reaction to English institutions that were blocking their own future prospects. Most of them would have

preferred to stay home; indeed, the list of the members of the Continental Congress is not overflowing with geniuses, as is shown in the chapter of Rakove's book entitled 'Ambition and Responsibility: An Essay on Revolutionary Politics'. The author, emphasizing the high rate of turnover among the delegates, argues that this situation was not due only to the whims of the State legislatures, for the same delegates were often reelected. He insists, rather, that the political experience of the Americans before 1776 was of another order and concerned other problems than those with which the Congress had to deal, such as military questions, inflation, foreign affairs.

As to the supposed democratic leanings of the future 'anti-federalists' who came to oppose the new national Constitution of 1787, a historian who is rather sympathetic to their cause, Jackson Turner Main, notes that they were often narrow-minded, prejudiced and anti-intellectual people who defended local authority which they believed was threatened by the new institutions. See *The Antifederalists. Critics of the Constitution, 1781–1788* (Chapel Hill: University of North Carolina Press, 1961). This viewpoint is confirmed by Cecilia Kenyon's 'Men of Little Faith: The Anti-Federalists on the Nature of Republican Government' ( *William and Mary Quarterly*, XII, 1955), which stresses also the influence of Montesquieu's demonstration of the impossibility of founding a republic on an extended territory. Their lack of 'faith' comes from their pessimism, and their Old Whig fear of all forms of power. They did not accept the idea, favoured by Madison and the authors of the Constitution of 1787, that politics can become a science.

2. I analyze neither of these issues in the text, which is concerned with the logic of politics. A few words here will have to suffice to provide the context. The war was often localized in scope, sometimes taking on the aspects of guerrilla warfare. The troops directed by General Washington suffered at the outset from rivalries between generals and especially from the lack of provisions which the confederated States were slow to provide. Every American child is familiar with the image of the tattered army spending the winter of 1777 at Valley Forge, Pennsylvania. Later, the efforts made by the army's commissaries and aid from France ameliorated the situation somewhat. The military's internal problems stemmed also from the fact that the Articles of Confederation provided for Congress to nominate the generals while allowing the States to name all other officers. When, in 1780, the officers of the army threatened to resign *en masse*, the Congress voted them lifetime retirement at half salary. This was resented by the States, which saw in it the beginnings of a national army. This fear was revived in 1783 when the Superintendent of Finance, Robert Morris, tried to win acceptance for his fiscal policy by waving the threat of a military *coup* . . . which Washington succeeded in quelling only *in extremis*. The formation after the war of an organization of ex-officers, the 'Society of the Cincinnatii', whose membership was to be hereditary, stirred fears of the creation of an aristocracy. The organization had to disband under pressure of public opinion. In short, the army functioned within the constraints of the Old Whig ideology.

As for diplomatic affairs, the rivalry between the American emissaries to France had disastrous effects as early as 1777, when Silas Deane was accused, among other things, of having given out too many military commissions and of having promised too much money to the ambitious French artistcrats whom he had recruited to serve in the American army. The polemic between Deane, who had been recalled to Philadelphia, and Arthur Lee resurfaced when Congress examined the possible terms for concluding a peace treaty after the defeat of the British at Yorktown. France's representatives, Conrad Alexandre Gérard and then the Chevalier de Luzerne, became involved both directly and through the intermediary of pamphleteers (including Tom Paine) whom they hired in order to pursue France's goals. Although the importance of this debate over the terms of the peace treaty should not be overestimated, it revealed a first fracture in American unity manifested in the deep differences in interests between the agricultural South, which was occupied and threatened by the English armies, the commercial North, which insisted that any treaty take into account its maritime interests, and the West, for whom the frontier and access to the Mississippi were of fundamental importance. The ideological context in which diplomacy was debated is discussed in Gilbert, op. cit.

3. This policy remained the basis for the colonization of the West (except with respect to the issue of slavery, which went from compromise to compromise until it reached the point of no return in the 1850s). Its reaffirmation in 1862 by the Homestead Act constitutes, among other things, the basis for the system of state Universities that still exists today. Peter S. Onuf's *Statehood and Union: A History of the Northwest Ordinance* (Bloomington: University of Indiana Press, 1987), appeared too late for consideration here.

4. We have already noted that to this classical idea of the City's inevitable temporal decline, the Americans could oppose the image of vast spaces yet to be conquered in the West, thus seemingly delaying the advent of this decline which was thought of as the result of the sclerosis of the political principle animating the republic. For the *ricorso* (or renewal) to which the classical authors appealed, America substituted the inevitable movement toward the conquest of the West.

## CHAPTER 8

1. In 'The Founding Fathers: Young Men of the Revolution', *Political Science Quarterly*, Vol. LXXVI, 1961, pp. 181–216.

2. In as much as the political thought of the 18th century considered private property as the prerequisite for the liberty that makes of man a citizen, the protection of private property is neither contradictory to it nor the sign of a counter-revolutionary coup. But, as has been noted, the very nature of private property was in the process of changing at this time. It was acquiring increasingly mobile and less autonomous forms. It was no longer the incarnation of pre-political natural law, as was imagined in Locke's theory, or the material basis of (aristocratic) freedom. The owner of the new kind of speculative investment is in fact dependent upon the opinion of others, as, to a lesser degree, are the merchant and the tradesman. Can he then claim to enjoy the liberty that citizenship presupposes? If the Constitution protects

this kind of mobile and commercial property, this is simply an affirmation that freedom of trade has taken precedence over pre-social natural rights as Locke conceived them. The authors of the Constitution could well have been seeking to protect a Lockean type of property, only to have their work overtaken by the new economic realities.

3. This nationalization of the debt did occur under Washington's presidency, in conformity with the financial policies of Alexander Hamilton, the *bête noire* of the progressive historians.

4. We have already cited Eric Foner's *Tom Paine and Revolutionary America*. He shows that Paine, who had proven to be the model interpreter of the American mentality in *Common Sense*, was later more and more marginalized by events. In a typically American reflex, Paine withdrew from public life in order to devote himself to the invention of an iron bridge. During a trip to France to sell his product, he found himself a participant in the French Revolution (though he hardly spoke French). His brilliant response to Burke's condemnation of the Revolution in his essay, *The Rights of Man*, will always be remembered for its stingingly ironic reply aimed at Burke's haughty tone: 'He pities the feathers, but forgets the dying bird'. A Girondist, Paine used his ten months in prison to write an anti-religious pamphlet, *The Age of Reason*. Following its publication and his return to the United States, Paine found himself totally alienated by the spirit of the times; his pamphlet disturbed his former friends and admirers, who ignored him on account of his criticism of religious superstitions. He died alone and forgotten in 1809.

5. 'The Convention as A Case Study in Democratic Politics', *American Political Science Review*, 1961.

6. Recall the first lines of the first chapter of the *Social Contract:* 'Man is born free, and everywhere he is in chains. Many a man believes himself to be the master of others who is, no less than they, a slave. How did this change take place? I do not know. What can make it legitimate? To this question I hope to be able to furnish an answer'. Similarly, when Kant seeks to understand the legitimacy of the French Revolution in his essay, 'On the Common Saying, "This may be true in theory but it does not work in practice"', he attacks the error of those who would justify a revolution by saying that some original contract has been violated by the present system. On these problems, see especially my *From Marx to Kant* (Albany: State University of New York Press, 1985), as well as *Defining the Political* and *The Politics of Critique* (both London: Macmillan and Minneapolis: University of Minnesota Press, 1988).

7. Ultimately, it poses also the question of the relation of the French and American Revolutions, but that is another topic.

# Part III

## CHAPTER 9

1. They do not contradict republican theory, but the Americans were trying to integrate republican thought into this Old Whig viewpoint. The resulting

dynamic, which we have already encountered, appears once again in the present case.

2. In truth, this problem was not totally unknown. Religious liberty was based upon this idea of minority rights. But, if freedom of conscience is a private matter, the liberty of a minority of wealthy people is rather a public one. Moreover, freedom of religious conscience and that of religious practice did not always benefit from the same protections. During the 19th century, certain aspects of an established church remained, for example in the form of taxes paid to the dominant denomination in a State.

Concerning the passage from popular sovereignty to the protection of minorities, see the interesting historical analysis of the right to free speech in the United States by Günther Frankenberg and Ulrich Rödel, *Von der Volkssouveränität zum Minderheitschutz* (Frankfurt: Europaïsche Verlagsanstalt, 1981). This study analyzes the development of the problem up until the present time.

3. The experience of this convention was to leave a small trace in the unfolding of the French Revolution. Brissot was touring the United States at this time. Upon his return, he published a pamphlet arguing that the Estates General did not have the right to draft a constitution and that this task ought to fall to a convention specially elected for this purpose. But Brissot could not count on the support of powerful and well-organized interests as his counterparts in the United States had done. (The episode is mentioned in Claude Fohlen, 'The Impact of the American Revolution in France', op. cit.)

4. This is the thesis of Douglass G. Adair, presented in two influential articles, 'Experience Must be Our Only Guide: History, Democratic Theory and the United States Constitution', op. cit. and 'That Politics May Be Reduced to a Science: David Hume, James Madison and the Tenth Federalist', in *Huntington Libary Quarterly*, XX:4 (August 1957) p. 343–60.

5. This paradoxical situation is worth emphasizing. The political dilemmas faced by the States are resolved at the national level, and the new Constitution is based upon an experience whose theoretical and political conclusions the States were unable to draw out by themselves. As Jack Rakove says, 'For it was in the creation of the state constitutions and ensuing appraisals of their success that American thinkers had most carefully developed their new conceptions of the separation of powers and representation. It was the experience of the States that had called into question the Americans' initial commitment to the supremacy of the legislature and the evisceration of the executive. It was in the States that the problem of protecting constitutional charters and rights from legislative encroachment had become apparent and that the doctrine of judicial review had begun to take shape. And it was there, too, that the difficulty of reconciling the traditional forms of mixed government with a republican conception of popular sovereignty had led toward a new understanding of the meaning of revolution' (op. cit., p. 395). Rakove pays tribute here in a note to the influence of Gordon Wood on this analysis. For the theoretical paradox, cf. my works cited in Chapter 8, n. 6, and the Afterword to this volume.

6. One could mention, of course, the equally rich reflections found, for example, in Jefferson's *Notes on Virginia* (which contain the rough draft of a new constitution intended to replace the one adopted by Virginia in 1776 but

which was never voted on because of the war), or of John Adams' *Defence of the Constitutions of Government of the United States.* Or, if one did not want to rely solely on illustrious authors, anonymous pamphlets, journalistic essays, and such like could be cited. In this regard, the remarkable work of Gordon Wood, op. cit., is a treasure trove.

7. Madison says no more here on the topic of slavery, a subject that Americans tended to avoid. This attitude may be explained first of all if a comparison is made between the conditions of American slaves and those under which the poor of Europe lived. Moreover, the importation of slaves had practically ceased since the inception of the struggle against England, and the extension of slavery to the northwest territories had been forbidden by the Northwest Ordinance of 1786. The 1787 Constitution forbad the importation of slaves, beginning in 1808, on a *de facto* basis but in timid language and without even employing the concept. Article I, Section 9 simply states: 'The migration or importation of such Persons as any of the States now existing shall think proper to admit, shall not be prohibited by the Congress prior to the Year one thousand eight hundred and eight . . .' A conceptual silence heavy with future consequences! One might recall that for classical theory the question is not political, slaves being dependent upon the *oikos* and not the *polis*. A rather weak defence, admittedly!

8. In the previously cited article, 'That Politics May Be Reduced to a Science', Douglass G. Adair attempts to show that these three arguments are only paraphrases from David Hume. To illustrate this thesis, Adair quotes the following passage from Hume's essay, *On the Independency of Parliament:* It is 'a just *political* maxim *that every man must be supposed a knave:* Though at the same time, it appears somewhat strange, that a maxim should be true in *politics*, which is false *in fact* . . . Honour is a great check to mankind: But where a considerable body of men act together, this check is, in a great measure, removed; since a man is sure to be approved by his own party . . . and he soon learns to despise the clamours of adversaries' (op. cit., p. 497).

Scottish thought (which Adair wants to find at the roots of American political thought) is, nevertheless, not the first to have thus opposed the public to the private in this way. This distinction is found as early as the time of Greek democracy, which sought to exclude the private from the public, since these two domains are conceived of as resting on different and opposed principles. On the other hand, Adair seems more convincing when he attributes to Hume's influence the solution that will be advanced by Madison. My disagreement bears simply upon the image of a Madison searching in texts for *solutions* to the problems of his country. Madison's method, along with that generally applied by the Americans, consists rather in seeking to understand general principles that they can then apply to their specific conditions in order to construct particular solutions that will then be verified in action. Adair admits, moreover, that Hume does not deal with the issue of economic interests, whereas it is an overriding preoccupation for Madison and his contemporaries.

## CHAPTER 10

1. Jackson's notes were published in 1818; those of Madison in 1840. Other delegates had also taken notes that have been collected along with those of Jackson and Madison by Max Farrand. The four volumes Farrand published in 1911 were revised in 1937; they are published by the Yale University Press (New Haven, Connecticut) under the title, *The Records of the Federal Convention of 1787*. A convenient set of excerpts, on which I have often relied, is found in Page Smith, *The Constitution* (New York: W.W. Morrow, 1978).

2. This idea is at the basis of the theory of 'concurrent majorities' advanced later by John C. Calhoun, who sought to defend the interests of Southern slave owners against the threat of an alliance between the North and the West. Calhoun's theory, developed in *A Disquisition on Government*, was published in 1853, after the death of the Senator from South Carolina. His goal could be generalized in the following terms: defend the interests of any minority against the tyranny of the majority. It should be stressed, however, that this idea is the *contrary* of the classical conception of the political, which seeks to exclude the private from the public sphere. Thus, as Cornelius Castoriadis notes, when it came to declaring war, the Athenians excluded inhabitants of frontier areas from voting, as their particular interests risked skewing their judgement. (See Aristotle's *Politics*, 1330 a 20; Castoriadis, 'The Greek *Polis* and the Creation of Democracy', in *Graduate Faculty Philosophy Journal*, New School for Social Research, 9:2, Autumn 1983, p. 102.) At the outset of their debates, the delegates were closer to this classical conception than the understanding which Calhoun was to develop on the basis of the conclusion to their deliberations.

3. Since the Convention had been called in the name of the Confederation and under its authority, voting was to be conducted by States although they were unequally represented and sometimes – during this long summer – not represented at all. The important thing, as Roche's 'reform caucus' thesis affirms, was not victory but unanimity and consensus. The Convention was confronted with the same need to search for unity as the Continental Congress had been in 1774 and in the two years that led to the Declaration of Independence.

   New York was regularly divided due to the fact that its governor, Clinton, in order to ensure his own local power, added two localists to a delegation whose other member was his political enemy, the nationalist Alexander Hamilton. This collision between local politics and Convention business was not unique, as could be shown by a more anecdotal history of the Convention – for example, that of Forrest McDonald. See his recent, supposedly theoretical work, *Novus Ordis Secularum* (Lawrence: University of Kansas Press, 1987).

4. The number of voting States had increased. Delegates continued to arrive as the debate progressed while others left, for personal reasons and sometimes for political ones (as with New York Governor Clinton's allies, who departed after this vote).

5. This fear was in no way imaginary. The idea of a monarchy had been bandied back and forth several times, the candidate often advanced for this position obviously being George Washington. His refusal to assume this role was later to prove important when it came to winning popular acceptance for the institution of the presidency, which was in some respects tailor-made for the former Commander-in-Chief. Many Americans were expecting aristocratic institutions to develop, and their current absence was explained simply by the relative youth of the country, as John Adams' *Defence* had asserted. Along the same lines, the difficulties experienced by the Confederation were sometimes explained by analogy with the elective Polish monarchy, whose divisions and paralysis led to the partition, and then disappearance, of that nation.

6. A proposal by Wilson on 2 June, which would have established something like the current presidential electoral college, was rejected. Franklin's speech on the same day – which expressed, in typically Old Whig political terms, his fear that the establishment of an executive might become the basis for erecting a new monarchy, in conformity with the lessons of 'all history' and 'a natural inclination in mankind to Kingly Government' – was listened to respectfully, but it did not provoke any further discussion. The Americans seemed to have learned the need to conceptualize their problems in terms of their own society and their own history.

7. This statement, which was frequently cited, is taken from Plutarch's *Life of Solon*. See Plutarch, *The Rise and Fall of Athens*, trans. Ian Scott-Kilvert (London and New York: Penguin, 1960) paragraph 15, p. 57.

8. The term 'president', which was finally accepted, does not suffice either, in so far as it designates someone who presides or directs the debates of a legislative assembly. As is well known, the history of the United States is punctuated by the alternating growth and decline of the powers actually exercised by the president.

9. Hamilton's long speech on 18 June was in fact a rejection of both plans under discussion. Praising the English model but recognizing that the conditions necessary for its implementation were lacking, Hamilton proposed a Senate and a governor, both elected for life, the latter being armed with an absolute veto. if this speech represents his true opinions, he would then have had to water them down in his apology for the 1787 Constitution published in *The Federalist*. This is not the place to conduct an analysis of this fascinating personality – a courageous republican to some, a potential Caesar to others – who shaped the economic policy of the Washington presidency, and then supported the hardcore wing of the Federalist party in its struggle against Jefferson's republicans before dying in a duel in 1803.

10. Nevertheless, history proved Hamilton right: subsequent domestic conflicts in the United States were based on differences between regional interests and not on the interests of the large States versus the small ones. The small slave State of Maryland had more interests in common with the large slave State of Virginia and the little State of Rhode Island with the large State of Massachusetts than the large or small ones had among themselves.

11. One should not think that the divisions within the Convention centred only on the divergent interests of the small and the large States. Others rejected the developing theoretical style, which I call sociological, trying still to

analyze the situation in terms of classical thought. Thus, before a committee was nominated, Gouverneur Morris made a final plea for a Senate elected for life. The proper qualifications and virtue are the necessary ingredients, he said, for the members of both houses; for the second, one must add: (a) a personal interest in counteracting the first house; (b) wealth, an aristocratic spirit, and the pride that motivates resistance to abuses; and finally, (c) independence, which would be guaranteed by giving candidates life tenure. In support of his argument, Morris noted first of all that, in the States, the senates had not proven capable of resisting the popular forces in the legislatures. If it was necessary to protect oneself against the abuses of the rich, he proposed their isolation in the Senate as a much surer method since presence of the rich in the first house threatened to corrupt the people and to profit from their passions – especially in a very large country. But Morris simply delivered these remarks without making a motion. Perhaps he knew that his cause was already lost, or maybe he counted, as did John Adams (who had made similar suggestions previously), on realizing his goal 'when the present states become . . . rich, powerful, and luxurious, as well as numerous . . . their good sense [will] dictate to them what to do; they may [then] make transitions to a nearer resemblance of the British constitution'.

12. Those who remember the Watergate scandal which forced President Nixon to vacate the presidency will recall that the bill of impeachment was to be voted by the House of Representatives while the trial that was to have followed would have taken place in the Senate (presided over by Chief Justice of the Supreme Court). The justification for this procedure in terms of checks and balances is found in *The Federalist*, numbers 65, 66 and 81.

13. This premonition proved correct when the fiscal power of the national government was invoked during the first Washington administration to tax alcohol produced by small farmers located too far from eastern markets to be able to transport their grain there. This tax gave rise to the Whiskey Rebellion. Federal troops had to be called in to put it down.

14. On the support given by artisans to the proposed Constitution, see, for example, Eric Foner's *Tom Paine*, op. cit. Foner notes, for example, that ship building in Philadelphia, which had reached 39 vessels in 1784, was down to 13 in 1786, a year when the recession was already ancient history.

15. There is a paradox here, due to the fact that the efforts of both the opponents of the proposed Constitution as well as the nationalists were aimed at allowing interests to have their place, the former by isolating them from the political, the latter by sacrificing the political to them. Cf. note 16 below.

16. Logically, such a bill was not necessary. Once the people are sovereign, there is no longer any reason to fear that the people will be oppressed since there is not power separate from them. Those who felt the need for such a bill therefore remained within the framework of the Old Whig logic in which liberty must be protected from a power that is opposed to it. The frequent recourse to this argument in the debates over ratification show that the new political orientation embodied in the Constitution did not yet express the common attitude of the American people.

17. It would be wrong to think that this pamphlet was the only book written at the time in defence of the Constitution or that it had an immediate impact on the debates in every State. Its role and its reputation have increased with

time. Already, when Jefferson sought to establish a list of important political books for students at the University of Virginia which he had founded, his letter to Madison began thus: '1) The Declaration of Independence, as the fundamental act of union of these states; 2) the book known by the title of *The Federalist*, being an authority to which appeal is habitually made by all, and rarely declined or denied by any as evidence of the general opinion of those who framed, and of those who accepted, the Constitution of the US on questions as to its genuine meaning'. Nevertheless, it is worth noting that the importance of number 10 of *The Federalist*, which we will soon be speaking about, was recognized only in 1913 when Beard carried out his critique of the Constitution.

It should be noted that Herbert J. Storing has recently published *The Complete Anti-Federalist* in seven volumes (Chicago: University of Chicago Press, 1981). The debates of the conventions of the various States have also been published. A summary of the most important speeches made during these debates as well as on other occasions may be found in the third volume of the collection by Max Farrand, op. cit. Those seeking a quick, documented summary may consult – as I have – Page Smith, *The Constitution. A Documentary and Narrative History*, op. cit.

## CHAPTER 11

1. I am treating *The Federalist* as if it were the work of a single author, following in this respect the interpretation of, among others, Albert Furtwangler in *The Authority of Publius. A Reading of the Federalist Papers* (Ithaca: Cornell University Press, 1984). Illness prevented John Jay from continuing this collaborative effort beyond nos. 3–5 (on the weakness of the Confederation in foreign policy), with the exception of no. 64 (which also deals with foreign policy). As to the contributions by Madison and Hamilton (who conceived the project), the scholars are still debating; Furtwangler cites, for example, a computerized stylistic analysis which discovered that a typical sentence written by Madison is 34.59 words long, whereas one by Hamilton is 34.55! That Hamilton and Madison later found themselves in opposing camps piques the curiosity of historians. But, as Furtwangler notes, the goal of *The Federalist* was to defend not ideal political principles but a political compromise that seemed to be the sole possible option. This allows us to interpret *The Federalist* as a reflection of the entire Revolution and as the work of a single hand.

Garry Wills' interpretation, in *Explaining America: The Federalist* (Garden City: Doubleday, 1981), which seeks to demonstrate a unity in the thought of Madison and Hamilton due, supposedly, to their mutual indebtedness to Hume, is not convincing. The parallels between *The Federalist* and some of Hume's essays had already been pointed out by Douglass Adair, who sought to make this into the foundation for a new political theory. In order to extend his 'Scottish thesis' to the entire history of the founding of the United States, Wills – whose 'Scottish' reading of the Declaration of Independence in *Inventing America* we have already mentioned – tries to counter the influence, which he deems pernicious, of the egoistic/individualistic abstractness of Lockean contractualism. This supposes that theory determines practice, a doubtful idea when we are examining a period as agitated as that of the American Revolution.

2. This sociological argument about the role of a republic on an extended territory was already suggested in Madison's essay on 'The Vices of the Political System of the United States'. Knowing that Madison is the originator of this theory and that he is the author of Number 10, many readers have been tempted to contrast Hamilton (the author of this ninth number) to Madison. Furtwangler is correct, however, to see in the thought of Publius a unity, noting that the reference to Montesquieu in Number 9 serves as an introduction to the remarks made by Madison in Number 10.

3. This is also the argument Tocqueville uses to explain the likely longevity of republican institutions in the United States. Tocqueville explains simply that 'What is meant by 'republic' in the United States is the slow and quiet action of society upon itself', *Democracy in America*, trans. George Lawrence, ed. J.P. Mayer (Garden City: Doubleday Anchor, 1969) p. 395. *The Federalist* explains how this social action is made possible by political structures.

4. Hamilton is known to be the author of Number 78, which is supposed to justify the doctrine of judicial review. That doctrine was first applied at the beginning of the 19th century when Chief Justice John Marshall presided over the Supreme Court while his political party (which was also Hamilton's) was no longer in power. One is tempted to conclude therefore that Hamilton's interpretation slants the intentions of the founders in a conservative direction. Yet, during the 1960s, the Court, presided by Earl Warren, played a key role in a radical extension of American civil rights. At that point, it was conservatives who sought to abolish the Court or to make it subject to political decisions. One should therefore avoid drawing theoretical conclusions from contingent historical facts. Cf. the Afterword to this volume for an interpretation of the theoretical source of judicial review.

5. The assertion that the selection of national Senators depended on the State legislatures until the adoption of the Seventeenth Amendment to the Constitution in 1913, resolves nothing with respect to the other representative functions. As we have seen, the question of representation was present throughout America's constitutional experience.

6. The political authorities which concretize the political sphere in its generality have not yet been specified on this level of the argument. Publius relies simply on the panacea of 'modern representation'.

7. Size will also favour the appearance of factions, which are a manifestation of liberty and something that encourages it. In a letter to Jefferson (24 October 1788), Madison expressed his regret that the Constitution did not include a national veto power over State laws, which he had vainly defended during the Convention. For he explained, if the Republic is too large, there will be too many factions and not enough unity, which will compel the government to furnish itself with the means to oppress these factions. The analysis therefore cuts both ways, a fact that Publius does not emphasize here for obvious polemical reasons.

8. Or else in a (pre-modern) democracy, for 'where a multitude of people

exercise in person the legislative functions and are continually exposed, by their incapacity for regular deliberation and concerted measures, to the ambitious intrigues of their executive magistrates, tyranny may well be apprehended, on some favourable emergency, to start up in the same quarter'. This argument is based on the modern theory of representation found in the discussion of the Senate in Number 63, to which we have already referred.

## CHAPTER 12

1. Obviously, the Civil War cannot be reduced simply to this. The change from a political theory in which liberty must constantly protect itself from power to one in which liberty must seek the power necessary to conserve itself in a society based on interests, has implications for the treatment of slavery by the Founders and their successors. It could be argued that the Civil War resulted precisely from the inability to find an adequate form of power to assure the liberty of all Americans. It would follow that the process of Reconstruction, including the elastic phrasing of the 14th and 15th Amendments to the Constitution, are an attempt to remedy this default. The further implication would be the growth of Big Government in the 20th century, which could be seen as a further attempt to create the power necessary to protect freedom. But the contemporary dilemmas of the Welfare State serve to remind us that, in our constitutional system, power is always representative, and that popular sovereignty cannot be incarnated in any government. Theodore Lowi's critique of the Welfare State warns against going to the opposite extreme; the issue is civil *rights* and not the entrance of yet another interest group into the game of social pluralism. On the latter point, cf. *The End of Liberalism* (New York: W.W. Norton, 1966).
2. See Laurent Cohen-Tanugi, *Le Droit sans l'Etat. Sur la démocratie en France et en Amérique* (Paris: PUF, 1985). The author's concern is contemporary, but the collection of quotations from Tocqueville with which he embellishes it justifies our placing his approach on the list of reflections upon American history that err because they pose poorly the questions they ask. For a critical account of how the use of the courts can stifle political energy, cf. Michael Walzer, 'The Pastoral Retreat of the New Left', in *Dissent*, Autumn 1979, pp. 406–13.
3. Robert A. Dahl, *A Preface to Democratic Theory* (Chicago: University of Chicago Press, 1956).
4. ·Cited in Farrand, op. cit., vol.3, p. 234, from the archives of the Secretary of State. United States. Correspondence. Supplement, 2nd Series, vol. 15, pp. 314ff.
5. Madison to Thomas Ritchie, 15 September 1821; cited in Farrand, op. cit., vol. 3, p. 447.
6. The chapter in which Wood lays out what he thinks of as the birth of a new politics bears the title, 'The Relevance and the Irrelevance of John Adams'. Wood, therefore, is aware of the persistence of the old rhetoric in the lived experience of the American people. Moreover, Pocock seems recently to

have watered down his propositions. The long introductory remarks on 'The State of the Art' in his new collection *Virtue, Commerce and History*, op. cit., distinguish between an orientation based upon the priority given to rights and another which privileges politics. Although Pocock does not return to or reconsider his previous writings here, the new American politics certainly gives priority to rights.

7. Wood, op. cit., p. 601.

8. We should emphasize that this interpretation of interest as a rational principle that justifies its being taken into consideration by the political sphere appeals neither to Locke nor to any theory of labour value. This does not mean that these notions were unknown to the Americans, but only that they were not indispensable to the elaboration of their political theory.

9. This argument has been developed for European revolutions by Claude Lefort. See especially his criticism of Marxist simplifications of these revolutions and his analysis of the relationship between the will to establish what some call a 'real democracy' and the explicitly modern phenomenon of totalitarianism, in *Essais sur la politique* (Paris: Seuil, 1986) and *L'Invention démocratique* (Paris: Fayard, 1981). A collection of translations of Claude Lefort's writings from these two books and elsewhere have recently been published by Polity Press as *The Political Forms of Modern Society* (Oxford, 1986). On Lefort, cf. *The Marxian Legacy*, op. cit.

## AFTERWORD

1. It should be stressed that I have inverted the Hegelian ordering which portrays the concept as integrating the moments of the immediate (being) and its reflexive mediation (essence). The reason for this inversion is that Hegel's system is not capable of thinking the autonomy of the political, as I tried to show in *From Marx to Kant*. For Hegel, the social poses the question of the political whereas it is the inverse relation which defines the true problem of modern societies, as we shall see in the case of the American Revolution.

2. It would be tempting to add to this double structure a third moment which would make explicit to themselves each of the first two moments. Such a third moment would present directly the institutional functioning of the political logic (*logique politique instituante*). The claim then would be that the autonomy won in the first period is explicitly conceived at the level of the individual lived experience during the second period; and that the particularity of the States is reflected explicitly at the social level during the third period. The result would be that the entire two hundred years' history of the republic would be considered as making clear the properly political logic which determines the elaboration of the Constitution of 1787. Thus, the lived experience of a socially fragmented Confederation would have become untenable once popular revolts broke out in the States. Shays' Rebellion would have catalyzed the energies of those who met at Philadelphia to create the new Constitution. That Convention represented diverse interests which refused to sacrifice their own particularity. The compromise proposed to popular ratification claimed, in the oft-cited phrase of Solon, not to offer the

best constitution but only the best that the citizens could accept. The result of this compromise would be the depoliticization of American life in a society where capitalism and the common interest are considered as identical. But this is precisely the thesis that I want to invert by reading reality in terms of its theory! Once again, a Hegelian dialectics cannot account for the political. The third moment is reflective, not reflexive.

3. It would of course be wrong to neglect the religious aspect of colonial thought. I do not emphasize it here insofar as it is the political form of the lived religious experience, particularly in the case of New England, which influenced the development of the Revolution as such. If the religious element is treated as if it were simply and integrally transferred to the political level, the result can only be abusive simplifications of the type which claim, for example, that the easy acceptance of political parties flows from the lack of an Established Church and from the plurality of religious sects in the colonies. More important is the fact that the religious reading of the political theory underlying the revolution would neglect the social aspect of English 'corruption' and the 'virtue' the colonists sought to oppose to it. The Revolution would then acquire a Manichaean or ahistorical character.

4. This does not contradict the earlier assertion that the constitutions of the States intended to represent *society*. The explicitly political form of representation incorporated in these State constitutions was assumed to be necessary in order to guarantee that the essence of society, its common good, would be correctly recognized. In this sense, the constitution of Pennsylvania and those of the other States do not differ; each assumes that there *exists* something called the common good, although they differ about the political institutions necessary for its discovery. We shall see that the federal Constitution of 1787 works in terms of a different, a properly political, logic.

5. A demonstration *a contrario* can be found in Martin Van Buren's *Inquiry into the Origin and Course of Political Parties in the United States* (New York: Augustus M. Kelley, 1967 reprint of the 1867 edition). Van Buren was the first professional politician to reach the presidency. Although his own practice was wholly pragmatic, and although he insisted that party loyalty is the most important of all political principles, his *Inquiry* is founded on the opposition of Good and Evil that is typical of pre-modern politics. (The only exception to this is his justification of the controversial Veto of the Bank Bill by Andrew Jackson. Interestingly, the constitutional theory which Van Buren applies to justify his president's choice is precisely the one presented here.)

One should note here that historians and political scientists distinguish between a first and a second party system. The first is said to be founded on political principle, the second on men and the positions they seek to occupy. The first party system is said to end with the presidency of James Monroe, called the 'Era of Good Feelings'. The election of 1824, which brought John Quincy Adams to power on the basis of the 'Corrupt Bargain', sealed the fate of the old system. The presidency of Andrew Jackson, with Van Buren as his vice-president, marks the new stage. The parties are routinized, rationalized, made into electoral machines which function to mediate between the elector and the government as well as being mediators between the executive and the legislative branches. These sociological distinctions would need to be reconsidered in the light of the *political* interpretation of the Constitution offered here. I suggest such an orientation at the conclusion of this discussion.

# Index